The War of Words

The Publisher and the University of California Press Foundation gratefully acknowledge the generous support of Jamie Rosenthal Wolf, David Wolf, Rick Rosenthal, and Nancy Stephens / The Rosenthal Family Foundation.

The War of Words

Kenneth Burke

Edited by Anthony Burke,
Kyle Jensen, and Jack Selzer

UNIVERSITY OF CALIFORNIA PRESS

University of California Press, one of the most
distinguished university presses in the United States,
enriches lives around the world by advancing scholarship
in the humanities, social sciences, and natural sciences. Its
activities are supported by the UC Press Foundation and
by philanthropic contributions from individuals and
institutions. For more information, visit www.ucpress.edu.

University of California Press
Oakland, California

Library of Congress Cataloging-in-Publication Data

Names: Burke, Kenneth, 1897–1993, author. | Burke,
    James Anthony, 1937– editor. | Jensen, Kyle,
    1981– editor. | Selzer, Jack, editor. | Preceded by
    (work): Burke, Kenneth, 1897–1993. Rhetoric of
    motives
Title: The war of words / Kenneth Burke ; edited by
    Anthony Burke, Kyle Jensen, and Jack Selzer.
Description: Oakland, California : University of
    California Press, [2018] | Includes bibliographical
    references and index.
Identifiers: LCCN 2018017668 (print) | LCCN 2018021744
    (ebook) | ISBN 9780520970373 (E-book) |
    ISBN 9780520298101 (cloth : alk. paper) |
    ISBN 9780520298125 (pbk. : alk. paper)
Subjects: LCSH: Semantics (Philosophy) | Rhetoric.
Classification: LCC B840 (ebook) | LCC B840 .B87 2018
    (print) | DDC 149/.94—dc23
LC record available at https://lccn.loc.gov/2018017668

Manufactured in the United States of America

26 25 24 23 22 21 20 19 18
10 9 8 7 6 5 4 3 2 1

Contents

Acknowledgments

The editors are grateful to staff members affiliated with the Berg Collection at the New York Public Library (notably Anne Garner and Lyndsi Barnes) and with Penn State's Eberly Family Special Collections Library (notably Sandra Stelts) for their expert and generous assistance. Jack Selzer's research on this project was made possible by a grant from the New York Public Library and by the Paterno Family Liberal Arts Professorship endowment; he benefited as well from conscientious research assistance by Megan Poole. Kyle Jensen's research was funded by a Scholarly and Creative Activity Grant by the University of North Texas, as well as a Dorothy Foehr Huck Travel Award provided by the Eberly Family Special Collections Library at Penn State; he further benefited from research assistance provided by Nicole Campbell. James L. W. West III, Michael Anesko, and Sandra Spanier offered invaluable advice on the preparation of an authoritative scholarly edition, but they are innocent of any errors or misjudgments that may appear here; we acknowledge as well the helpful comments of reviewers for the University of California Press, Barry Brummett and Edward Schiappa. Dore Brown and Paul Tyler provided expert guidance during the production process. Quotations from Kenneth Burke's letters and manuscripts are published with the permission of the Kenneth Burke Literary Trust, and the photograph of Burke taken at the 1949 Western Round Table on Modern Art is reproduced with the permission of William R. Heick, Jr.

The editors thank the participants at the 2015 Rhetoric Society of America Summer Institute seminar on *The War of Words* and *The Rhetoric of Motives*—notably co-leader Krista Ratcliffe—for stimulating conversations; and we thank many others—notably Steve Mailloux, Ann George, and Ron Fortune but also our students and those present at our conference presentations and other occasions—for conversations about *The War of Words*. Michael Burke and Julie Whitaker have been unfailingly helpful and hospitable during our several trips to Andover to work on *The War of Words:* these trips have been among the highlights of our careers. Finally, we thank our families for their loving patience and continuing support: they make possible everything we do.

Editors' Introduction

When Kenneth Burke was preparing *A Rhetoric of Motives* for publication early in 1949, he inserted a footnote to signal the existence of a prospective second volume of his book: "The[se] closing sentences were originally intended as a transition into our section on The War of Words. But that must await publication in a separate volume" (294). Surprisingly, no one has so far paid much notice to these sentences, even though *A Rhetoric of Motives* (*RM*) is the most significant work by the prolific writer and theorist whom W. H. Auden described in 1941 as "unquestionably the most brilliant and suggestive critic now writing in America" and even though *RM* has remained especially popular among rhetoricians as the most intriguing, original, and stimulating contribution to rhetorical theory since Aristotle's treatise on the subject.

And why should people pay much attention to the footnote? There is plenty enough to take in and remark upon in *RM* already, since Burke in his book was delivering elaborately and famously on the promise he had made in his Introduction: to extend the range of rhetoric to include literary and scientific discourses (not just explicitly persuasive prose); to review the many traditional principles of rhetoric that have gathered around the term "persuasion" since ancient times; to offer as a complement to those traditional principles Burke's central concept of "identification" as it operates as an inducement to cooperation; and finally to illustrate his principles and his concepts with numerous rhetorical analyses of literary, political, pedagogical, scientific, and philosophical texts, many of them erudite. Who could ask for anything more—even something with a title as intriguing as *The War of Words?*

And who could have guessed, based on that modest footnote, that Burke's *The War of Words* had indeed been developing from a section entitled "The War of Words" into a very substantial book-length manuscript of its own, one that had been conceived of from the start as a central part of *RM,* and one that remains timely today for its trenchant commentary on the belligerent aspects of contemporary American culture that operate in both conscious and unconscious realms? And yet that separate volume has never appeared until this one. Quite frequently Burke described the various iterations of what is published here as *The War of Words* in the letters he sent between 1946 and 1950 to his life-long friends Malcolm Cowley and William Carlos Williams, to his friend and patron J. Sibley Watson (a.k.a. W.C. Blum), and to his friendly colleague Stanley Hyman,[1] and the editors of this edition have located the various versions and parts of *The War of Words* in the Berg Papers of the New York Public Library, in the Kenneth Burke Papers at Penn State, and in the Burke papers that Anthony Burke has personally overseen. At the NYPL is a one-page introduction that overviews what Burke had in mind for the four chapters of *The War of Words:* "The Devices" (in which Burke would "classify and describe characteristic rhetorical forms employed in the struggle for advantage that is essential to the Human Comedy"); "Scientific Rhetoric" (a catalogue of "the typical rhetorical resources available to journalism and other mediums that deal in the distribution of information"); "The Rhetoric of Bureaucracy" (designed to "deal with instances where administrative or organizational factors are exceptionally prominent" in persuasion); and "The Rhetorical Situation" (an "attempt to state what we consider to be essentials of present conditions implied in the characteristic rhetoric of social relations, the press, and administrative persuasion. It should be as extra-verbal in reference as we can make it").

Those first two chapters of *The War of Words,* as we will explain in greater detail later in this introduction, derive from manuscripts that are complete, polished, and in ready-to-be-published condition; they are the result of Burke's continuing thoughts and revision processes as he composed *A Rhetoric of Motives* over the period between 1945 and 1950. The lengthy "Devices" chapter itself has two parts: "Of the Devices in General" is a detailed accounting of eleven "modern" rhetorical tactics that Burke had noticed in contemporary discourse and felt to be roughly complementary to Aristotle's catalogue of rhetorical devices in his *Rhetoric;* and "Theory of the Devices" is an enlightening overview designed to show that his analysis was as transhistorical as it was timely—*The War of Words* takes as its exigence the developing Cold War but it also seeks to explain past discourses as well as current ones, private discourses as well as public. "We have not been trying to approach the Devices pragmatically, as a rhetorical manual for instructing students in their use," Burke wrote in the "Theory of the Devices" segment. "Rather, we aim at an ethical approach to them, a method of meditation or contemplation that should be part of a 'way of life'." "Scientific Rhetoric," the second substantial, finished chapter, has little to do with science but everything to do with the media: its seven sections amount to a sustained rhetorical analysis of postwar journalism that demonstrates the "interested" (i.e., anything but objective) nature of print news. Burke's comments on the use of "facts" in media accounts make his comments especially timely to twenty-first-century reflections on "fake news," "alternative facts," and the like.

Although "Devices" and "Scientific Rhetoric" are complete and in ready-to-be-published condition—Burke left them in their own folder and called attention to them as special items intended for future presentation—the other two chapters in this volume are less finished. The first is "The Rhetoric of Bureaucracy," which we have entitled "[Notes toward] The Rhetoric of Bureaucracy" to indicate its fragmentary condition; included is an introductory passage that elaborates Burke's important concept of identification. Chapter 4 of *The War of Words* we are calling "[Notes toward] The Rhetorical Situation," again to underscore its fragmentary nature: it includes beginning efforts by Burke to sketch out his thinking on "Nation vs. Nationals," "Merger and Division," "War," "Policy," "Politics and Economics," "Contradictions," "Ambiguities of Capitalist Expansion," "Hierarchic Motive," "Identification," and "Church." In addition to the four chapters of *The War of Words,* we include in this edition three appendices. Appendices 1 and 3 provide facsimiles of two previously unpublished documents that are directly related to *The War of Words:* an outline of "The Rhetorical Situation," which offers an illuminating preview of what Burke had in mind in terms of a complete chapter 4 of *The War of Words;* and "Foreword (to end on)," which supplies some of Burke's reflections on *The War of Words* from the perspective of the 1970s. Appendix 2 is a word-for-word transcription of the Appendix 3 document.[2]

What exactly did Burke want to accomplish in *The War of Words?* Who and what did the book address—what was the book's cultural context? How did the manuscript of *The War of Words* take shape over the course of Burke's drafting process and what is its relationship to the rest of *RM*? Why did Burke never publish *The War of Words* after all, and what became of it after *RM* was published? What is the status of *The War of Words* if Burke never saw fit to publish it as he promised? And how have we prepared this edition? In what follows we address these questions.

We begin by introducing Burke and the professional and personal circles in which he was operating just after World War II in order to suggest the cultural context out of which *The War of Words* emerged. Then we overview Burke's process of composition and manuscript preparation between the years 1945 and 1949, as "The War of Words" grew into *The War of Words* within the framework of *A Rhetoric of Motives*—an overview that stresses how fundamental *The War of Words* was to Burke's developing conception of *RM*, as well as the value of conceptualizing Burke as a writer who was attempting to solve rhetorical problems intimately connected to the argument of *RM* and to the historical moment in which he was writing. Viewing Burke in this manner permits us to explain how *The War of Words* evolved out of "The War of Words" during the composition of *RM* without our advancing an interpretation of the work (we leave that to the reader).[3] Following that we offer a brief textual apparatus, explaining the editorial issues that we addressed in putting together this edition. Finally comes *The War of Words* itself—a book that offers perspective on *A Rhetoric of Motives* but which, more importantly, is a significant independent addition to the Burke canon that discloses numerous contemporary rhetorical tropes while also exposing how conventional and uncritical journalistic and bureaucratic communications condition Americans to accept the possibility of ruinous wars.

KENNETH BURKE, 1945–50: THE CULTURAL CONTEXT
FOR *THE WAR OF WORDS*

No wonder *A Rhetoric of Motives* and *The War of Words* are among Burke's masterpieces: in terms of both his personal and professional life, he was at the top of his game in the years after the conclusion to World War II.

Take, as a representative moment, Burke's circumstances on his fiftieth birthday, May 5, 1947. He no doubt marked the date by attending to his usual routines: doing the spring chores required (even on that rainy day) by the small Andover, New Jersey farm that he had acquired in 1922; reading his voluminous mail and answering letters; playing his own music and improvising on the piano; and writing and doing research and clipping excerpts from newspapers toward what would become *The War of Words* and *A Rhetoric of Motives*. Nine days earlier, on April 27, 1947, he had described the prospective contents of *RM* in a letter to J. S. Watson, and the manuscript was developing nicely; after wrapping up a semester of teaching at Bennington College in December 1946, he had turned his full attention to his book—at the moment he was determining how to frame what would become the opening argument. Deeply conversant with the political and social events that distinguished the late 1940s, he reflected in that letter to Watson on the final disposition of the Paris Peace Treaty and the recent "export[ation]" of progressive Henry Wallace and "import[ation]" of cold warrior Winston Churchill.

Living with his second wife, Libbie, and their two young sons, Burke and his family subsisted by means of a frugal lifestyle, support from his regular patron Watson and regularly irregular teaching assignments at Bennington (he had contracted for continuing arrangements in 1945), and royalties from his recent books and articles and speaking engagements. Burke was financially secure enough to own a 1936 Pontiac (virtually necessary for rural living), to take on a gas-powered lawn mower (known as "Putt-Putt"), and to plan on spending the following winter in Melbourne Beach, Florida, completing his *Rhetoric*. (In 1950, the Burkes would acquire a new and reliable Pontiac, and in 1949, even electricity would come to Andover, though inside plumbing could wait until the 1960s.) His three daughters by his first wife, Lily, now growing independent, would live nearby in the summers and were forming families of their own, supplying Burke with many grandchildren. Perpetually hypochondriachal, Burke was already beginning to complain of an all-too-real "Migratory Symptom," a "gulpo-gaggo-gaspo" reflex that would plague his body and his imagination for years (was it lung cancer? or possibly asthma? or what?), and he regularly complained in his letters about everything from an infected cut on his toe to impetigo to a stiff neck to nosebleeds to hypertension. And yet his body was firm from outdoor exercise and hale enough to eventually get him to the age of 96, so when he went to the doctor in May 1947 to check out what Burke thought might be "cancer in the ear," his physician just laughed.

In his professional life Burke on his fiftieth birthday was proficient and productive, respected and admired. Over four thousand copies of *A*

Grammar of Motives had already been sold (the source of those royalties) since its publication by Prentice Hall at the end of 1945, and mostly laudatory reviews of the book had been appearing regularly. A couple of months earlier the American Academy of Arts and Letters had surprised him with a $1,000 grant, and on December 19, 1948, he began a three-month paid residency at the Institute for Advanced Study at Princeton, overseen by Robert Oppenheimer. (That T. S. Eliot had also been invited for September, October, November, and December 1948 speaks to the esteem in which Burke was held at this time.) Vassar (1944), the University of Iowa (1945, 1948–49), the University of Chicago (1946, 1947–48), the University of Washington (1948), and the University of Minnesota (1946–47) were all trying to interest him in joining their faculty. (Although resistant to the idea of full-time teaching because it would interrupt his writing, he eventually signed on for two semesters of duty at Chicago in 1949–50.)

On May 3, 1947, two days before that fiftieth birthday, he had been among the guests invited by the Frick Museum to hear Eliot speak on Milton—against his expectations, given his political misgivings about Eliot, he enjoyed it immensely—and his other professional associations were impressive as well. The Fugitives and New Critics John Crowe Ransom, Allen Tate, and Robert Penn Warren (whose novel *All the King's Men* had been published in 1946) were all corresponding with Burke, often in connection with Burke's contributions to *Kenyon Review* or *Sewanee Review*. He remained connected with the literary leftists he had consorted with during the Great Depression (and indeed his plans for "The War of Words" included additional thoughts on the "literary wars" of the 1930s). The sculptor Alexander Calder and artist Peter Blume were in Burke's circle of friends, along with the writer-critics Malcolm Cowley (whose *Portable Faulkner* had been published in 1946), R. P. Blackmur (whose poetry collection *The Good European* came out in 1947), and Francis Fergusson (just then finishing his book *The Idea of a Theatre*). Burke would speak to an overflow crowd on James Joyce at the December 1948 meeting of the Modern Language Association, would lecture that year and the next at Amherst (1949), Drake (1950), and Iowa (1950), and in April of 1949 participated in the Western Round Table on Modern Art in San Francisco along with Gregory Bateson, Marcel Duchamp, George Boas, and Frank Lloyd Wright (see figure 1).

Auden and Theodore Roethke had been teaching with Burke at Bennington, Howard Nemerov would join the faculty in 1948 (having pub-

FIGURE 1. Western Round Table on Modern Art (San Francisco, 1949). Seated are (left to right) George Boas, Frank Lloyd Wright, Kenneth Burke, Marcel Duchamp, and Andrew C. Ritchie. Source and credit: William R. Heick.

lished a friendly essay on Burke in the summer 1947 issue of *Furioso*), and William Carlos Williams (often) and John Berryman (occasionally) were visitors to Andover—Williams's poem "At Kenneth Burke's House" appeared in the *Yale Poetry Review* in August 1946. Another frequent visitor, the scholar and cultural critic Stanley Edgar Hyman, was now teaching at Bennington too, thanks in part to Burke's intervention, and his 1948 book *The Armed Vision* would include a chapter on Burke that would spread Burke's fame. Hyman's wife, Shirley Jackson, usually accompanied her husband on trips to Andover, and her famous story "The Lottery" appeared in the *New Yorker* in July 1948. On November 23, 1945, Hyman's friend Ralph Ellison had written to thank Burke for recommending him (successfully) for a Rosenwald Fellowship and for "the many things I've learned (and continue to learn) from your work. . . . I am writing a novel now and perhaps . . . it will be my most effective means of saying thanks." Burke had read Ellison's essay "Richard Wright's Blues," an extended review of Wright's novel

Black Boy that Ellison had published the previous July, and on several occasions Ellison read portions of his novel-in-progress at Andover, including its famous opening: "I am an invisible man."[4]

There was just one catch: the war and its aftermath were as traumatic for Burke as they were for so many others. Burke's son-in-law Ricky Leacock had returned from Burma and China in one piece, but millions of others were less fortunate. The base statistics are so stark as to be numbing: war in Europe and the Pacific claimed between 60 million and 80 million lives (depending on which estimate you prefer), about three percent of the world's population. Over four hundred thousand of the dead were Americans. The full extent of ethnic cleansing across the vast territory occupied by wartime Germany had come to light because of the 1946 Nuremberg Trials (Anne Frank's diary, first published in Germany, would appear in English in the summer of 1947), and the Pacific war had had deep racial overtones as well. Many other millions of people across the world and in the United States were maimed; damaged victims of the carnage were visible everywhere; displaced persons were wandering unsettled and famished across the globe; and when the British left India in August of 1947, sectarian violence between Hindus and Muslims led to hundreds of thousands of deaths, the partition of India and Pakistan, and the largest mass migration in human history. Political unrest everywhere existed alongside the postwar rubble, and of course the economic costs were staggering.

The war had ended, in August 1945, with a horror among horrors, the catastrophic atomic bombings of Hiroshima and Nagasaki, a terrifying "conclusion" to the war that to Burke only seemed to presage even more catastrophe. "The era of the Mad Scientist of the B movie now seems with us in a big way," Burke told Cowley in an August 9, 1945 letter from Andover, on the day the second bomb leveled Nagasaki: "There seems now no logical thing to do but go on tinkering with this damned thing until they have blown up the whole damned world." Burke was equally concerned that the unstable international situation and developing Cold War would lead to another major war, as indeed they did when the Korean War erupted on June 25, 1950, while Burke was beginning a six-week residency at Kenyon College's Summer School of English for college teachers, an event designed by John Crowe Ransom, supported by the Rockefeller Foundation, and including William Empson, L. C. Knights, Robert Lowell, and Delmore Schwartz, among others.[5]

"The atomic bomb has made me sputter with wrath," Burke complained to Dr. Watson on August 13, 1945, a few days after the bombs fell on Japan: "Give civilization another fifty years with this new toy and the 'marvelous' world that results will be such a boring clutter of super-gadgets as would make a present Woolworth's counter look in comparison like Hayakawa's Ming period." When the Cold War hardened and brought forth a Red Scare, a new nuclear arms race, McCarthyism, bomb shelters, and the fearsome prospect of Mutually Assured Destruction, Burke sputtered with more wrath, again and again. The actions of the House Committee on Un-American Activities caught his attention in October 1947, and again in August of 1948 when Whittaker Chambers would accuse Alger Hiss of disloyalty (Cowley testified at the subsequent Hiss perjury trials); and Burke fretted too about the forced exportation of capitalism around the world. On August 14–18, 1950, Burke took part in an interesting event at Harvard called "A Defense of Poetry," one that had drawn Roethke, Ransom, Robert Lowell, John Ciardi, Marianne Moore, Richard Wilbur, Stephen Spender, Randall Jarrell, and other notable poets and critics to an open discussion of the supposedly ahistorical role of poetry in the Cold War environment: when Burke spoke passionately about the need for poets "to turn the world away from the cult of ultimate destruction," his talk was interrupted for its alleged disloyalty.

Burke had been too old to participate directly in the war effort, though he had served for a time as a reporter of plane sightings and had tried unsuccessfully to land a job in Archibald MacLeish's Office of Facts and Figures; and his loved ones emerged from the catastrophe intact. Also on the plus side, the wartime crises energized him intellectually. On his fiftieth birthday he had a renewed sense of professional purpose as well as a brilliant new approach to offer for understanding human interactions—an approach designed to reveal and resist the wartime and Cold War mentality that was (and still is) infecting his nation.

THE COMPOSITION HISTORY OF
THE WAR OF WORDS

If Burke decided, in the end, to conceive of *The War of Words* as a volume separate from *A Rhetoric of Motives,* then why have we been discussing the two works in tandem? The answer is that from the beginning Burke had conceived of them together, as part of one sustained argument, and until the last minute he expected "The War of Words" to be a section within the published *A Rhetoric of Motives.* In other words, the story of *The War of Words* is intertwined with the larger story of the development of *A Rhetoric of Motives.* Taken together, the *War of*

Words manuscript and the recountal of its compositional evolution provide an opportunity to outline Burke's vision of modern rhetorical studies as a coherent project. While it is somewhat artificial to treat the development of *The War of Words* and *A Rhetoric of Motives* as proceeding through discrete stages, nevertheless the two did develop together across four overlapping phases. Informing each of the four phases was the backdrop of World War II and its aftermath; each phase offers witness to Burke's obsession with the problem of "purifying war."

Preliminaries: 1942–45

After his *Attitudes Toward History* was published in 1937, Burke began conceiving of a third volume that, along with *Permanence and Change* (1935), would complete a kind of trilogy. His plan was at first interrupted by the successful side-project entitled *The Philosophy of Literary Form,* but once Burke finished the lengthy title essay to that collection of articles and reviews in the spring of 1939, he returned to complete his trilogy with a book that he was calling "On Human Relations" (Burke to Watson, November 22, 1939). That book would deal both "[in] human relations and in a rhetoric of human relations" (Burke to Watson, January 24, 1940); it would be concerned with "the subject and quandaries of motivation in general—and with a critical and tentative point of view that cannot be felt as relevant at the moment, but should seem quite relevant when the war is over, and people are more poignantly facing the 'what next'" (Burke to Hyman, June 3, 1942). As Burke began work, the explicitly rhetorical parts of "On Human Relations" took a subordinate place to material on constitutions, to what he was calling "the four master tropes," and to the five terms, his famous pentad, that would become the core construct known as "dramatism" in *A Grammar of Motives.* By the spring of 1941, as the pages were already piling up on his analysis of the internal laws governing human motives (i.e., "the grammar"), he was giving up on the idea of "On Human Relations" as a single book. Not everything could fit into one volume. And as he wrote to Malcolm Cowley on March 8, 1941, "I seem to be shifting my linguistic analysis from a *rhetoric* to a *grammar.*" A year later he had a lengthy independent manuscript that had taken shape as the foundation of what we know as *A Grammar of Motives.*[6]

In other words, for a time Burke thought he was completing one trilogy—*Permanence and Change, Attitudes Toward History,* and *On Human Relations*—only to end up conceiving of another: his "motives trilogy." As late as June 3, 1942, he wrote to Hyman that he had completed 110,000 words "to my speculations on the imputing of motives," which was to "be followed by sections on 'Rhetoric' and 'Symbolic'," all in one volume; but in November, a year after the attack on Pearl Harbor, he had still not finished the lengthy "grammar" portion and it was clear that to do justice to the three topics, he would need separate volumes. In May 1943, he was telling his friends that "On Human Relations" would now indeed be three separate books: *A Grammar of Motives, A Rhetoric of Motives,* and *A Symbolic of Motives.*

Burke calculated that he could complete all three by the end of 1944 (Burke to Watson, December 11, 1943), but as it turned out he couldn't even complete the first by then. Amid the uncertainties of a wartime economy, it proved difficult for Burke to find a publisher for the *Grammar,* and in the midst of his search, in the summer of 1943, he contracted to teach at Bennington College for the next three terms—from September to December of 1943, from April 1944 to the end of June, and from September 1944 through December. These two factors forced Burke to put aside plans for the *Rhetoric,* especially because the search for a publisher took time and because Burke renewed his association with Bennington for April to July 1945. In November of 1944, just as he was giving a talk at Vassar on "Grammar, Rhetoric, and Symbolic," Burke at last placed *GM* with Prentice Hall, thanks to his connections with Gorham Munson, his collaborator and colleague from two decades earlier in Greenwich Village. Burke received a $500 advance to produce a finished manuscript of *GM*—and the contract also included a provision for Prentice Hall to publish Burke's promised *Rhetoric of Motives* and *Symbolic of Motives.*

During the first three months of 1945, winter break at Bennington, Burke therefore threw himself into finishing off *GM* according to specifications and left his ideas for *RM* percolating. It wasn't easy: "What I have done," he wrote Cowley (April 16, 1945), "is throw out big sections of the accepted version [of *GM,* because they had to do with *RM*] and add bigger chunks of a totally new version [of *GM*]." But while he didn't quite finish *GM* before the spring semester began at Bennington around April 1, 1945, he was close enough that he got the finished manuscript off to the publisher later that month. From there it was a matter of seeing *A Grammar of Motives* through production, of getting through the April–June Bennington term, of rolling out over the summer the many promotional materials that Prentice Hall was cooking up for *GM*—and beginning to resuscitate and refine at last his thoughts for

RM. With the war concluding in August that summer, with *GM* galleys under review in September and page proofs in November, and with *GM* off the presses in December 1945, Burke was ready at last to turn his full attention to his *Rhetoric.*

What kind of book was he conceiving at that point?

Focusing on the relationship between war and words had always been the plan for "On Human Relations" in general and *A Rhetoric of Motives* in particular. After all, *A Grammar of Motives* itself had been published with the motto "Ad Bellum Purificandum," a motto that just as easily could serve for the entire motives trilogy. However, the introduction of atomic bombs into world history during the summer of 1945 added urgency to Burke's rhetorical vision. Now he set out to explain "the lore of The Scramble," he told Watson (September 10, 1945), "to find ways whereby working and loving may be done without warring" (December 27, 1945). Anticipating "a whole new era (with wholly new areas) of international intrigue and individual warped ambitions" centered on the strategic eradication of enemy populations (August 13, 1945), Burke resolved to give special attention to how the news media were portraying the defeated enemies following their surrender: "Presumably, if we are to spread our influence internationally, we can't plan just one hold at a time, as Rhetoricians in control of a press dearly love to do. It must be adjusted to several antagonists variously placed" through the use of various rhetorical devices (September 10, 1945). He could be explicit about articulating his goal for *RM:* "Have been battling away at the *Rhetoric,*" he told Williams on November 19, 1945. "It will become . . . a study devoted to showing how deep and ubiquitous are the roots of war in the universal scene and the human psyche—a study extending from our meditations on the war of words. . . . Rhetoric. The War of Words. Logomachy."

After the difficulties he had encountered with *GM* ("I wonder whether there has ever been a more revised and rerevised book?" he asked Watson on April 12, 1945), he predicted to Cowley on October 13, 1945, that "The Rhetoric should be the easiest volume of the three to write. My main problem is to keep the book from disintegrating into particular cases (so that it becomes in effect a disguised way of saying repeatedly: 'another instance of this is . . . and still another instance is . . . etc.'). I want it to be rather a philosophizing on rhetoric (as the main slant), though the particular instances should be there in the profusion."[7] Accordingly, after four months of gathering his thoughts, making beginnings, and knocking "off, none too exactly, a first rough draft . . . to be used as an outline" (Burke to Cowley, November 25, 1945), he prepared a formal prospectus for Prentice Hall, dated January 2, 1946, that described his initial thoughts about contents and arrangement. (See box on pages 14–15.)

The prospectus offered that *A Rhetoric of Motives* would be "a treatise on the 'art of persuasion'," "probably" with five major parts:

> Part One (on the War of Words, the "Logomachy") is designed to show how deeply the military ingredient [is] in our vocabulary. . . . The Second Part ("The Rhetorical Situation") . . . review[s] in a general way the grounds, or resources, available to the Rhetorician in giving urgency and poignancy to his utterance. . . . The Third Part ("The Boundaries of Rhetoric") considers in particular certain literary battles of recent years that hinged on confusion about the relation between Rhetoric and Poetic. . . . [A] Fourth Part ("Landmarks of Rhetoric") . . . review[s] the various works of the past and present [that] I consider particularly useful as contributions to the study of Rhetoric. . . . [And] Part Five: "Catalogue of Rhetorical Devices."

The first four sections would be "concerned with general theory"—Burke's "philosophizing"—while the last, "mainly technical" section would "list, classify, and analyze the many examples of rhetoric [that he had] been assembling over the years," examples that he been culling from the *New York Times* to show "the ingredients of war lurking undetected in language that may seem on its surface to be the language of peace." Note that none of these proposed section titles appear in the version of *A Rhetoric of Motives* that was ultimately published in 1950—the only section that bears a resemblance to what appears in the published version of *RM* is "Landmarks of Rhetoric," which would eventually morph into "Traditional Principles of Rhetoric" as "a kind of long review [of] the various works of the past and present [that] I consider particularly useful as contributions to the study of Rhetoric." But also note that the promise of a book on the theory and practice of persuasion did materialize in *RM*, and that "The War of Words" (or "Logomachy," as Burke often called it) as well as "The Rhetorical Situation" and "Catalogue of Rhetorical Devices" were all central to this earliest conception of the book. All ended up in the version of *The War of Words* that is published here in this edition.

In his general description of the chapter "The War of Words" in the prospectus, Burke promised to theorize (i.e., to produce what would become an "upward way"): "This section is intended to place the whole subject, and to show why Rhetoric is not just a matter for specialists, but goes to the roots of psychology and ethics, including man's relation to his political and economic background." Already positioning rhetoric as a

Prospectus

Herewith is my statement of plans for the Rhetoric, a treatise on the "art of persuasion." I am fairly sure that the outline is substantially the one I shall abide by, since it is the result of about six weeks' work spent on a tentative draft made for purposes of organization.

The book is probably to be in five parts. The last is mainly technical, and the first four are more concerned with general theory, the philosophy and background of rhetoric.

Part One (on the War of Words, the "Logomachy") is designed to show just how deeply the militaristic ingredient in our vocabulary goes. This section is intended to place the whole subject, and to show why Rhetoric is not just a matter for specialists, but goes to the roots of psychology and ethics, including man's relation to his political and economic background. It deals with two main trinitarian clusters (Love-War-Work and Mine-Thine-Ours), showing how each member of a given cluster implicates the other two, and how basically such interweaving affects the formation and use of the communicative medium. Above all, we seek to disclose the ingredients of war lurking undetected in language that may seem on its surface to be the language of peace.

The Second Part ("The Rhetorical Situation") expands such concern with the philosophy of rhetoric by reviewing in a general way the grounds, or resources, available to the Rhetorician in giving urgency and poignancy to his utterance. We here review, in broad generalizations, both the formal and the extra-literary factors that contribute to the persuasiveness of rhetorical expressions.

The Third Part ("The Boundaries of Rhetoric") considers in particular certain literary battles of recent years that hinged on confusion about the relation between Rhetoric and Poetic, or between Rhetoric and Esthetic. I could write a whole book on this alone, by simply recounting my own experiences during the literary squabbles of the Thirties. Instead, I intend confining myself to what I consider to be a few of the more representative moments.

Mainly for pedagogical reasons, I have planned a Fourth Part ("Landmarks of Rhetoric") that treats in a kind of long review the various works of the past and present I consider particularly useful as contributions to the study of Rhetoric. I am still not quite decided to do this as a separate section, however, I may find, by the time I have finished, that I have made sufficient reference to those works in passing, so that a separate chapter on them would be unnecessary.

Part Five: "Catalogue of Rhetorical Devices." Here I intend to list, classify, and analyze the many examples of rhetoric I have been assembling over the years. I have enough of these to make two or three books, if I were to use them all without selection. But my plan is to weed them out drastically, keeping only the ones that I consider intrinsically most interesting, or that can be given effectiveness by reason of developments purely internal to the book. In order that these devices do not merely jump from one to another, like words in a dictionary, I am working to group them as variations and combinations of a greatly reduced set of principles.

As with the Grammar, there will be frequent reference in this book to the two other members of the trilogy, illustrating how the area covered here impinges upon the subjects treated elsewhere. But also as with the Grammar, the Rhetoric will be designed to be complete in itself.

Kenneth Burke
Andover, New Jersey
January 2, 1946

Word-for-word reprint of the January 2, 1946 prospectus that Kenneth Burke submitted to Prentice Hall. Source: Burke 3 [P23], box 7, folder 5, Kenneth Burke Papers, Penn State Special Collections. Credit: The Kenneth Burke Literary Trust.

general area of study that could uniquely expose the complexity of humanity's political and economic background, Burke was proposing to extend the influence of rhetorical studies, to "disclose the ingredients of war lurking undetected in language that may seem on its surface to be the language of peace." By identifying such ingredients lurking undetected in "peaceful" language, particularly that which was appearing in contemporary news media, Burke would by means of "The War of Words" expose to scrutiny what he would come to call the "downward way" of actual rhetorical practices while creating the conditions required for more responsible forms of contemplation and deliberation. In sum, therefore, from the start *A Rhetoric of Motives* was designed to include "The War of Words" and to extend rhetoric's long tradition of educating audiences to participate in public debate with greater attention and insight and effect.

"The Upward Way": January 1946–March 1948

By the summer of 1946, however, as Burke got down to drafting particulars, his prediction that *A Rhetoric of Motives* would be easy to write proved naïve. He dedicated himself conscientiously to his writing, but, as he confessed to Stanley Edgar Hyman on July 21, 1946 (three weeks after the United States tested an atomic bomb at Bikini Atoll in the Pacific and five weeks before the *New Yorker* devoted an entire issue to John Hersey's *Hiroshima*), "There are many pressing reasons why the writing of a Modern Rhetoric is not a joyous undertaking—and I am finding every one of them, the hard way." For one thing, as he began to compose, his thoughts changed several times; and instead of beginning with "The War of Words," as he had implied in his prospectus, he started drafting various pieces of the entire project. The tension between "philosophizing about rhetoric" and analyzing specific rhetorical practices was already becoming apparent. As he complained in a letter to Cowley on April 3, 1946,

> First draft of the Rhetoric goes bumping along. Instead of writing it from start to finish, I seem to be writing it from the middle out. Each day I drive in more wedges that push the two ends farther apart. And there's just the possibility that I may, this time, be lambasted for being too easy to read. The book is as anecdotal as T.B.L. [*Towards a Better Life*, Burke's 1932 novel], except that this time the anecdotes are strung along an idea instead of a story. The clothesline method. Except that there is a shortage of clothespins, so that you have to hang several items at each spot along the line.

The passage intimates that the most difficult challenge Burke would face in completing *RM* over the next two-plus years would be managing the book as a project both ambitious and coherent. Moreover, Burke was also unsettled about the style of his presentation. On the one hand, he explained to Cowley, he was approaching *RM* and "The War of Words" with a "benevolently caustic" tone; but on the other, he was now also experimenting with an "ironically irenic" style that could address the dangers of the popular press less aggressively.

In any event, while there was always a common thread tying his disparate analyses together (i.e., the fundamental relationship that exists between war and words), Burke's target of analysis as well as his tone would undergo constant evolution. And yet through it all, *The War of Words* and its component chapters, as we have them in this edition, would remain central to his developing vision. If the pragmatic "downward way" of his book ("The War of Words") would catalogue the unfortunate details of the abuse of rhetoric in postwar America, his more theoretical "upward way" (a term derived ultimately from Plato) would promote a set of more positive principles for encouraging human cooperation.

Burke articulated the changes in his developing approach in a new outline for his book (available at Penn State in Burke 3 [P23], box 7, folder 2), which he formulated in September 1946 as he was trying out his ideas with Bennington students and as he described in a September 21, 1946 letter to Watson. (See figure 2.) *RM* would now have three

Andover,
New Jersey,
September 21,1946.

Dear dr.,

        Home after sally no. 2. Finally got warmed up
somewhat this time. And am beginning to discover some good modifications for the book. In the fourth two-hour lecture, I finally hit
upon the proper way to begin! (That's trying it out on the dog,
no?) I.e., took a whole batch of rhetorics, apparently quite at
odds with one another, and showed how they could be derived from a
common definition (being but the stressing of one or another of its
possibilities). So, as things look now, the enterprise is beginning
to fall into three major divisions (vive la tinity): The Range of
Rhetoric, Rhetoric and Poetic, the Logomachy. Section One wd. contain a survey of the field, ending on our specialty, generalizations
and particulars concerning "The Rhetorical Situation." Section Two
wd. deal with the shift btw. the study of the internal relations of
a work (poetic) and the study of its relations to audience. Best
sort of material for consideration here: good plays. Section
Three wd. deal with all the variants of malice and the lie, the
thumbs-down side of rhetoric, and wd. contain our specialty, analysis
of rhetorical devices (operated about the ambiguities of competition
and cooperation). Here also wd. be analysis of news, literary
polemic, etc. (I see a chance to smack at some of my old enemies,
under favorable, even enjoyable, conditions.) ... Problem still
to be decided: The Rhetoric, considered in itself, should end on
Section Two, and the War of ░░░░ shd. be the transitional stage
btw. the section on Range and the section on Rhetoric and Poetic.
But considered as member of a trilogy, the book shd. end on the
theme of the Logomachy, as the best lead into the "neo-pacifism" of
the third book, on Symbolic. That is, if one ends Book Two on the
theme of the Universal Wrangle, as goaded by unnecessary itches and
appetites, then one has the best lead into Book Three, which is
the study of these Itches and Appetites in themselves (as grounded
in motives not competitive or invidious at all).

                      . . .

        The Rhetoric, as now piled up in first draft, had
been taking a wrong tack in that it was becoming too negativistic.
In part, this was due to my morbid gloom over the ░░ homicidal and
suicidal ░░░░░░░ corruption of the concemporary press, which is doing
almost as much as is humanly possible to prepare us for a ░░ cult of
devastation and desolation that will leave practically no one in
a position to attain ░░░░░░░ rudimentary ░░░░░ amenities. And in
part it was due to the fact that all the various material on communication scattered through my books was itself a stress upon the
positive side. of rhetoric. Hence, the tendency to stress the other
side, the what-is-left. But I think that a systematized treatment of
the relation between internal structure and external address, ░░░
as exemplified in the study of. good plays, can restore the balance in
the book, without requiring me me to peddle my previous stuff over
again.

        But I must back to the grind. Best wishes,

                          K B.

FIGURE 2. Paragraphs 1 and 4 of Kenneth Burke's letter to James Sibley Watson,
September 21, 1946. Ellipses indicate that paragraphs 2 and 3 have been deleted. The first
sentences of the letter indicate that Burke had returned to Andover after his second week
of teaching at Bennington, having finally gotten the semester well under way. Source: The
Henry W. and Albert Berg Collection of English and American Literature, New York
Public Library, Astor, Lenox, and Tilden Foundations; Dial Papers, Series III, Papers
Related to Kenneth Burke, box 7. Source and credit: The Kenneth Burke Literary Trust.

sections. The first, "The Range of Rhetoric," would outline his subject, "ending on our specialty, generalizations and particulars concerning 'The Rhetorical Situation'." The second, "Rhetoric and Poetic," would now emphasize and rationalize Burke's belief that literary discourses were also thoroughly rhetorical in nature: for the benefit of the literary critics in his audience who were firmly committed to the autonomy of art and to its felicity, he had decided in July that "Rhetoric and Poetic" would permit him to defend his belief that poetry is fundamentally persuasive in that it has designs on readers' beliefs, attitudes, and actions, and to address the difference between analyzing a work on its own "intrinsic" terms and doing so in "extrinsic" ways. (The distinction between "intrinsic" and "extrinsic" criticism was much on the minds of Burke and other literary critics as the New Criticism was being formulated in the 1940s. See for example Burke's "The Kinds of Criticism," published in *Poetry* in August 1946.) With all that in place and with several sample analyses of "the good side of rhetoric" on the table, he would then turn to another angle, organized around the bad side: "The War of Words" (Burke to Watson, September 21, 1946). Consistent with Burke's original plan, "The War of Words" would in several sections "deal with all the variants of malice and the lie, the thumbs-down side of rhetoric, and wd. contain our specialty, analysis of rhetorical devices. . . . Here also wd. be analysis of news, literary polemic, etc." While Burke was still not firmly settled on this arrangement, one benefit would be its promise of an elegant transition at the end: instead of beginning with reflections on the war of words, "the book shd. end on the theme of the Logomachy [i.e., "war of words"] as the best lead into the 'neo-pacifism' of the third book, on Symbolic" (the *Symbolic of Motives* being the projected third volume in the motives series). Another benefit of such an organization would be its advance of a more even-handed approach to the study of rhetoric, allowing his audiences to become more educated readers of contemporary popular news media.

But what could unify these two dimensions of his *RM* project, the "positive" side and the "negative"? What would be "requirement no. 1, ye olde generating principle," that would convert "a clutter of loose ends" (Burke to Cowley, September 27, 1946) into a unified treatise on rhetoric? As Burke tried out his ideas on his Bennington students that fall and as he worked on a review of Ernest Cassirer's *The Myth of the State,* he was concluding that *identification* would be his key concept. "Have got it all down to three words," he wrote Watson on January 27, 1947: "For the Grammar, Substance. For the Rhetoric, Identification.

For the Symbolic, Identity. . . . The rest is but to draw out all the implications, transform them into explications." Burke's key notion of *identification* had already made brief appearances in his previous books and articles, notably in "Revolutionary Symbolism in America" (1935) and "The Rhetoric of Hitler's *Battle*" (1939) but also in "Reading While You Run" (1937), "The Calling of the Tune" (1938), the "Dictionary of Pivotal Terms" in *Attitudes Toward History* (1937), and passages explaining the pentadic ratios in *GM*. Yet Burke's incipient realization that identification could be the organizing principle for *A Rhetoric of Motives* indicates that his treatment of the concept would be far more elaborated than anything he had previously realized. As readers of *RM* well know, over the course of 1947 and into 1948, identification would develop into Burke's most notable and original contribution to the understanding of persuasion. Focusing as it would on the "intermediate area of expression that is not wholly deliberate, yet not wholly unconscious" (xiii), that is, on intermediate, nonvolitional areas of rhetorical expression, Burke's version of identification would eventually extend the insights of Freud (who theorized identification in *Group Psychology and Other Works*) into rhetoric by explaining how group perspectives could be organized through the circulation of rhetorical devices. But there still remained, at this point in his drafting process, a considerable distance for Burke to travel before all the constituent parts of *A Rhetoric of Motives* would be connected.

As a January 26, 1948 letter to Cowley indicates (Burke by mistake typed the date as "1947"), Burke was seeking to draw out the implications of identification and to transform them into explications according to a structure that again would place "The War of Words" in a central position. With the controversy over "intrinsic" and "extrinsic" criticism abating and with Burke's thoughts on identification taking hold, the chapter on "Rhetoric and Poetic" was now put aside (and eventually reserved for *A Symbolic of Motives*), though the relationship between rhetoric and poetic would remain an important focus of *A Rhetoric of Motives*. What Burke was coming to call the "Upward" portion of *A Rhetoric of Motives* would now include three movements: "The Range of Rhetoric" would extend the domain of rhetoric to include literature and science; "Traditional Principles of Rhetoric" would overview the contributions of the ancients and feature their anticipation of the concept of "identification"; and "Dialectic, Ideology, and Myth" would extend the range of rhetoric into territory that it had never before inhabited (i.e., into myth and mysticism). The

"Downward" portion, for the moment entitled "The World of Public-ity" or "Logomachy" instead of "The War of Words," persisted as planned, with the section "Catalogue of Devices" (to detail the modern rhetorical moves that Burke had been noticing in contemporary dis-course), and others on "Scientific Rhetoric" (to deal with the analysis of journalism), "The Rhetorical Situation" (to comment on the scenes of rhetoric that govern social relations), and "The Rhetoric of Bureau-cracy" (to review institutional factors in persuasion). In other words, as we noted in our opening paragraphs, these four chapters were remain-ing coherent and stable through Burke's conception of *RM:* they became *The War of Words.*

And on this scaffold Burke continued to draft *A Rhetoric of Motives,* concentrating first on "The Upward Way" and his meditations on iden-tification but always maintaining a commitment to "The War of Words." It is tempting to recount in detail Burke's thinking between January of 1947 and March of 1948 because *RM* evolved in great part during that period and because his thoughts are documented so thor-oughly and interestingly in his letters and notes. But in order to main-tain our focus on *The War of Words,* here we distill Burke's work dur-ing this period into five episodes.

First, as is apparent in the published version of *RM,* Burke spent considerable time during 1947 thinking through the complexities of myth as they govern and are governed by identification and persuasion. As Burke told Watson on February 11, 1947, "Resolved: that property is (a) the very core of moral integrity; (b) the very core of war. Hence, if we are not to carry out the logic of the new weapons, the need for a 'New Myth'." Of course Burke had long questioned the U.S. national myths that sanctioned warfare and supported capitalism, notably in his 1935 speech at the First American Writers' Congress, but now he seized on Virgil's *Aeneid* in the hope that it would serve as an ideologically neutral model for the creation of a new, less martial American myth. In a significant lecture entitled "Ideology and Myth" that he delivered at Bennington College on March 31, 1947, Burke pointed out the "many important correspondences between Virgil's situation and the situation today" and outlined a twelve-step method for creating a new political myth, appropriated from J. W. Mackail's *Virgil and His Meaning to the World of Today.* Accordingly, as reflected in an unpublished outline dated April 27, 1947 (Burke 3 [Q22], box 12, folders 33–34), Burke considered including all of "Ideology and Myth" at the beginning of *RM* because it "gives . . . a panoramic opening; yet without recapitulating former writings on rhetoric; and without avoiding main subject." In the end Burke rejected that idea (while including some revised portions of "Ideology and Myth" into the opening of the "Order" section of *RM*); but by establishing myth elsewhere in *RM* as the nonpolitical grounding for political discourse, he could bring to light in *The War of Words* the particular ideological manifestations that distinguish any local rhetorical situation.

Second, Burke continued to parse the distinctions and commonalities between rhetoric and poetic. He created new sections entitled "Rhetoric of the Drama" and "While They Last": the former would help him to place identification as the systematizing principle of *A Rhetoric of Motives,* while the latter, as we mentioned earlier, was focused on "the litry racket [in the 1930s]; a kind of Inferno, where we might consign enemies and theories to hell; attack, intermingled with litry theory."[8] Burke had been compiling notes for "While They Last" in the earliest stages of his drafting process, as evidenced by his January 2, 1946 prospectus (where "The Boundaries of Rhetoric" are described) and by the contents of a letter he wrote to Watson on November 2, 1945: "Am now thinking of including a section that goes over some of the literary squabbles I went through. I was recalling the other day, for instance, how things went about the time of the first Writers Congress," when the relation between literature and politics was a central concern. "While They Last" would thus potentially serve as one of Burke's anticipations of the local rhetorical debates that he planned to address in "The War of Words."

Third, in the summer of 1947 Burke substantially revised "The Range of Rhetoric" to conform to his commitment to identification as an organizing concept. In a September 1946 outline of his plans for "The Range of Rhetoric" (Burke 3 [P23], box 7, folder 2), Burke had proposed a "[s]urvey of the field, about Aristotle's definition as a point of reference [and] treating other views of rhetoric as derivations from that." But with his focus now on identification and with a resolve to give up teaching for the rest of 1947 to concentrate on his writing, Burke revised his survey so that it would center not so much on the concept of persuasion but more on identification. As he explained to Stanley Edgar Hyman in a July 31, 1947 letter, "After many attempts to find the ideal start for my Rhetoric, I finally found the ideal start. Wrote it. . . . Opening section: 'The Range of Rhetoric.' Home, home on the range of rhetoric. Where hammer and anvil sway. Where never is heard an encouraging word, and the sky is not cloudless all day."

In particular, he "began, for my anecdote, with Milton: Samson Agonistes, and the cantankerous old fighter's identification with same."
While interpreting "Samson Agonistes" rhetorically, as "literature for
use," Burke through "Samson" also disclosed the complexities associated with identification as the systematizing principle of his rhetoric.
Burke's brilliant analysis would remain the opening of "The Range of
Rhetoric" because it would accomplish all kinds of rhetorical work for
RM: among other things it erases clear differences between rhetorical
and poetic works; it illuminates the important role that myth plays in
structuring rhetorical identification; it reveals factional identification
as a struggle over property; and it offers the possibility of sanctioning
and forestalling violence through the war of words. In dramatizing
the processes by which one could disclose the complexities of identification through the elaborated analysis of a specific work (whether poetic
or otherwise), Burke was beginning to teach his readers how to carry
out similar interpretive processes within their own local, rhetorical
circumstances—an activity that he would develop further in *The War
of Words.*

Fourth, with the first major section in place, Burke turned to the next,
which he tentatively titled "Landmarks of Rhetoric," a selective account
of the history of rhetoric that claimed Burke's attention during the fall of
1947. In a letter to Watson on September 28, 1947, Burke described how
he was currently in the Landmarks section "wrestling with the job of
telling about Aristotle's *Art of Rhetoric,* Cicero's *De Oratore,* Quintilian's *Institutio Oratoria,* and fourth book of Augustine's *De Doctrina
Christiana* (with side-glances at Longinus on the Sublime)." Burke cut a
new angle on those works by reading "the whole five books as stages in
one 'curve'," the curve being the principle of identification. By establishing these works as core demonstrations of identification's role in rhetorical history, Burke could present new works as "off-shoots of the
principles already stated." On January 13, 1948, Burke was telling
Hyman that he had completed the "Landmarks of Rhetoric" chapter,
now renamed "Traditional Principles of Rhetoric," and he had given it
considerable new prominence in the structure of the book. When Burke
included the "Landmarks of Rhetoric" chapter in his original prospectus, he was imagining it mostly as a small, pedagogical section, one that
might even eventually be cut. But now the complete "Traditional Principles of Rhetoric" had grown to "over 50,000 words" (Burke to Watson, January 13, 1948); so comprehensive was its argument that Burke
in the same letter reported that he had decided to relegate "most of my

stuff on Rhetoric and Poetic to the third volume (being transitional btw. Rhetoric and Symbolic, it fits equally well in either)." "Traditional Principles of Rhetoric" would undergo some additional revisions before its publication in *A Rhetoric of Motives* in 1950, but Burke's descriptions of the drafted chapter indicate that it was not far from the published version. (As we will indicate, the length of "Traditional Principles of Rhetoric" would have the effect of making it difficult for Burke to include in *RM* his even longer section, "The War of Words.")

Fifth, Burke worked on one additional segment of "The Upward Way" during 1947 and the first months of 1948: he began to contemplate a segment entitled "Dialectic, Ideology, and Myth" that would eventually become Part Three of *RM*, "Order." The idea was to distinguish his theory of identification (which included the concepts of mystery, myth, and hierarchy) by placing it within a broader dialectical framework ("The Upward Way"). This move would substantiate Burke's claim that the rhetorical motive is a transhistorical phenomenon that is fundamental to the human condition as well as establish the theoretical infrastructure necessary to track implicit hierarchical identifications through what he would eventually call "socioanagogic analysis." This conceptual synthesis would sharpen the book's philosophical teeth and create the conditions for the sophisticated, particular, and situated analyses of the contemporary news media that Burke planned for *The War of Words*. As Burke noted on page 278 of the finished version of *RM:*

> As students of rhetoric, we concede the great persuasive power of mystery (indeed, even to the extent of wondering whether those journalistic apologists of capitalism may be most ironically defeated in their own purposes when they attempt to build up the notion that the motives of the Kremlin are "enigmatic," and "inscrutable," that the ancient mysteries of the "East" are threatening to sweep across the enlightened "West." . . . However, when we hold that there is a hierarchic incentive (with its "mystery") embedded in the very nature of language, when we insist that one would deceive himself who derived "mystery" purely from its institutional sources, we are not arguing for or against any particular set of institutions.

Burke's focus in the as yet unwritten chapter on "Order" would be on how the study of myth exposes the complexities of the rhetorical motive, and eventually that section on "Order" would enrich the philosophical vitality that accounts for the success of Burke's remarkable *Rhetoric of Motives*. (But by its very length, "Order" too would compromise Burke's plan to include "The War of Words" in *RM*.)

Burke with his family had repaired to Melbourne Beach, Florida, on December 15, 1947, to escape the New Jersey winter and to give Burke leave to write. In the letter to Cowley on January 26, 1948, he summarized his progress: "Of the said Rhetoric, there are now 75,000 words in final order. . . . In about another 25,000 words, I hope to have finished the entire 'Upward' section (of three parts, probably to be called, 'The Range of Rhetoric,' 'Traditional Principles of Rhetoric,' and 'Dialectic, Ideology, and Myth,' though the last of these [eventually entitled "Order"] is still yearning for improvement)." The book's argumentative burden is evident in Burke's characterization of the first three chapters as the "upward section"—it was the first time in his correspondence that Burke used such terminology to describe the arrangement of *A Rhetoric of Motives*. By mid-February Burke was telling Richard McKeon about these plans for the book, confirming its organization into an "Upward Way" and "Downward Way"; was sending Watson his finished "The Range of Rhetoric" and "Traditional Principles of Rhetoric"; and was explaining to Watson that he had already drafted 20,000 words on "Order" (with another 10,000 or so to go). On March 7, he promised to send Watson the first hundred pages of "Order," his elaboration of the ideas first expressed in his "Ideology and Myth" lecture. And on the last day of winter 1948, Burke could announce that he had finished "The Upward Way" in principle (he would fine-tune some additional details on "Order" later, while at the Institute for Advanced Study) and was now going to complete his *Rhetoric of Motives* by finishing up "The War of Words."

"The Downward Way": March–December 1948

Not that Burke had ever forgotten what he had in mind for "The War of Words." As we have noted and as the published version of *RM* indicates (vestigial references to "The War of Words" appear, for example, on pages 23, 45, 63, and 161 of *RM*), Burke was keeping "The War of Words" firmly in mind throughout his drafting of "The Upward Way." And so in his January 26, 1948 letter to Cowley, Burke outlined his specific plans for "The War of Words," his "downward section." It would include " 'Catalogue of Devices,' 'The Rhetorical Situation,' 'Scientific Rhetoric,' and 'The Rhetoric of Bureaucracy',", and involve the "sorting, revising, and arranging of notes already written," a reference to the notes he had been taking on the postwar rhetorical situation as early as the summer of 1945 and through 1947. Other documents in the archival record indicate that Burke composed those notes in consultation with and sometimes directly on excerpts from newspaper media, particularly the *New York Times*. While Burke's actual writing had been given over in 1947 to "The Range of Rhetoric" and "Traditional Principles of Rhetoric," and the winter of 1947–48 to "Order," he was still collecting raw materials toward "The War of Words," and during most of the spring and summer of 1948, he sought to put those notes into words.

The first order of business was "The Devices." Back in Andover after his winter in Florida, Burke reviewed his notes on rhetorical devices and began to compose in earnest. By May 5, 1948, he was in a position to tell Hyman about his early progress: "Only today have I finally got into manageable shape my notes for the Catalogue of Devices. (Or rather, for the opening 15,000 words or so.) Have made several beginnings, some of them quite extensive. But now at last I think I have hit upon the right approach." Two days later, Burke could announce to Watson that he had finished the first section of "The Devices," on the "Bland Strategy" device, and would soon turn to the closely related "Shrewd Simplicity"; and once "Shrewd Simplicity" was complete, Burke would set his sights on "Undo by Overdoing," "Deflection," and "Spokesman." Burke also requested Watson's feedback on sections of the Devices chapter that outline a general theory, sections that were complete but open to further revision if Watson saw a need for it.

> I am back at the part of my project where, some several years back, when I began to write up these same notes (though many have been added since), I found all the other stuff interposing itself. So now, after the Grammar, and the Mlbrn Bch section of the Rhetoric, I am caught up. The puffed-upness has now abated. The particular kind of tension and impatience that went with these unwanted but necessary preliminaries is gone. The writing becomes more of a driving, less of a being-driven.

By the third week of May, Burke had driven forward the first half of the "Devices" chapter. In addition to the five devices that Burke had discussed in his May 7, 1948 letter to Watson, Burke was now thinking about a number of others, all of them enumerated in a May 17, 1948 letter to Watson: "Yielding Aggressively," "Reversal," "Say the Opposite," "The Nostrum (Spiritualization)," "Say the Word," "Say Anything," "Putting Two and Two Together," "The Pointedly Unsaid," and "Failing to Make the Connections." (These titles endure in the final contents, except that "Failing to Make the Connections" became "Making the Connection" and "The Pointedly Unsaid" was relegated to a segment within "Making the Connection"; "Making the Connection" also gathered up the topoi "Putting Two and Two Together," "Say the Word," "The Relevant Association," "The Quid Pro Quo," "Letting the Situation Speak for Itself," and "The Imagistic Inundating of the Negative.") Burke continued to elaborate these sections of his "Devices," one after the next and all of it quite smoothly, until a more-or-less finished version was complete by the middle of July (Burke to Hyman, July 15, 1948).

And six weeks later he had finished "Scientific Rhetoric" as well, though not without misgivings. In a letter to Watson dated July 29, 1948, Burke reported on the prospects and challenges in front of him with "Scientific Rhetoric." He remained fixed enough on his aim: to point out how contemporary print media (especially in excerpts from the *New York Times* and *Christian Science Monitor*), wittingly or not, were misrepresenting the political situation and advocating for a persistent wartime stance—so persistent that it has continued to the present day. But the challenge would be to avoid getting bogged down in overly topical cases that could potentially alienate readers and reduce the book's shelf life. "Stylistically, it is perhaps the most difficult problem in the book. For one must look closely at things that don't deserve a glance. So it is a search for subterfuges" (Burke to Watson, July 29, 1948). Burke had become generally satisfied with the tone of his chapters, but Hyman still worried, along the same lines that Watson had taken, that "the political logomachy will just about get you tarred and feathered by the reviewers, and to the glory of no one" (Burke reported Hyman's words to Watson, May 30, 1948). And so on the same day Burke explained to Watson that he would remove any topical invective by means of a generalizing stylistic move, according to which the illustrations of each device would "be de-localized, exactly as I de-localized the personal anecdotes. They should be about subjects such as the Ambassador of Preenland, His Excellency of Pronia, The Grand Apex of Onlychurch II, etc. Factions shd. be not Democrats and Republicans, or Stalinists and Trotskyites, etc., but Ins and Outs, or Innables and Outables, or Perfectists and Loathesomites, etc." In this way Burke would also "more clearly point up the form (that is, the 'permanent element') in each anecdote." But Burke undertook this revision reluctantly. As he explained to Watson in a June 19, 1948 letter, "I don't think I have completely solved the resistance problem that Hyman made so much of (I think too much of—but if he kicked some, others will kick much more)."

Having addressed that problem to his temporary satisfaction, Burke announced to Watson on September 1, 1948, that he had completed all seven subsections of "Scientific Rhetoric": "'Facts' are *Interpretations,* Headline Thinking, Selectivity, Reduction (Gist), Tithing by Tonality, News as Drama, and Polls, Forums, and Accountancy." Burke considered the completed chapter "the most dogged accomplishment of [his] areer-cay" [i.e., his career] because over the course of its composition, he had managed to treat the material less polemically than he had in the initial note-taking and drafting stages. There were "still a few flare-ups here and there," Burke acknowledged, but these could be tossed out or moderated during the final revision process. Burke sent a typed, finished manuscript of "Scientific Rhetoric" to Watson on September 25, 1948, explaining in his accompanying letter that he was still concerned about its style—that the chapter was working dangerously on "the edge of platitude."

But the chapter was essentially behind him, and as he turned to his teaching at Bennington that September, he needed only to tidy up some details and to complete "Bureaucracy" and "The Rhetorical Situation" to be finished with *RM*. He had collected his thoughts and made beginnings on both chapters, planned to try out his ideas on his Bennington students, and imagined that a term at Princeton's Center for Advanced Study between late December and March would give him the time he needed to complete "The War of Words." At last.

The End Game: December 1948–April 1949

So why didn't "The War of Words" get finished and included in *A Rhetoric of Motives* after all?

To begin with, Burke got distracted as usual by the fall semester of teaching at Bennington. Burke always wrote comparatively little while he was engaged with his students, for his pedagogy often required the preparation of formal lectures and demanded that he devote attention to individual students. Burke was thus able to tinker a bit with "The War of Words" that fall, but not much more, and so in December, just after Harry Truman's unexpected victory in the presidential race, he wrote to Cowley that while most of *RM* was now complete, with some 200,000 words (about the same number as *Moby-Dick!*), he still had those final two chapters (and 30,000 more words!) to go. Nonetheless, he expected to be able to finish by the beginning of spring.

Then Burke's plans were further modified by his experiences at the Institute for Advanced Study between December 19, 1948 and March 27, 1949. The original idea was that the residency at Princeton would give Burke the leisure and comfort to complete the remaining chapters of his *Rhetoric,* i.e., "The Rhetoric of Bureaucracy" and "The Rhetorical Situation" within "The War of Words." Burke had become fond of getting away from the rigors of Andover during the winter months, when Bennington was between sessions, and so when his friends R. P. Blackmur and Francis Fergusson began lobbying (in the spring of 1948) for Burke to be invited to Princeton for the next winter, Burke figured that the arrangement would afford just the circumstances he needed to finish his book. Burke had known the amiable Blackmur for nearly two decades, ever since he had placed parts of his novel *Towards a Better Life* in Blackmur's little magazine *Hound and Horn* in 1929, and over the years, after Blackmur caught on at Princeton in 1940 and after *Hound and Horn* itself went under (in the process inspiring its successors *Southern Review, Sewanee Review,* and *Kenyon Review*), Blackmur and his wife had made several visits to the Burkes at Andover. Fergusson, an expert on drama and equally amiable, had been on the faculty at Bennington after 1934, so he knew Burke well after Burke began teaching there too. In 1947, Fergusson was accepted for what became a residency at the Institute for Advanced Study at Princeton, in part because he had been the college roommate of Robert Oppenheimer, who had just been appointed the director of the institute. The two of them, Blackmur and Fergusson, thus put Burke forward to the institute so that he could complete *A Rhetoric of Motives* while offering a handful of lectures at Princeton as the price of admission.[9] On June 24, 1948, Burke received an official invitation from Oppenheimer for a membership at the institute: Burke would stay on campus during the winter of 1948–49 and be paid $1,200. Burke therefore explained to Watson at the end of his November 23 letter that he would devote the next three months to "putting . . . the final revision" to *A Rhetoric of Motives,* hoping that the Princeton residency would give him the needed footing for executing the book as he had planned. On December 19, 1948, Burke, his wife, and their two sons moved into the living space provided by the institute.

For a time things proceeded as planned. There is no indication that the working conditions stalled Burke's efforts to complete "the Rhetorical Situation" or "The Rhetoric of Bureaucracy." Quite the opposite: he enjoyed meeting new colleagues (including Jacques Maritain), went to parties and threw one, and reported putting in long hours of writing, characterizing himself as a downright "revision machine" (Burke to Cowley, January 17, 1949); and the space and time afforded by the institute helped him make important improvements to *RM*. "We are in a very comfortable place," Burke told Cowley (January 3); "I am set up in a roomy office all to the self—all new and shiny." In a letter to Hyman (January 18, 1949), Burke elaborated: "Instead of revising by omission, I've tended to revise by addition. Some parts don't have the fuoco they had while I was writing them. They seem so tame, it's hard to think that during some of the said elucubrations the author was puffed up like a pouter pigeon." Some of the additions were no doubt to "The War of Words," but Burke was also touching up other things, "putting in sub-titles, pointing up the arrows," and so on. On January 20, he told Watson that "The Range of Rhetoric" and "Traditional Principles" were absolutely finished, but that still left tune-ups to "Order" and those last two chapters of "The War of Words."

Yet despite the setup at Princeton, Burke complained to Watson that "nobody could continue productive work here for any length of time." For one thing, the five lectures that he had committed himself to deliver-ing at Princeton were proving more distracting than Burke expected. On February 16, 1949, Burke told Watson that "I'm so damnably dizzy I don't know from nothing. I let Dick Blackmur book me up for five lectures," one of them to Blackmur's undergraduates, the others to insti-tute colleagues (as well as to Princeton faculty and students), and the lectures had "started falling due, and my book is still in need of quite some revision." Three weeks later Burke had completed the lecture series, offering sections from "Order" having to do with "The Rhetori-cal Radiance of the Divine" and courtship (*Venus and Adonis,* Casti-glione, Kierkegaard, and Kafka). Either the lectures were drawing Burke back to making additions and revisions to "Order" or he was adding them as planned.[10]

For another thing, at Princeton Burke was coming to concede that the developing *RM* was becoming unwieldy. As early as January 3, 1949, Burke acknowledged to Cowley that *A Rhetoric of Motives* had grown "into two sizable tomes," not one, and by the first days of March, in the midst of his lecturing responsibilities, Burke had firmly resolved to postpone the completion of "The War of Words" on practical grounds. He admitted to Watson on March 2 that while he was "batting away at a good clip" on revisions to "Order," he had also grown "weary" from the work and at the prospect of the final two chapters of "The War of Words." He would turn to a "grand finale" to *RM* instead ("The Rhetorical Radiance of the Divine"), hope that Watson would permit Burke to dedicate the book to him, and turn the book over to the publisher without "The War of Words"—but with that footnote on page 294 promising that *The War of Words* would be published "in a separate volume" (namely, this one). Hyman's concerns about the anticipated response to all the topicalities in "The War of Words" were lingering with Burke as he made the decision (reinforced when Watson expressed some of the same reservations as he responded to Burke's chapter on "Scientific Rhetoric" in December[11]), and no doubt the unexpected amount of energy it would take to complete "Rhetoric of Bureaucracy" and "The Rhetorical Situation" likely factored in as well. Perhaps the political fears associated with developing McCarthyism figured in too. At any rate, with spring term responsibilities at Bennington looming and with his publisher getting impatient, no wonder Burke decided to send what we now think of as *A Rhetoric of Motives* to press and to hold off on sorting out how to proceed with the now-book-length *The War of Words*. The relative hastiness of Burke's decision helps explain in part why some readers have had such a hard time making coherent sense of *A Rhetoric of Motives*: "The War of Words" was designed from the start to be the analytic realization of Burke's theory of the rhetorical motive, which constituted the first half of the book. Without *The War of Words, RM* remains incomplete.

In any event, on March 19, Burke pronounced *RM* "finished" (Burke to Watson). He was concerned that his conclusion had been rushed— "At the last minute, a whole new last chapter engrafted itself onto the organism ["The Rhetorical Radiance of the Divine," an extension of the socioanagogic analysis that he had developed in "Order"], and maybe I'll some day kick my pants that I let it do so, since it's the only one I haven't had time to let mellow"—but he would also proceed with some confidence because he had tried out several portions of that chapter during his lectures at Princeton and because he knew that his "Upward Way" was original, innovative, and persuasive.

Apparently the editors at Prentice Hall (or their in-house reviewers) were somewhat baffled by what Burke sent them. The archival record is silent on the matter, except for this comment by Burke in a letter he sent to Cowley on April 26, 1949: "I sent in the Rhetoric to the publisher some weeks ago—and he seems to be undergoing sorrows of some sort. Last week, one of the editors said, plaintively, 'But you have to *study* the book!' Whereupon rearranging my lines hastily, I came back indignant and thunderous. 'Of course, you have to study all my books.' Presumably he's still studying." Whatever the case, Burke did make additional small refinements to *RM* even as he completed his residency at Princeton at the end of March 1949 and before he resumed teaching at

Bennington through the end of June. (The Bennington term was interrupted only by the April 7–10 trip to the Western Round Table of Modern Art that we mentioned earlier; by a May 7 speech at Amherst; and by a Father's Day weekend seminar back at Princeton.) By November 1949 *RM* was in production. Burke was approving galleys in December and reviewing page proofs in February 1950, and *A Rhetoric of Motives* was published in April. The *War of Words* manuscript, which Burke had promised to provide "in a separate volume" in that footnote on page 294 of *RM,* remained unfinished. Burke didn't even tell his Prentice Hall publishers that it existed.

THE WAR OF WORDS AFTER 1950

What became of *The War of Words?* How did Burke's apparent indecision about it in 1949 turn into an ostensible decision to leave the work indefinitely unpublished? Definitive answers to these questions are difficult to provide, but letters and additional archival materials produced after 1949 offer some clues—as well as evidence that Burke never abandoned *The War of Words.*

What we do know is that after April 1949 Burke turned to *A Symbolic of Motives* instead of to the unfinished *War of Words.* He devoted much of the summer of 1949 to working out a long essay, "The Vegetal Radicalism of Theodore Roethke," that he imagined as one piece of the *Symbolic;* further, his seminar at Princeton in June 1949 allowed him the time to outline in more detail his plans for the *Symbolic* (Burke to Hyman, June 1949), and on June 20 he wrote to Watson that he was indeed "thinking more than ever of holding the War of Words section until after the Symbolic has appeared. Also, by then, things should have swung around a sufficient number of times for me to be surer of my over-all perspective. Meanwhile, I think I'll try to carve out bits of the material [in *The War of Words*] for possible magazine publication, lest someone else get a scoop on me."

Burke often published pieces of his books in various periodicals in order to promote his work, as he had done in the case of *Permanence and Change* and *A Grammar of Motives,* but only one such article excerpt from *The War of Words* actually made it into print, a piece entitled "Rhetoric—Old and New." In April 1949, just as Burke was submitting the final manuscript of *RM* to Prentice Hall, Burke received and accepted an invitation to spend two semesters at the University of Chicago. During the first term (late September until Christmas break) he would teach one course while mainly leading a Carnegie Foundation seminar for University of Chicago English teachers who wanted to invigorate their required freshman writing course by grounding it in rhetoric. During the second term (January through late March) Burke taught a graduate seminar—an opportunity to test-drive some of his ideas for the *Symbolic*, including his ideas on *Othello* (Burke to Watson, January 14, 1950)—as well as to offer some lectures to colleagues on the "Devices" (Burke to Watson, April 7, 1950) and to advise under-graduates on their projects.[12] As something of a grand finale, Burke served as a keynote speaker for the first meeting of the Conference on College Composition and Communication, at the insistence of Chicago English chair Henry Sams and John Gerber of the University of Iowa. For the occasion he offered to those teachers of freshman composition the remarkable "Rhetoric—Old and New": it was a précis of the con-cepts he had developed for the forthcoming *RM*, with comments on the "old rhetoric" that he had formulated for "Traditional Principles," on the "new" concept of identification, and on several of "The Devices" that he had discovered in the course of writing *The War of Words*. When that essay appeared in the *Journal of General Education* in 1951, readers without knowing it were getting the first published inklings of what Burke had in mind for parts of *The War of Words*, including an overview of "The Bland Strategy" and "Deflection." "Rhetoric—Old and New" remains an accessible and instructive introduction to Burke's full vision for *A Rhetoric of Motives*, to both the Upward Way and Downward Way. Other than that, however, Burke did not try to publish parts of *The War of Words*—though he did on occasion continue to promote its ideas. For example, at that August 1950 Harvard confer-ence on "The Defense of Poetry," he made a strong case (drawing from *The War of Words*) for poets to turn their energies to resisting the war machine; and as late as January 27, 1972, he was including excerpts from "The Devices" in a presentation at the University of Texas at Aus-tin entitled "Some Thoughts on the Rhetoric of Human Relations" (Burke to Cowley, December 10, 1971).

But mainly he kept his eyes out for opportunities to publish the full manuscript or large parts of it (typically minus "The Rhetorical Situa-tion" and "The Rhetoric of Bureaucracy"), although his initial hopes must have been tempered when Prentice Hall on May 31, 1950, point-edly invited him to publish his future books elsewhere.[13] One of his first thoughts was to expand the motives trilogy into a motives tetralogy: the *Grammar*, the *Rhetoric*, and the *Symbolic* would be followed by a book about ethics that would draw on *The War of Words.* "As things now look," he wrote to Hyman on May 7, 1951, "there'll have to be a fourth volume [in addition to the *Symbolic*], probably called 'On Human Relations,' combining the lore of The Devices and our still unpublished and still unorganized material on what we tentatively call 'affinities'." That idea persisted: a letter to Cowley on September 17, 1956, refers to Burke's "notes for the fourth book (the damned trilogy having become a godam tetralogy)"; on January 20, 1962, he reported to Watson that the ethics book, now two thirds finished, would "probably use the Devices which were the start of the whole bizz and which I never got around to revising and developing"; on July 5, 1965, Burke told Watson that he was still pondering the *Symbolic* and an *Ethics,* "including the lore of 'The Devices' in the second half"; and on April 26, 1969, he told Hyman that he been offered contracts by the University of California Press to publish four of Burke's books—one of them "The Devices," which "I've been sitting on long before you were wet behind the ears."

The University of California Press opportunity nearly came to fruition in Burke's lifetime. In 1965 Burke had connected with the press, and when their reissuance of Burke's novel *Towards a Better Life* went well, other volumes followed. *Language as Symbolic Action* was published by California in 1966, and the first printing (2,500 copies) was exhausted by February 1968. In 1967 Burke contracted with the press for his *Collected Poems, 1915–1967* (based on his Hermes Press *Book of Moments*) and *The Complete White Oxen* short stories, both of which appeared along with a new edition of *Counter-Statement* in 1968—the occasion for Denis Donoghue's omnibus review of those books (and the LSU Press's new 1967 edition of *The Philosophy of Literary Form*) in the *New York Review of Books* on July 11, 1968.[14] On September 8, 1968, Libbie Burke—already in great distress from Lou Gehrig's disease—suffered a serious stroke, but Burke was still able to arrange for California to republish *A Grammar of Motives, A Rhetoric of Motives,* and *The Rhetoric of Religion*—and to turn once again to the possibility of issuing *The War of Words*: "Incidentally, we once talked somewhat aimlessly about my showing you that MS on Devices (I fondly refer to it as De Virtues and Devices)," he wrote to Bob Zachary on October 17, 1968. "I had withheld it, at various times, for different reasons, including the need of later editing. But I now see how the editing could be kept at a minimum. . . . Are you interested in my sending along a copy, for your experts to meditate on?" Zachary, his Cal editor, responded favorably, and Burke sent the manuscript off on

December 2, 1968, accompanied by a December 4 letter explaining Burke's brief description of what he had in mind: "Basically, my dream is of this sort: They [the parts of *The War of Words*] should be included as part of a volume that GETS SHIT (watch it!) of the Motivorum outpourings for good." On December 8, Burke elaborated, as indicated in figure 3.

Burke's intellectual excitement about possibilities is apparent in this letter. Running over options as he writes, he ponders adding a revised version of "The Rhetorical Situation" (based on a talk he was preparing to deliver in Appleton, Wisconsin, on February 19, 1969)[15]; offers to consider updatings of "The Devices" and "Scientific Rhetoric"; and plans "to surround all this, before or after, with a summarizing statement about the project as a whole" and its relation to his *Symbolic* and possible *Ethics,* thereby "attempt[ing] to 'wrap up' my Treatise On Human Relations."

And yet a month later, Burke was expressing second thoughts. Discouraged by Zachary's tardy reply and much more "suicidally dispirited [by his wife's condition], I have figured out many compelling reasons why the Devices should be beyond rescue. So heck, jes send 'em back—and that's that. But I still do dare to hope that the Grammarhetorica Motivorum project still moves forward."[16] Zachary did not give up, however. "Please don't lose heart or decide against publishing them [i.e., the Devices] before I can say something halfway intelligent about them. The only question, it seems, is whether they stand alone or should have forematter and aftmatter, but they must see the light" (Zachary to Burke, January 23, 1969). In the ensuing months and then years, Burke and Zachary went back and forth. As Burke indicated in the letter to Hyman cited earlier, Zachary issued four contracts for four books, including what he called *Devices of Rhetoric,* just before Libbie's death on May 25, 1969, but Burke never returned the *Devices* contract with his signature. The two occasionally exchanged comments about the *Devices* in their letters of 1970, and in the spring of 1971 Burke got enthused about publication once again when he tried out "some of the Devices on the class" he was teaching at Clark University (letter to Zachary, April 27)—but again nothing materialized. In 1972 Zachary again expressed interest in the project after Burke's Austin presentation on January 27, but Burke couldn't settle his ideas about the contents. And on May 11, 1973 (after a Zachary visit to Andover) Burke wrote to both Zachary and Cowley that he was turning his attention to finishing the book, but by the end of the year his wish was still unconsummated.

Dear Bob,

Orm do I, after all, just mean mm eerie?

Best greetings from Ignatius Panallergicus.

I now grow more and more worried, lest my studipity in nut insuring the Devices may have undone me. (I have another copy, but it is unsightly, a dirty yellow. And it's poss. that my frenn Watson may still be able to dig up the copy I sent him, many years ago. But I'd feel much better, if the copy I levitatingly sent you reaches you.)

The general idea I have is this: I'd mmhimm for this ptikla portion of the project, the writing up of my talk on "The Rhetorical Situation: Congregation and Segregation." I'd introduce a few (quite a few) references to observations and formulations made since these pages were assembled). But basically I'd hold to my notion (admittedly a belated one) that, except for minor, incidental changes, I should leave the pages as they are. For, as I see things now, these things gain by distance. They're much better if, while cleansed of immediacy, they are felt to be in mmmmmm principle immediate all over again. Also, I could, if it were so desired, get out my packs of further clippings, and add a section mulling over mmmmm developments since mmmm the time when the present pages were immediate.

ALSO, I'd like to surround all this, before or after, with a summarizing statement about the project as a whole, discussing in particular the relation btw. Poetics and Ethics in the whole line-up. (Psst. I can now, as it were, SUM UP by LOOKING BACK on the project, even to the extent of saying what further step might ideally be needed here and there along the way.)

This would amt. to showing (a) just wherein the "equations" of a book coincide and diverge, as regards the character of a book mmm (Poetics) and the character of a person (Ethics). And (b) the "equations" (as embodied in mmmmm De Virtues and Devices) move questions of Ethics into the realm of practical finagling (and Ethics is par excellence the realm of thepractical). Here I'd love to add some pages looking back on Aristotle in the light of Machiavelli, who himself in turn is looked at in the light of my would-be COMIC study of finaglings. (I should remind: My chapter on "The Rhetorical Situation" is focal mm here, since it aims to show how beautifully and fatally Aristotle's concern with the principle of antithesis, purely as a stylistic device, merges with the sheerly practical resources of identification by segregation. And though recourse to this mm built-in device is not at any time inevitable, it is the perennial temptation of the human animal.)

In brief: I would here attempt to "wrap up" my Treatise On Human Relations, bymm not merely asseverating, but also retrospectively qualifying, and sometimes being frankly septuagenarian in my inclinations to both give and ask for quarter.

Herewith I rest my restless case. I thinkmthat, in winding up, I'd have a tale to tell (and maybe much more mellow a one than I often feel like, when lying awake at night). But there it is.

Sincerely,

FIGURE 3. Facsimile of a Kenneth Burke letter to Bob Zachary, December 8, 1968. Source: Kenneth Burke Papers, Penn State Eberly Family Special Collections Library. Source and credit: The Kenneth Burke Literary Trust.

As late as May 30, 1974, and again in August 1976, Zachary was still expressing interest in "the Devices," but when he left the press early in 1977 that was essentially the end of it.[17] In one of his later letters to Zachary (March 3, 1974), Burke expressed thoughts that are realized in this edition: "Heck. I got to taking a hard look at the MS, . . . and I see no grounds for its publication now. . . . Troubledness lies behind it, . . . [so] it shd. be published posthumously."

A NOTE ON THE TEXT

The authorized version of most of what we reproduce here as *The War of Words* has been in the possession of Anthony Burke because Kenneth Burke maintained that he eventually wanted it to be published. That authorized version, completed in 1948 and typed by Libbie Burke at Kenneth Burke's direction, consists of a fair copy of "The Devices" and "Scientific Rhetoric" chapters, with occasional short insertions, reformulations, and emendations penciled in later by Kenneth Burke. (This authorized version is included as items J34 and J35 in the Index of Catalogued Items prepared by Anthony Burke for Penn State's Special Collections staff; the manuscript remains in his possession.) The editors have incorporated those insertions and emendations; in a handful of instances the editors have also deferred to Burke's emendations on a carbon copy of the original manuscript that is also in the possession of Anthony Burke. Yet another copy of the 1948 typescript of the "Devices" and "Scientific Rhetoric" chapters is held in the Berg Collection of the New York Public Library—James Sibley Watson / The Dial Papers, Series 3, Papers Related to Kenneth Burke, box 10, folder 15J ("Devices") and box 10, folder 15I ("Scientific Rhetoric"). That version is identical to the chapters presented in this edition, except that Burke's insertions are missing and except that the "Devices" chapter leaves off after page 56—that is, 141 pages before the end of the authorized complete version of the "Devices." These chapters in New York were sent to James Sibley Watson on July 29, 1948 ("Devices") and September 25, 1948 ("Scientific Rhetoric").

The editors have reproduced "The Devices" and "Scientific Rhetoric" from the text that Kenneth Burke authorized, with only minor differences. Spellings have been regularized: e.g., "theater" for "theatre"; "Czechoslovakia" for "Czecho Slovakia"; "whereupon" for "where upon"; "maneuver" for "manoeuvre"; and so on. In some cases compound terms have been modernized with respect to removing a hyphen, adding a hyphen, or joining two words into a single word: e.g., respectively, "firearm" for "fire-arm"; "willy-nilly" for "willy nilly"; "warmonger" for "war monger." Certain variations in capitalization have been made consistent: for example, "Truman administration" instead of "Truman Administration." Some marks of punctuation have also been regularized to conform to current conventions, and a few paragraph divisions have been eliminated for the sake of reading ease. References in the text to "*NYT*" (to acknowledge quotations from the *New York Times*) were included by Kenneth Burke. Obvious typographical errors (e.g., "word" when "world" was intended, or "principle" in place of "principal") have been corrected. All other textual interventions by the editors are noted in the List of Textual Emendations and Explanatory Notes, at the end of this volume.

"[Notes toward] The Rhetoric of Bureaucracy" and "[Notes toward] The Rhetorical Situation" derive from documents at Penn State's Eberly Family Special Collections Library: Burke 3 [P20a], box 6, folder 22; Burke 3 [P18], box 5, folder 17. We emphasize that these two pieces derive from unrevised and incomplete manuscripts; while quite readable and quite interesting parts of *The War of Words,* they are nevertheless draft materials, and we emphasize that fact in the editors' headnotes at the beginning of the two chapters. We have again regularized spelling, compound terms, and punctuation and eliminated obvious typographical errors. Again, all other textual interventions by the editors are noted in the List of Textual Emendations and Explanatory Notes, at the end of this volume.

Appendix 1 presents a facsimile of "Outline of 'The Rhetorical Situation'," the original document of which can be found in the Burke Papers at Penn State: Burke 3 [P18d], box 5, folder 17; we include it for its relevance to Burke's intentions for the chapter to be entitled "The Rhetorical Situation." The numbers before each entry in the "Outline" correspond to the paragraph numbers indicated in brackets at the end of each paragraph of "[Notes toward] The Rhetorical Situation." Appendix 2, "Foreword (to end on)," as well as its facsimile (Appendix 3), is in the possession of Anthony Burke; it is noted as item J34 in the Index of Catalogued Items prepared by him.

Kenneth Burke's books rarely employ explanatory footnotes, so the editors have generally followed that practice here with *The War of Words* and the appendices. But in a few cases, for the convenience of readers we have identified contemporary references (e.g., "Garfield Oxnam" or details about the 1948 death of Jan Masarek) when they are not clear from the contexts in Burke's chapters, and added those identifications to the List of Textual Emendations and Explanatory Notes. Burke only occasionally offered his readers an index, and he prepared no index for *The War of Words,* and so the index at the end of this edition was prepared by one of the editors, in keeping with current practice at the University of California Press.

NOTES

1. Some of the letters to Cowley are included in Paul Jay's *The Selected Correspondence of Kenneth Burke and Malcolm Cowley* (Berkeley: University of California Press, 1990), though for the sake of accuracy we quote from the original letters (most of them not included in Jay) that are archived at the Newberry Library and in the Kenneth Burke Papers within Penn State Library's Special Collections. Burke's letters to Williams are quoted from *The Humane Particulars: The Collected Letters of William Carlos Williams and Kenneth Burke,* ed. James East (Columbia: University of South Carolina Press, 2003). Burke's letters to Hyman are in the Library of Congress, and the correspondence to Watson is in the Berg Collection at the New York Public Library. This introduction also cites *Letters from Kenneth Burke to William Rueckert, 1959–1987,* ed. William Rueckert (West Lafayette, IN: Parlor Press, 2003) and a letter to Richard McKeon archived at Penn State. Other letters to Burke referenced here are at Penn State. References to *A Grammar of Motives* and *A Rhetoric of Motives* in this Editors' Introduction are to the University of California editions published in 1969.

2. Without providing them here, we also invite readers to examine other essays that Burke conceived of as he was composing *The War of Words* but that he finally published separately—"Ideology and Myth" and "The American Way"—as well as the relevant unpublished lecture notes and drafts that are retained in Burke's papers at Penn State and in the files of the Kenneth Burke Literary Trust; consult the Index to Catalogued Items. In 1973 Burke published an essay entitled "The Rhetorical Situation" that is very different from the "[Notes toward] The Rhetorical Situation" that we include in this volume.

3. Throughout this Editors' Introduction we refer to "The War of Words" as the working title of what Burke was thinking of as a section within *A Rhetoric of Motives,* and to *The War of Words* as the title of this book, which became its own document over time, separate from *RM.* The title *The War of Words* likely derives from Jeremy Bentham, who used the phrase in his *Table of the Springs of Action,* in the section "Explanations of the Table." (We thank Ann George for pointing out this connection.) Readers of Burke (and of *RM* as well as this edition) will know that he was greatly interested in Bentham's writings; to this day, a visual representation of the *Table of the Springs of Action* hangs on a wall in his Andover home.

4. Michael Burke recalls hearing Ellison read the brutal passage from the "Battle Royal" section of *Invisible Man* in which sweating young black men are forced by white men to scramble for coins on an electrified carpet—as Michael and his brother lay on a carpet in the Burke living room.

5. While at Kenyon Burke fielded questions about *RM;* he and Empson offered a kind of debate over *Othello;* and Burke lectured on "Poetry as Symbolic Action"—"a treatment of the logical, rhetorical, and aesthetic aspects of literature" that drew from the book he was planning to write after *RM, The Symbolic of Motives.*

6. Burke recounted the whole process in a May 3, 1950 letter to Cowley, to assist Cowley in writing a review of *RM:* "Had originally intended to write a third volume to P&C and ATH. It was to be called On Human Relations. Had been taking notes (social strategies, diplomatic devices, ways of outwitting others and oneself, etc.). Began to write these up. Found they needed a general theoretical introduction. Thought a few thousand words would do it. But the project grew into the *Grammar.*" Burke confirms this account in the "Curriculum Criticum" that appears at the end of the Hermes edition of *Counter-Statement,* published in 1953 (pp. 217–18).

7. These are Burke's ellipses.

8. See Burke to Watson, April 27, 1947 (Berg Collection) as well as notes Burke made on his outline for the book on the same day: Kenneth Burke Papers, Burke 3 [Q22], box 12, folders 33–34.

9. To be precise: Walter W. Stewart formally recommended Kenneth Burke to Oppenheimer on March 30, 1948. Stewart was a Permanent Member of the School of Economics and Politics. Fergusson and/or Blackmur must have approached him to do so, as institute politics required that nominations be made by permanent faculty.

10. Incidentally, the lectures that Burke delivered at Princeton University in February and March of 1949 served as the model from which the Gauss Seminars in Criticism were developed. They continue to this day. Blackmur initiated the series, he and Fergusson served as the directors of the Gauss Seminars, and Burke returned to deliver others in 1952 and 1969.

11. Watson actually "doubt[ed] that there is much to worry about" concerning the topicalities, but he also suggested that Burke might "shift your attack from the Truman administration to Wall Street" (letter to Burke, December 5, 1948).

12. One of those undergraduates was Susan Sontag. Burke described her as "the best student I ever had" (letter to Hyman, August 13, 1963).

13. L.H. Christie, a Prentice Hall editor, somehow disappointed in the very early sales and reviews of *RM,* wondered if "we are the right publisher for you." He not only ignored Burke's expressed wish to publish *The War of Words* "in a separate volume" (and probably never read Burke's footnote on page 294) but instead remarked that if Burke wanted to publish the *Symbolic* elsewhere, "we would be cooperative." There is no evidence that Burke offered *The War of Words* to Prentice Hall.

14. This account of Burke's relationship with the University of California Press vis-à-vis *The War of Words* is intertwined with the complicated story of his dealings with Mildred Ligda and her Hermes Press. Having met Burke at the Kenyon College Summer School of English in 1950 and possessed of a printing press, Ligda during the winter of 1952–53 hosted Burke and his family at her place atop a mountain overlooking Los Altos, south of San Francisco and near

Stanford University. For the next several years Ligda through Hermes repub-
lished editions of *Counter-Statement* (1953), *Permanence and Change* (1954),
and *Attitudes Toward History* (1959), as well as Burke's *Book of Moments*
poems (1955). Burke even wrote an introduction to a projected Hermes edition
of Bentham's *Table of the Springs of Action* that ultimately fell through. Suffice
it to say here, however, that although Ligda knew about *The War of Words*, saw
its first two chapters, and was willing to publish it, Burke's relationship with her
grew more distant in the 1960s, especially after Ligda fell into financial difficulties and Burke turned his attention to Bob Zachary and the University of California Press. Burke always retained the rights to the Hermes editions, refused
Ligda's late 1967 offer to publish *The War of Words*, asked Ligda in March
1967 to return the copy of the manuscript that she had seen, and never made
any substantial effort at all to publish *The War of Words* via Hermes. Ligda's
extensive correspondence with Burke is in the Kenneth Burke Papers at Penn
State.

15. It would eventuate in the 1973 article by Burke, "The Rhetorical Situation," in *Communication: Ethical and Moral Issues*, ed. Lee Thayer, 263–75
(New York: Gordon and Breach Science).

16. By the "Grammarhetorica Motivorum project," Burke meant the plan
for California to publish *A Grammar of Motives* and *A Rhetoric of Motives*, a
development that indeed transpired in May 1969. In 1984 California published
new editions of *Permanence and Change* and *Attitudes Toward History*, completing the effort to make Burke's major works available from a single source.

17. Zachary was passed over for the press directorship in 1977 and drifted
toward retirement, partly due to health concerns and partly to avoid conflicts
with the new director. But he and Burke continued to correspond and commu-
nicate by phone well into the 1980s. On August 8, 1976, Burke even sent Zachary a "quickie Preface" for the Devices manuscript—it may (or may not) be the
document included in this volume as Appendix 3: "Foreword (to end on)."

The War of Words

Introduction

In the opening chapter of this section, we classify and describe characteristic rhetorical forms employed in the struggle for advantage that is essential to the Human Comedy.

Next we shall consider the typical rhetorical resources available to journalism and other mediums that deal in the distributing of information.

In both of these chapters, we shall lay stress upon the verbal element in Rhetoric. However, since the examples we consider involve human relations, a measure of non-verbal material will also figure. The third chapter, on the rhetoric of bureaucracy, will deal with instances where administrative or organizational factors are exceptionally prominent.

And the fourth chapter will attempt to state what we consider to be essentials of present conditions implied in the characteristic rhetoric of social relations, the press, and administrative persuasion. It should be as extra-verbal in reference as we can make it; for it concerns what we consider to be the ground of the Logomachy today. Since so much of Rhetoric is Symbolism *for use,* and the use applies to factors that often are not mentioned in the Rhetorical expression itself, the import of much Rhetoric can be grasped only by considering the non-verbal reality behind the verbal appearance.

CHAPTER I

The Devices

OF THE DEVICES IN GENERAL

In this section, we hope to deal with many sorts of examples, as though they were all on an equal footing. That is, for our purposes, relations between a man and his dog, or a bully and a toady, or a big imperialist country and a small overwhelmed one, might be treated as alike. Hence, if we illustrated a device by using examples chosen from all three orders of subject matter, we should be abiding wholly by our rules.

The political example might stir up passions which the other two did not. Or even worse, it might seem more "timely" than the others, hence more ephemeral. But by bringing out the formal element in a political maneuver, however a matter of the passing moment that maneuver was, do we not isolate the universal ingredient in it? The particulars change from day to day, but the principle they embody recurs constantly, in other particulars. For this reason, we consider a passing phase of politics, such as a typical pronouncement of the Truman administration, to be as permanent as fleas.

The aspect of the Scramble will change with changing conditions. These conditions themselves can be better or worse. But the human relations expressed through the Scramble will, *mutatis mutandis,* prevail under all historical conditions. "Human nature changes," in the sense that the means of livelihood, the quest for advantage, and the idea of order change. But "human nature cannot change," in the sense that we can abstract from various situations an essence common to the lot, transcending all details. Yesterday's sneeze is gone forever? The "principles" of that sneeze are eternal.

The Bland Strategy

In *The Idiot,* Ippolit accuses Mishkin of learning how to "make use of his illness." Mishkin, he says, has managed to offer friendship and money "in such an ingenious way that now it's impossible to accept under any circumstances." Mishkin's behavior has been "either too innocent or too clever." Ippolit is here in effect giving the formula for blandness.

Irony, in its simplest form, says one thing to imply the opposite (exclaiming "Splendid!" when meaning "Abominable!"). Blandness is a practical application of this principle. It is irony for use. Irony that never quite shows its hand; hence there is always the possibility that the surface meaning is the true one.

Warlike gestures made in the name of peace are bland, as when a "trouble spot" receives a "goodwill" visit by the fleet of a foreign power. Or would one nation call attention to the fact that she is moving troops near another as a threat? She can do so blandly by announcing the troop movements along with the statement that the troops are not intended as a threat. Or troop movements can be given significant pointing by special announcement of their dispatch, along with assurances that they are merely a "routine action."

A friend said: "I once had an uncle who was gentle enough, but enjoyed watching fistfights among children. Each Saturday he would get a dollar of his pay changed into pennies; and calling the children of the neighborhood, he would toss the pennies one by one, while saying unctuously: 'Just scramble for the pennies, and each of you can keep as many as he gets. But no pushing, no shoving, boys—*and above all, no fighting.*' While thus setting up the conditions of the Scramble that almost automatically made for a fight, he could blandly call for peace, confident that war would come before he had tossed a dozen pennies."

One can blandly "forget," as when Miss Prone was recalling vividly a memorable visit at Miss Preen's. Feeling warm at the memory of that past happy occasion, Miss Prone told of it in detail. Seeing an opponent thus off guard, Miss Preen enthusiastically praised Miss Prone's memory, "confessing" that she herself could not remember the occasion at all. The implication was, blandly, that Miss Prone's life must have been a starved one, in comparison with Miss Preen's, if Miss Prone thus cherished as a rich memory an occasion that Miss Preen had quite forgot.

A slightly deaf dowager was victimized by the blandness of the Misses Preen and Prone, thus: She *burned* with curiosity, wanting not to miss a single syllable and often humiliating people by making them repeat pointedly in a loud voice remarks that were worth only a low, diffident mutter. As a result, those who lived with her gradually began to conceal from her things that they would not mind telling to anyone, if only their remarks were not followed with avidity. She put such a high value on even casual gossip that the gossiper came to cherish his remarks for their value as rarities. The Misses Preen and Prone had lived with this situation long enough to become demons at it. As they conversed, while the dowager was ostentatiously reading a book, one of them reassured her obligingly: "We'll speak in a low voice, so as not to disturb you." And a little later, "We're not talking too loudly, are we?" Speaking low, so as not to disturb the deaf.

It is somewhat like the blandness of an overeagerness to please, as with Miss Preen's constant expression of concern for the health of Miss Prone, from whom she had detached an admirer. Miss Preen's solicitousness was meant to announce that she had scored. Miss Prone might be counter-bland, in thanking Miss Preen warmly for her generosity.

Or there was the case of Joseph who, without funds, had married a rich Josephine. At first, in all simplicity, he paid for his keep by being assiduously attentive. Then slowly over the years, a perverse, and even morbid blandness emerged in his treatment of her, unbeknownst to them both. Joseph began to plague Josephine with his worries for her welfare. He did not let her live a moment without the feel of a doctor's hand on her pulse. He was so attentive that no one could fail to comment on his devotion. And in her unexpressed and inexpressible desire to poison him, she felt so guilty that each day she became more sickly. Here was a situation worthy of the André Gide who wrote *The Immoralist*. Blandness could go no farther.

Japanese officialdom exploited a blandness of this sort. Soon after the surrender, when the U.S. army of occupation moved in, the local bureaucrats confounded the victors by being painfully meticulous in the desire to cooperate. They never tired of asking for "clarifications" of military orders, so that they might obey to the last letter. They were even "scrupulous" in reporting their own violations and misunderstandings of any order. They were so anxious to please, the very thoroughness of their compliance led our newsmen to fear a ruse. It was a ruse, and a particularly complex one. First, it allowed the imperial bureaucracy to bide its time. In this respect it was experimental maneuvering for a good position from which to feel out the enemy, without necessarily having any definite plan of future action in mind. Eventually, it could hope for the state of affairs that later developed, when the capitalists would again begin building up the very interests they were now tearing down. Meanwhile, the officials could take bland satisfaction in making the conqueror sick of his own regulations. For instead of attacking these regulations, they tirelessly thought up bothersome questions supposedly intended to "help put the regulations into effect."

An ironically bland kind of "cooperation" is said to have taken place during the German invasion of Czechoslovakia. The Nazis had been sending spies among the Czechs. These spies would spot anti-Nazi patriots by going to Czech cafés and talking "confidentially" against Hitler. Soon the Czechs learned of the ruse. Hence, next act: Nazi spy comes to café where Czech patriots are gathered. In the role of *agent provocateur*, he talks against Hitler. Whereupon the Czechs virtuously pummel him "for saying such things against the Führer."

There is a common variant that works well in charges of political corruption. It runs: Our opponents should invite this investigation of them, for if they are innocent, the investigation will prove it.

Bland irony also permits insult by hospitality. Thus, Prone comes to visit Preen. Preen promptly invites him to the corner saloon for a drink. Nothing more hospitable than being invited to have a drink on your host. But you are in effect being *asked out*. After the drink, Preen begs earnestly to be excused, hurrying away "to another engagement." The blandness is in the fact that this insulting sequence can also be enacted in all simplicity and goodwill.

A housewife provided the deftest instance we ever found of blandness that unmistakably made its meaning clear and attained its purpose, yet did not show its hand. Mrs. Prone and Mrs. Preen were next-door neighbors. Though their husbands earned about the same income, Mrs. Prone used much better tea than Mrs. Preen. This fact became clear when Mrs. Preen once came to borrow tea, which she later repaid in kind, with her own inferior brand. So she began to borrow tea quite regularly, always repaying in the same quantities of inferior quality. Though Mrs. Prone soon recognized the pattern, she made no protest. She merely kept some of Mrs. Preen's tea in a separate canister, and gave it back to her the next time Mrs. Preen came to borrow. Neighborly relations were strained for a few days, then, thanks to the blandness, a new *modus vivendi* was established, and without further traffic in tea.

In one variant of blandness at a meeting of the U. N. Security Council during the Iranian controversy, the American chairman sat silent while the Iranian ambassador was allowed too much latitude in presenting his case against the Soviet Union, and then severely called him to order *after* he had used his opportunities.

Or recall the occasion when our navy "inadvertently" let out the information that the Russians had been inefficient, non-cooperative, and repressive while supposedly helping us establish bases for meteorological observations in Siberia "in accordance with the Potsdam conference agreement." The implication was that they were thus blocking the normal progress of science. But at the end of the story one learned that the disruption came at a time when our military forces were conducting "cold weather combat testing operations" jointly with Canadian units, and when the navy was sending its giant carrier Midway on an expedition to the Arctic. So, in the name of international science, we had been blandly asking the Russians to help us assemble meteorological data for possible use against them if conditions worsened. And there was doubtless a counter-blandness in the Russians' ineptitudes and interferences.

When our Ambassador to Poland was inaugurating a tour of the United States, to work up feeling against the new Leftist government in Poland, he resigned his office, according to the story in the *New York Times,* "for the purpose of letting the American people know more of conditions than was proper for the State Department to reveal through publication of his official records." He then gave an interview where "it was insisted that the former Ambassador was speaking personally." But though now a private citizen, and stressing the fact that he had no differences with the White House or the State Department, he held his interview in the reception room of the Secretary of State, the room where the Secretary of State holds news conferences. And "officials of the press relations office of the State Department were present and from time to time prompted him on points as they arose in the course of his observations." Technically, we'd call this arrangement bland, since the official stamp was being presented in terms of the unofficial, without sacrificing of the official significance. But the Department did make certain that it wouldn't be *too* bland. In keeping with the genius of the Truman administration, this diplomacy had the subtlety of a blackjack. Recall the old saw of the father winding the clock as a hint that the daughter's admirer was staying too late. Truman diplomacy would amend the device delicately by having the father add, "This isn't meant as a hint," while he next went to put out the cat.

Blandness is sometimes close to hypocrisy; yet we would not call Tartuffe bland. One can even be so bland that he need not be sure just where the line between simplicity and cunning is to be drawn, in judging his own motives. To praise the valor of those you vanquished can be downright "noble," though its blandness, as a roundabout way of paying tribute to oneself, is revealed when, after a game of tennis, a gratified but embarrassed victor burlesques his enthusiasm about the "insuperable playing" of the opponent he has just beaten.

It was out-and-out hypocrisy when a host, to discourage a prospective guest, told him of the forbiddingly bad conditions into which he would be plunged. But what of the guest? Did he suspect that the circumstances were misrepresented, so that they might act as deterrents? He answered, saying: Where things were in such a deplorable condition, there he should be. And so he arrived, with the zeal of a missionary. And after arriving, he expressed his surprise at finding that, though he had anticipated a very bad state of affairs, to his great relief things were quite calm. Where are we? He really *was* sacrificial-minded. He really *would* take on problems. At the same time, he sensed a certain overdoing of the report. So he was bland in his way of announcing that he would come, and bland in announcing his surprise. This was not Tartuffism; it was true blandishment.

We go farther afield, though still remaining within the outer confines of the bland, with the formula, "our hands are tied," whereby a mighty nation can supposedly be deterred by "solemn pledges" its statesmen have at some time given to some petty chieftain or other. Thus the British were "prevented" from agreeing to the return of certain colonies to Italy because of promises made to the tribe of Senussi in North Africa. The tied-hands device under such conditions is particularly convenient because it need not tie the hands except when so desired. For obviously, when the hands of a large nation are tied by some very small one, the mere granting of minor favors, or the threat of withholding such favors, would be enough to get agreement for the revision of a pact. For a cartoon, one can imagine a diplomat crying, "Our hands are tied," while kicking away a kindly wayfarer who naively offered to untie them.

Or, you can go a step further, and tie your own hands, if there is no one to help you. It was thus with the Truman administration's policy in first killing the distribution of European relief through the United Nations and then bypassing the organization on the grounds that it was unable to deal with such problems. The first step "tied our hands" in making UNRRA unworkable, so that we could not work with it. The same diagnosis, but without reference to rhetorical devices, is in a report from Lake Success by Thomas J. Hamilton (*NYT,* 3/19/47): "As the United States also prevented the United Nations from establishing an agency to continue supplying food to war-devastated countries, it is felt here that Washington is responsible for the fact that unilateral action is necessary."

Blandness is par excellence the menace of a friend. Given blandness enough, one person might "cooperate" another off the map. Where lion and lamb are in the same "co-prosperity sphere," each will have its kinds of foxiness. Here we impinge upon such devices as popularly go by names like "Trojan horse policy" and "boring from within."

Shrewd Simplicity

Question III, Article VII of the *Summa Theologica* explains that God is "altogether simple" (*omnino simplex*). All that exists divisively in the multiplicity of nature (*divisim et multipliciter*) preexists in God's unity and simplicity (*unite et simpliciter*). Here is the Grammatical ground for those paradoxes whereby the devout man was asked to make himself "a fool for Christ" (as in Chapter XVII of Thomas à Kempis on *The Imitation of Christ*), or of those transformations whereby a pagan clown could become Parsifal of the Holy Graal. Here is the Grammatical ground for Rhetorical devices that equate the simpleton with the lovable, the stupid with the wholesome.

Obviously, we are still on the subject of Blandness. But usually there is more of a "front" about Blandness than marks many instances of Shrewd Simplicity. "Blandness" refers to the looks from the outside; "shrewd simplicity" names from within. The line readily becomes obscured because we are considering the reality behind appearances. So, if you prefer, think of this section simply as "Blandness—continued."

But our present term seems more direct for describing the "place," for instance, which Al Smith exploited for invective when in a St. Patrick's Day talk (1939) he called the Nazis "just plain stupid," and "original boneheads who will never get to first base." But the Communists were "cunning," there were "smart babies . . . past masters of the art of roping them in." Sum total of Smith's equations: Don't worry about Fascism; it has the harmlessness of the comedian (hence furtively also something of the comedian's lovableness?); keep your attention focused on Communism. We could hardly say that Smith was being "bland." But he was certainly shrewdly exploiting the resources of simplicity.

Similarly, a lawyer defending a man of Fascist sympathies on trial for sedition assured the jury that whereas his client had been piously worried about Leftist attacks upon the Church in Spain, he "isn't the smartest man in the world, by any manner of means." The defendant was contrasted with the Leftists, who were pictured as shrewd, keen, skilled in plotting.

The dangerous intelligence. In a syndicated column by a financial dopester, we read that the author had "just returned from a conference on wages," where "labor was represented by a very smart lawyer," and "management was represented by a kindly employer." Under the circumstances, one could not match the ominously bright with the reassuringly stupid, so instead of "stupid" one finds the adjective "kindly" which, in the device of shrewd simplicity, it is meant to suggest.

The device was carried through an entire book in Jaroslav Hašek's *Adventures of the Brave Soldier Schweik in the World War,* where the hero avoids unpleasant military duty not by rebellion but by being the soul of stupid good nature, a man with deftness in his daftness.

And there is similar simplicity for use in the ways of one who is magnificently careless about money matters, but somehow it turns out that he short-changes others much more often than they short-change him.

Unquestionably, here is the point at which the ideals of Christianity meet the essence of secular comedy. In his role as a "stumble-bum," the comedian so bungles that, by comparison, the stupidest member of the audience is bright and competent. (We sense what grave misgivings about themselves people must have, when we see what extremes of stupidity the comedian must simulate to make his audience feel reassured.) And by the paradox of substance, along with such curative comparison between comedian and audience, there is the relief of having stupidity thus vicariously confessed, through the audience's "wholesome" identification with him as the lovable comic scapegoat, the fool of Christlike simplicity.

The "good n*****" in the South is expected to play this role of the lovably harmless, to master the art of being perennially "childish." And he can gain certain restricted advantages by living up to the part. But as an ironic reflex of this attitude, members of the ruling class become so sympathetically affected by their norm for Negroes (equating stupidity with wholesomeness) that they expect their own women to be as free of political, economic, and sociological enlightenment as they want the Negroes to be. Sexuality, poetry, grief—vs. politics, sociology, grievances.

Likewise, women often perfect a device of "creative innocence" that would induce through unconcern. And for every woman who delights a man by her strength of character or companionship, a hundred charm and flatter their purchaser by simulating a stupidity that reassures him, and would make a successful marriage impossible if it were really as genuine as they both take it to be. Financially unsettled American men love a stupid woman almost as much as they love a raise in salary. In fact, her supposed stupidity makes amends for his failure to get the raise. Some women, born rhetoricians, can manage a large family with almost fantastic efficiency while being the butt of all the family jokes. Their secret competence, unavowed even to themselves, is masked by a fiction of incompetence that makes all the other members of the family feel good by comparison, makes them love themselves so much that they can love everybody.

Might not the story of Benjamin Franklin in France be the perfect instance of shrewd simplicity, exploited as a rhetoric device? The sly Franklin, a banker of bankers, expert in the nascent lore of capitalism, taking the role of a Rousseauistic noble savage, exploiting Europe's identification of all Americans with the Indians and the primeval forests, though Franklin actually represented a property structure having ways of thought wholly alien to the aboriginal societies it was obliterating. Ironically, the decadent French court, in its ritualistic motives, was probably nearer in essence to the Indian culture than was the new utilitarianism of finance and applied science which Franklin represented. Knowing that he could not qualify by proficiency in the norms of France, our wily ambassador apparently made a virtue of necessity, gallantly breaking all the laws of gallantry, and outraging ceremony by improvising ceremonies of his own. This "naïve," "comic" character got what he came for, having made all France laugh in contentment at his delightful bungling as he applauded a speech in his own honor.

But perhaps the most ingenious variant of shrewd simplicity, in international relations, appears in a statement made by Lord Salisbury in the nineteenth century: "British policy is to float lazily downstream, occasionally putting out a diplomatic boat-hook to avoid collisions." Or there is the remark of similar tenor, about the Empire's being founded "in a fit of absent-mindedness." This air of lackadaisicality in the spreading of British might imperceptibly suggests that the blasting of native spears by cannon, the swamping of native canoes by dreadnoughts, was the antics of a comically harmless clown, lovably irrelevant, wholesomely stupid.

The traces of the Christlike in shrewd simplicity can lead into a related device we have elsewhere called "Christian vengeance." Thus, you can accuse a man roundabout by constantly "forgiving" him. Or you can be *too* zealous in his defense (an out-and-out weak defense would lack the added "Christian" ingredient). When Voltaire said, "I can take care of my enemies, but God save me from my friends," he doubtless had the ways of Christian vengeance in mind. Soviet politicians are subjected to an effective dosage when the Church prays "nonpolitically" for the welfare of the Russian people.

Perhaps because women make greater efforts to be sympathetic than men, while at the same time there is the tradition of internecine warfare among themselves due to conditions of the marriage market, they seem to have a greater incentive for using the appearances of sympathy as a means of combat. Women's most telling blows at one another are through words of endearment, or by what popular speech, in a mood of rhetorical analysis, calls "backhanded compliments." This is the formula for the "catfight" at its best. Thus, knowing that the hat is Mrs. Prone's, Mrs. Preen acts as though she thought it belonged to someone else, and whispers to Mrs. Prone confidentially that she considers it an atrocity. (Hedda Gabbler: "Oh, it was a little episode with Miss Tesman this morning. She laid down her bonnet on the chair there . . . and I pretended to think it was the servant's.") However, since the game is played without an umpire, the contestants sometimes get out of bounds, and fall to using outright invective (changing from "cat" to "fishwife") rather than abiding by the rules of blandness according to which one must never quite show one's hand.

As for Christian vengeance "properly" used, a friend, a teacher in a girls' school, said: "One student, Preeny, in great distress, begged me to do something for another, Prona, who she feared was going to pieces from overwork. For she had found Prona in a positive rage, complaining bitterly of her assignments. Since I was responsible for most of these assignments, I hurriedly phoned her, but found her quite calm and affable. She explained that Preeny had been overanxious about her, and the matter was dropped. Not until later, when I discovered that Preeny and Prona were no longer on speaking terms, did I understand what elaborate schemings had been involved here. Previously I had publicly praised Prona for her patience and affability (in implied contrast with Preeny, who was bellicose); and Preeny's air of sweet solicitude had been designed to inform me of Prona's bad temper."

And thus when Q had told a dear friend about a compliment he had received from an elderly man of importance in academic circles, a man whom they had both greatly admired in the past ("one of our country's grand old men," Q now said, glowing with praise of the man who had praised him), his friend answered earnestly, "I am glad you saw him. How is he holding out? Are his faculties still sound?" The question was so spontaneous, so genuine. Was malice discovered by accident?

There can be the vengeance of charity, too. Envy wanted Lucky to get a little. / Lucky got a lot. / Lucky, gloating, said to Envy, / "Guess how much I got. . . ." So much for the situation. Knowing how ungenerous Envy was, Lucky had expected him to make a low estimate. But Envy was more complex than that. By the device of Christian vengeance, he realized, this was the time for him to be exceptionally generous. So he named an estimate much higher than Lucky could possibly have got. Hence, when Lucky told the exact amount, by comparison with Envy's handsome estimate it looked niggardly.

Our previous stories of Joseph plaguing Josephine with attention could fall neatly under the head of "Christian vengeance"; and, lest the expression be interpreted too literally, we should also note that the principle figures in the incident of the Japanese who made their helpfulness a hindrance.

In another variant: If your audience considers A an obnoxious object, and you would damn the thing under discussion by calling it an A, you may do so suavely by praising it as an *excellent* A. Thus, whereas you might ungenerously damn a statement as a lie, you could treat it "generously" by praising it as a very able lie. Accordingly, when Soviet Deputy Minister Vishinsky in meetings of the U.N. Assembly was attacking "warmongers" of the United States and Britain, the *New York Times* published an article by James Reston, "Vishinsky in Difficult Role Wins Support as an Actor," in effect calling it a weak case by praising him for his skill in upholding it. Confronting such "appreciation," we understand why a Demosthenes, eager to make a point, will concede that Aeschines is really better at words than he is, while he himself must try to make up for his own shortcomings by a somewhat slow-witted earnestness.

But here we come close to devices of "attack by weak defense," as when, in *Tom Sawyer Abroad,* Tom is disgusted with Huck and Jim for their inability to understand why the slaughtering done by the Crusaders was so noble an example of religion. Or there was the bepuzzlement, in *Alice in Wonderland,* because the watch clogged with butter wouldn't run, though "it was the best butter." Here we move into areas more directly treated under other heads.

An effective variant, an ironic admission of bewilderment when the user of the device has already established himself with his audience as a person of perception, is discussed by Stanley Hyman in his chapter on T. S. Eliot (in *The Armed Vision*). The method is to attack a not difficult thing by declaring that it is beyond one's understanding. Thus Eliot, he says,

> has protested that he is able to make no sense whatever of the fifth stanza of Shelley's "To a Skylark." . . . He has maintained that Keats's line: "Beauty is truth, truth beauty," "means nothing to me," and so on. It is obvious that this sudden pose of dullwittedness is meant as Socratic irony, both from the examples he chooses (always the fuzzier sentiments of romantic poets), and from the fact that he has praised F. H. Bradley for "his habit of discomforting an opponent with a sudden profession of ignorance." It is ironic that one of his bitterest critics, Yvor Winters, should have attacked him almost exclusively in that fashion.

A shrewd teacher, polemically inclined, may use a device of this sort in efforts to discredit a colleague in the eyes of students. For his "admission" that the colleague's doctrines are "too much for" him to understand, suggests *a fortiori* that students should not expect to get profit there either. The device has further value: when the user really cannot understand the work he is disparaging, his overeagerness to say so can suggest that not he, but the work alone, is to blame.

Meanwhile, to round out our remarks on shrewd simplicity in general: Think of the promoter, who was of so contagiously trusting a nature that he could swindle others with false promises through being able to swindle himself. Or consider the admonitions of the Angelic Doctor on "voluntary mental blindness" (*voluntaria caecitas mentis*). Where our relations to God are concerned, he says, any deliberate closing of the mind to reality is a sin. But we should note that, in secular matters, judged by the tests of rhetorical devices, bland blindness can have much in its favor.

At times, were the principle of Shrewd Simplicity endowed with utterance, it might express itself thus: "Why be a plotter? By merely forgetting to stir the milk, you can pour yourself cream."

Undo by Overdoing

A toastmaster, concealing malice beneath a show of generosity, could subtly turn an audience against a man of *much talent* by praising him as an *exceptional genius*. Formula: Since a buildup prepares for a letdown, assure the letdown by making the buildup vulnerable.

Similarly, one who begins by not complaining may in time learn to not-complain with great unmistakableness. The victim of such a powerful, though inaudible rhetoric will grow dizzy, whereas the more vocal sorts of complaint will make him deaf.

A friend, a psychologist, said: "One patient made unnecessary trouble for herself by trying to be the center of every gathering. I advised that, just as an experiment, she try being in a group of people for an entire evening without making a single bid for attention. She tried it— and was aggressively retiring. She was as unnoticeable as if she had carried a sign announcing, 'I am being unnoticeable.'"

We once heard a speaker making a partial defense of Communism before an audience of Catholics. This was before the period when anti-Communist animus had reached a high pitch. The speaker began by saying that he had no intention of pitting Marxism against Catholicism. First, he had no desire to do so; second, he realized that by the nature of his audience any such effort would be bound to fail. He assumed that they were good Catholics, and that they meant to remain so. But he did think that the Marxist critique could be of help in guarding against the *misuse* of religion. And he assumed that a truly religious person will welcome any criticism, from even the unfriendliest of sources, if it could admonish the devout as to ways in which religion might be misused. He then proceeded to show how, as economic conditions gradually change, the hierarchy of a Church, even in all simplicity, can become aligned with sinister social and political forces. He dealt mainly with instances of the remote past or in foreign countries where the hierarchy had become aligned with large absentee landowners. Analogies suggested themselves, but he did not point them up. He next went on to show how a kind of religious motive can infuse the conduct of a Marxist despite the formal effort to disclaim them. At least, he pointed out, the average churchgoer is usually much less zealous than the Communist in his self-sacrifice and devotion to what he considers human betterment.

The speaker was making some headway. No great amount, probably, for he was speaking in a Catholic Church, in the presence of many priests, and to an audience of the faithful. But at least he had cut into the areas of strong antagonism. The audience was tolerant. Perhaps some members were even sympathetic, perhaps too sympathetic. For of a sudden, someone in the audience shouted fervently, "Thank God for the Communists!" Immediately the rapport was snapped. A roar of protest went up. The mood of "both-and" was gone; things were bluntly back in the realm of "either-or."

Having no clear idea of the motives in the mind of the person whose fervent exclamation had unloosed the avalanche of protest, we shall make no attempt to account for it. But if, for our present purposes, you hypothetically imagined planting confederates in an audience, with instructions to prevent an undesired response by an overzealous expression of it, you would have a perfect instance of undoing by overdoing. The exclamation made the speech unfit for the situation by creating a situation for which it was unfit. It got its effect by forcing the violation of a major dramatic law: it introduced a resolution that had not been prepared for.

Benedetto Croce once brought down such an avalanche upon himself, through an error in procedure that called forth an unprepared resolution. The irony in this case was that he had, grammatically, prepared for his next remark by asking a rhetorical question, which he intended to answer himself. But in form a rhetorical question is addressed to the audience—and his audience promptly roared out the answer, the *wrong* answer. He was talking in Naples, at a meeting held in his honor, during Allied occupation soon after the fall of Mussolini. He asked rhetorically, "Do we want to abolish the monarchy?" He had intended to answer the question himself, by proposing a regency; but before he could say his "No," the audience shouted a thunderous "Yes!"

Demosthenes, in one of his battles with Aeschines, is said to have deliberately led his audience into an apparently unruly response, which he could then turn to his purposes. He was asking whether the Athenians considered Aeschines a hireling of Philip. But he slightly mispronounced the word for "hireling," whereat the audience, insistent upon good Greek, shouted back at him the correct pronunciation. As they thus shouted "Hireling! Hireling!" he remarked with satisfaction, "You hear what they say." They had loudly proclaimed Aeschines the tool of a foreign power.

Croce, as a speculative philosopher, might be expected to make oratorical mistakes which an actor, skilled in the theater, would naturally avoid. It takes no Demosthenes to know that a faulty preparation for a line is in effect its undoing (an undoing, if not by overdoing, then by an under-doneness that has the same result). And the next step is, as with the Demosthenes tactic, deliberately to make a move that looks like a blunder, thereby drawing out the audience as preparation for one's next move. Thus, during Roosevelt's fourth campaign for the Presidency, Orson Welles seems on one instance to have got exactly the effect he wanted, by deliberately using a faulty preparation. At a time when the press was working up popular feeling against strikes (unjustly giving the impression that they were widespread and were causing a disastrous drop in production), Welles addressing a conservative audience declared that no American soldier had to go without implement or weapon because of strikes in the United States. After his statement was vigorously booed, he disclosed that he was quoting from General Marshall, who was then at the height of his reputation. The speaker thus tricked the audience into an overdoing. And one can easily imagine that he could have had confederates in the audience primed for that one, making sure that the audience booed by starting the demonstration themselves.

In Ibsen's *An Enemy of the People,* does not the fourth act utilize a subtle variant of this same principle? His *Ghosts* having aroused public indignation, this play was his answer. And the Dr. Stockmann who is presented as being persecuted for his support of a righteous cause is also allusively spokesman for the author of *Ghosts.* In the fourth act, Dr. Stockmann confronts an unfriendly audience on the stage (as the playwright with his play was confronting a potentially unfriendly audience in the pit). But the unfriendly audience on the stage is overprompt in its clamor against Dr. Stockmann. Hence, by allusion, they overdo the attack against Ibsen. And their rowdyism thus serves as a lightning rod to draw off the possible charge of Ibsen's audience. By overdoing their protests, the members of the stage audience turn the real audience in the other direction, arousing furtive sympathies with Dr. Stockmann as the underdog (having Christlike connotations); hence allusively the audience is moved towards sympathy with the scheming playwright whom the hero represents.

As for the trials, during the recent war, of persons charged with Fascist conspiracy against the United States, we assume that the prosecutors honestly intended to get a conviction. But our thoughts about the device of undoing by overdoing suggest that, had they wanted to be sure of failure, they should have acted exactly as they did. They should not have begun by selecting for trial what were obviously the most vulnerable cases. Rather, they should have lumped the whole batch together (as they did), trying those accused of major offenses along with those accused of very trivial offenses. And by thus overdoing the process, they could be reasonably sure of undoing it. As it was, the only victim of the trial was the judge, who was apparently so undone by the overdoing that he was exhausted, and died within a few months. We might contrast this lump trial of the Right with the separate trials of the ten persons accused of contempt in refusing to testify before a Congressional committee concerning their alleged membership in the Communist

Party. Here, at least, there is to be no risk of an undoing by overdoing. (We should also note that, under certain conditions, mass trials are not a weakening of the prosecution, as with the Moscow trials of "The Anti-Soviet Bloc of Rights and Trotskyites" and the various war-guilt trials after the Second World War. In such cases, one gets the advantages of what Trotsky called an "amalgam," whereby the guilt of each scores against the others. In such cases, the "undoing by overdoing" may figure in a different way, however. With many persons, for instance, the very effectiveness of the Moscow Trials was taken as evidence that they were themselves a conspiracy.)

Where much might be gained by joining forces with a good ally, the proposal can be attacked on the grounds that he is not better. Thus, the pro-Nazi forces in the United States used isolationist sentiment (against *all* foreign entanglements as bad) to aid the rise of Hitler. And the fiction of the non-intervention in Spain was used as a device to help Franco suppress Spanish republicanism. Preventing the good, in the name of the best. "Perfectionism" as excuse for inaction. In heretical violation of the proverb, Better a snotty child than his nose wiped off.

Standard bargaining practice: to price at five when you hope to sell for not less than three. But by the subtleties of undoing by overdoing, in some situations the result can better be got by asking for too little. Thus with the old sea-captain, now retired. He tended a dock for pleasure boats, living nearby in a little cabin stocked with supplies for yachtsmen, etc. A man of wealth asked him to cane a small seat in a canoe. When the work was finished, the charge was twenty-five cents. This wealthy man, who was used to being overcharged and had become almost a fiend at inspecting bills for possible mistake of a nickel in the sums, was thrown off his balance. And to make up for an absurdly excessive undercharge, he handsomely overpaid. Had the wily old seadog himself overcharged, he would have met a fury of resistance. Had he made the proper charge, he would have got just that. But by asking for much too little, he got far too much, plus the wealthy man's praise of him as one of nature's gentlemen, of rare simplicity.

Or, applying a Kierkegaardian expression, we might say that, since his income and that of his wealthy client were "incommensurable," he found a way of turning this disparity to his advantage. He also set up a kind of expectancy wherein future overcharges might go unquestioned, as with the rustic who did a small repair job on his city neighbor's country house, not for a little, but for nothing, refusing to accept any pay whatever, insisting that he did the work purely to "help out." By establishing such "incommensurability," he set up a situation that enabled him later to overcharge without arousing even a murmur of protest.

Yet there may have been some point to the wealthy man's admiration of the old sea dog. At the basis of such roundabout bids for advantage, there can be fears and pieties almost magical in motive. Understatement can have its origins in the sense of cosmic drama, in the uneasy appreciation of the technical fact that, for the most effective drama, pride must go before a fall. It can be as with those primitives who, lest their children excite the envy of heaven, give them humble, or even repugnant names. For no god, desiring a fit victim, would deign to consider, say, even a couple's favorite son, if he happens to go by the essence-bearing name of Little Loathesome Stench. (However, recalling our previous concerns with hierarchy, we should also note that such pious humbleness towards heaven seems to have been most prevalent in cultures like that of India, where the magic of the caste system was most extreme.) In any case, as with those who belittle themselves to elicit praise, whether the device arises out of a feeling for dramatic irony, or pious humility, or superstition, or caste, from it can emerge a shrewd simplicity, a cunning advantage which, though not the kind for empire-building, can materially benefit a certain modest percentage of peace-loving souls in an empire-building society.

Another variant of undoing is by the weak defense, damning with faint praise. A friend said: "While out of sorts, I was walking with two of my friends who were in most irritatingly high spirits. Finally they decided that they should in some way penalize me, on the grounds that I was not in sympathy with them. When I pleaded that my disgruntlement had nothing to do with them, and that I was actually quite in sympathy with them, they decided I should be penalized because it was unpardonable for anyone to approve of their foolishness. In sum, I should be penalized because I was either in sympathy or out of sympathy. Things looked bad for me until I thought of this argument: I swore that I was unsympathetic only with those aspects of themselves which they themselves so discerningly condemned. But I greatly admired them for their admirable qualities, such as their imaginativeness, their intelligence, and above all their scrupulous love of justice tempered by mercy. At this they were stumped for a moment. Then they decided to relent. They admitted that I had not been given a fair trial, for I had been denied the services of an attorney. So, still touched by my tributes to their high qualities, they appointed one of themselves to defend me—and he promptly lost the case."

Mrs. Q tells Mr. Q how badly the children behaved while he was away. She gets Mr. Q so aroused that he paddles them. Later, when he is absent, Mrs. Q consoles the children. And she puts in a good word for Mr. Q, explaining to them that he works hard for their good, and that he was irritable from overwork.

Or a Secretary of State in one nation calls upon his people to be calm about events in another nation—and he describes these events as a "reign of terror."

An inversion of the principle was worked in an article by a journalist who was building up a possible candidate for President. First, a long panegyric. Then, to temper the panegyric, the writer also added some "admissions" of "shortcomings." The great man had shifted his policies; and he had made mistakes. However,

> If he was wrong, so was his country. If in the Nineteen Twenties and Thirties he was a little too cocksure, a little too proud, a little too vain, so also was America. If he has swung round with honesty and sincerity and tried to work hard to avoid mistakes of the past, he has done no less and no more than his country has done.

Thus, when the writer comes to admitting his hero's "faults," they turn out to consist in his having been exactly in tune with the temper of his country as a whole. The "faults" of this man, as a possible candidate to represent us, are that he is thoroughly representative. The example belongs here only by antithesis. It reverses the process of damning by faint praise, as with the man who "confessed" about himself that he was "too sincere."

In the way of more overt sparring: Preen was not content with telling Prone of successes. He incidentally kept suggesting comparisons with Prone, who had a much lower income, and he made sure that Prone didn't fail to get the implications. Prone suffered in silence, until one day a demonic idea struck him. He said, indignantly (with an indignation leveled not at Preen but at the world in general): "You are not being paid enough. I know men with less enterprise than you, and with nowheres near the ability, who are getting much higher incomes. Look at So-and-so, and So-and-so. Compared with me, it's true, you are getting a lot already. But compared with them, you're still not getting anyways near the amount that your kind of work can bring." Prone had rebelled; he had undone Preen by overdoing Preen's own line. And he got respite. The subject of comparative income was dropped.

There is blandness in overdoing, when the trickster does not show his hand. But as you apply the device for purposes of farce, burlesque, satire, caricature, the irony becomes obvious, the animus is clearly indicated.

In satire, the effect can be got quickly by merely turning things around, treating the to-be-avoided as the to-be-desired. Thus, an article calling attention to the drastic wastage of our soil could be turned into satire by taking as its theme, "A Treatise on the Most Efficient Methods to Effect the Depleting of Our Soil."

Or often, when the principle of undoing by overdoing is satirically applied, it could be said to get its effect by an excess of consistency. This is the basis of many cartoons. Thus, to cite from the *New Yorker:*

A holdup in a modern antique shop. Burglar in courtly, eighteenth-century costume, with ancient firearm. . . . Couple standing upside down, on roof of cave, suspended like flies. Surrounded by enormous stalactites and stalagmites. Caption: "I never could tell the difference between a stalactite and a stalagmite." . . . An undertaker, teaching his dog to play dead. . . . A family coming from a Quonset hut, their bodies of the same hemispherical shape. . . . Pickets of a typographical union, their signs in fancy type. . . . Pickets before a cut-rate store, their signs showing markdowns in their demands. . . . Governor Dewey when, as Presidential candidate, he was dodging as many controversial issues as possible. He counts sheep as he goes to sleep. The sheep are not jumping the fence, they are walking along it. . . . Horses stretched along a race-track. Their order in the race corresponds to the numbers on their saddles. . . . A row of houses all alike. In front of each, there is a tree, of identical size and shape. Every tree is bare, but for one leaf, which is in the same corresponding place on each. . . . Woman shopper, on stretcher, being carried by attendants in department store. She exclaims "Where am I?" just as they pass the clerk at the Information booth. . . . Three soldiers, camouflaged with leafy branches. Two are standing erect; their camouflage is similarly erect. The third is bent and dejected; and his camouflage is drooping, as he says, "I don't know—I've just felt miserable all day." (This last is an excellent burlesque instance of what, in the *Grammar,* we call a "scene-agent ratio," as states of mind are "analogously present" in the surroundings.)

Yielding Aggressively

Closely allied to the previous strategy. Indeed, "excess of consistency" could equally well fit under either head. Sportswriters have a similar behavior in mind, when they speak of a fighter who "rolls with the punch." When the poet calls upon the rolling sea to roll on, O Sea, he embodies a principle which, if used for advantage beyond the confines of pure utterance, makes for aggressive yielding. Or when Margaret Fuller announced that she had "accepted the Universe" (the occasion that made Carlyle exclaim, "By God, she'd better!"). Or when the wrestler converts his antagonist's attack into a device for throwing him. Blake had the same principle in mind when writing, "Dip him in the river that loves water." The story of Midas is another variant. The popular expression, "You asked for it," is grounded in this principle. Likewise saying, "Have it your way," when the speaker proceeds to use this ruling against you.

Like the leader following his mob . . . or like the medium who, before a congregation of elderly people, announced that she saw the spirit of a "little old lady," and asked whether perchance any of those present had lost a mother, or like the critic who wrote to a poet, "I believe your book has not yet received the careful treatment it deserves." . . . Or as with the stories of the Westerner among savages when, knowing that a solar eclipse is due, he establishes his prowess as a magician by calling upon monsters to eat up the Sun god.

Yielding aggressively, in its most prevalent form, becomes merely the rush for the bandwagon, or the politician's haste to identify his measures with any cause that happens to be in popular favor at the moment. Defiance of a weak or distant enemy. Convincing the convinced. Propagandists winning battles at home. The cock bold on his own dunghill.

The device is clearly like excess of consistency when it says in effect, "Very well, if you would have it so, let's have it thoroughly so." Thus: Recall the days of Hoover's presidency when, during the Depression, the destitute built themselves shacks of old boxes, tin, and other junk, on empty lots, and when, as a tribute to the exponent of "rugged individualism" who let them go unaided while bailing out big financial institutions handsomely with public credit through the Reconstruction Finance Corporation, these communities came to be called "Hoovervilles." Some years later, during the reaction against Roosevelt, some Congressmen proposed to change the name of Boulder Dam to Hoover Dam. Democratic Senator Glen Taylor then suggested that they go a step further in the ex-president's honor, and change the name of Boulder City to Hooverville.

W. C. Fields used the device in a motion picture where he played the role of a cardsharp who, to outwit other cardsharps, posed as a tyro. We forget the details, but here is the design: They taught him poker, in order to swindle him—and he "learned" with bungling slowness. Once, when he had a high hand, in aces, and was about to rake in the pot, they explained to him that aces were low. He raised no objection, bided his time, and finally he dealt one of the cardsharps four aces, while dealing himself, none too imperceptibly, four deuces. Of course, the other man bet heavily, on the strength of his higher hand. Fields then blandly put down his four deuces and took the money. He had let them have their way. They had made their bed, let them lie in it.

Girl-less, girl-minded boys loafing on the corner. Girl walks by briskly, disdainfully oblivious of the gents inspecting her. They whistle a tune in time with her pace, and thereby have her keeping step to their tune. A gallant kind of forcing. . . . Motion pictures adapting the motions of animals to human fictions sometimes embody the same principle, in taking "shots" of the animals at random and then supplying plausible human commands which the animals can seem to be obeying. Occasionally the obedience is made too pat, to get not merely a personalizing effect, but a comic excess. . . . Or when a child is being teased to laugh against its will, the child may force an artificial laugh as a way of stifling an involuntary one.

The promoters of a somewhat dubious venture requiring that investors "furnish references" before their money would be accepted. Surprise! All applications met the requirements. . . . Sometimes, of course, limitations *are* maintained. The property is worth twenty dollars an acre? Then call it "restricted," and sell it for a hundred. . . . The customer would buy but one? Let the sign read, "Not more than two lots to a customer." . . . In priestly magic, where the thing is worthless, guard it, to make it valuable. (Mark Twain's burlesque variant: Tom Sawyer making the boys pay to whitewash the fence for him.)

Primus, knowing that Secundus has something on him and is about to strike, goes to him, saying, "Frankly, I am in an embarrassing situation. I need your advice and help," thereupon telling him "the truth," which he knew already. If Secundus does strike, things are no worse than they would have been had Primus not asked for help. And his act may clear the air, change the situation, reform the alignments sufficiently to forestall the blow.

Thus the employee, fearing that his employer was beginning to lose confidence in him, interrupted the dangerous continuity by saying, "Frankly, I am not satisfied with my own work of late. And I was hoping you might give me some advice as to how I can improve it."

Where there is no retreat, meet your pursuers like a host welcoming a guest. . . . If a burglar has you covered, invite him to make himself at home. . . . In all such cases, you would be "yielding aggressively."

When indications were that all the workers would abide by the union's call to strike, the company published a request that the "loyal" employees stay away also. . . . The public being apathetic about a clash abroad, officials issue a statement earnestly calling upon them to remain calm until the matter has been investigated. . . . Soon after the Nazis began their occupation of France, spokesmen for the "free French" called upon the people to stay indoors at a prearranged hour, as token of their sympathy with the Resistance. The time chosen was siesta hour on Sunday, when a maximum number would normally have been indoors—hence, by this demonstration *in absentia,* there was no way of spotting the "demonstrators."

When someone objected to the blackness of the sails in Turner's "The Burial of Wilkie," the painter answered that he wished there were some color to make them blacker. In form it is the typical rejoinder of all artists. The novelist avows that he aimed to get the very effect which the critic objects to. Burlesque variant: Sculptor, looking at his production, musing, "The head seems out of proportion. Maybe I'd better call it 'Woman With Large Head.'"

A very effective variant of this device in the field of partisan politics is got by *demanding what is about to be given.* One faction learns that another faction is planning to grant a bounty for the purchase of goodwill among the voters. It immediately starts demonstrations *demanding* the bounty. Hence, when the bounty is voted, the demonstrators can claim that it was granted because of their agitation. . . . In accordance with this principle, we often thought that the European Left, in their attacks upon the Marshall Plan, would have been much more effective if, instead of thundering against it, they had clamored for ten times more.

Or if a measure has already been agreed upon, but time is needed to work out its details, any opposition voiced in the interim can be interpreted as "making sure" that the measure will pass. Thus, the passage of the first Greek-Turkish aid bill in the spring of 1947 was a foregone conclusion; but after Henry Wallace spoke against it in England, his speech could be interpreted as having "lent great assistance to a project he opposed." Similarly, during preparation for the granting of the first big "Marshall Plan" fund for Western Europe, the final passage of the bill was so certain that, for weeks at a time, there was not even a quorum present during Congressional speeches, which were made for the Congressional Record alone, and often before a nearly empty chamber. Yet repeatedly during that time, whenever the Leftists in Europe made any notable move, this could be effectively interpreted here as an act that was sure to cause retaliation by an overwhelming approval of the funds. Until finally, after the establishment of a Leftist regime in

Czechoslovakia, our public was encouraged to have the impression that our entire program in Europe was formed in response to that event, which had "made certain" that the foregone conclusion would come about.

A friend said: "Once a traffic policeman whistled me down for passing a red light. He motioned to me indicating where I was to park, while waiting for him to give me a ticket. But I misunderstood his directions, which he took as evidence of further infractions. He came rushing up in fury, announcing ominously, 'Now you *will* get a ticket.' I was going to get a ticket anyhow, but as a result of my error I would get a ticket with twice the assertiveness. I think of the incident when considering the psychology of national defense. Thus, one nation builds air bases that threaten the security of another. The other nation takes steps to protect itself against the danger. Spokesman of first nation then announces grimly: 'Now we *will* build bases.' "

Obviously, in diplomatic, political, and legal battles, precedents can be used for this purpose. A nation that sets a precedent when it suits their purposes is reminded of this by foreign diplomats when it would violate this precedent for other purposes. "Last year you laid down such-and-such a principle. You had it your way. Very well, now recall the same principle, on this occasion when it would tell against you." Hence, in meetings of the U.N. Security Council, where precedents are only now being established, the majority decided that "each case should be settled on its merits"—which means that precedents cannot be a source of much embarrassment to them so long as they retain their majority.

A child offered the subtlest variant we know of aggressive yielding. He was upstairs, playing with his fire engine. His mother called for him to put away his blocks, in a box that was downstairs. When she came upstairs some time later, she found him still playing with his fire engine. Mother: "Why haven't you put your blocks away?" Child: "The fire engine is going back and forth looking for the box I keep them in." Mother: "You know very well that the fire engine can't find it there, when the box is downstairs." Child: "Yes, but the fire engine doesn't know it." Here the blandness seems to have been attained through three stages: (1) In his game, he is having things his way; (2) the mother answers, without impairing the rules of his game; (3) the child then answers by treating his way as her way, and thus "using her way against her."

In relations between the United States and the Soviet Union, the Russians aggressively yielded on a grand scale when (in May 1948) they transformed a very blunt statement of United States grievances into a bid for peace. According to James Reston's interpretation (*NYT*, 5/12/48), four-fifths of the note "dealt with the United States determination to pursue its present policy toward the Soviet Union." And the remaining fifth, which referred to "the possibility of talking things over," was nothing more than a "routine gesture of good-will." Yet the Russians published the note, with their reply, and with such international trumpetings as for a day startled the whole world into sunny hopefulness, and gave us a few hours of perfectly idyllic living, until our spokesmen got into their stride again and dragged us back into our dungeon.

Acting *as if* a movement were on, and swinging into the movement. " 'Accepting' what was not offered" (Arthur Krock's formulation). Blandly interpreting a diplomatic formality as a bid, perhaps somewhat as though you were to get a letter addressed, "Dear Sir," and were to treat it as evidence that your correspondent loved you. (Except that in this case our spokesmen wanted the thing both ways at once, explaining that while the remark was routine, yet it was to be taken as genuine evidence of our good intentions, regardless of the recent great increases in our preparations for war.)

Deflection

More of an end than a means—and so general an end that nearly all of the Logomachy could be included under it. In a sense, any slightest bias in presentation is a deflection. Since even the most imaginative, intelligent, virtuous, and fortunate of men must err in their attempts to characterize reality, some measure of deflection is natural, inevitable. Insofar as special interests can gain advantage by deflections in the vocabulary of criticism, no great unimaginativeness, unintelligence, viciousness, or bad luck is necessary to set the conditions for the Rhetorical coaching of deflection. Add now the fact that there is a woeful lack of imagination (as evidenced by the radio, cinema, and popular magazines), that intelligence is rare (as evidenced by the quality of the journalism by which people are goaded to action), that if men are not more vicious than normally, at least their vices are better organized ("rackets" being but organized crime), that the very newness of our modern complexities and powers is in itself a misfortune as judged by the needs of cultural adjustment—and you find little reason why the Rhetoric of deflection should not be everywhere. Deflection is so perennially effective when deliberately used, because it arises so spontaneously. The

Freudian notion of "displacement" in dreams indicates how close it is to the roots of natural human evasiveness.

Thus a child, provoked when made to give his brother something that he wanted to keep, began crying bitterly because his brother hadn't said "thank you." His brother promptly said "thank you," whereupon the child cried all the louder, "because he didn't say it soon enough." He replaced a *what* with a *how*, like aestheticians who find an alien politics "unbeautiful."

Similarly, a variant of deflection is used in many satiric jokes, where there are two infractions, one large and one small, and laughter is elicited by placing the stress upon the small one, thereby implying that the large one is not important. Thus with the anti-Roosevelt joke of the man who asked the Court for authority to change his name. When the Judge heard that the petitioner's name was Franklin Delano Stink, he promptly agreed that a change was justified, and asked what name the petitioner chose to take instead. The answer was: "Joseph Stink."

Or there is a "universal" kind of deflection in the antics of the comedian who, interrupted just as he is about to kiss the heroine, in lonely hunger turns and passionately embraces a marble statue posturing nearby. . . . Such "universal" deflection is likewise recognized and its recognition made comic when, the villain having shot the comedian's stooge, the comedian complains, "Everything happens to me!"

Instance of unintentional deflection: In his *Ideology and Utopia*, when trying to illustrate the deceptions in perspective and the ways of correcting these, Karl Mannheim uses the example of a peasant boy who, had he remained in the country, would have taken the local perspective as "reality," but who comes to the city, and by his experiences there greatly widens his perspective. The instance is adequate, offered in all goodwill. Yet note how it subtly reinforces a narrow perspective in the very plea for a wider one. For it leaves out the converse example, of the city dweller who might, in coming to the country, widen his perspective (*fortunatus et ille deus qui novit agrestes*). The distinction is tenuous. But in choosing one of these examples as your model, you deflect attention from the other, giving your theory of motives a metropolitan or agrarian bias respectively. (Indeed, considering the close traditional relations between "nature" and "God," one could even say that the author's choice implicitly contains the design of the book itself, which proceeds from religious to secular terms for human motivation.)

Henry Adams says of John Bright: "He struck, in succession, pretty nearly every man in England that could be reached by a blow, and when he could not reach the individual he struck the class, or when the class was too small for him, the whole people of England." The thought suggests kinds of deflection that are grounded in the most typical convenience of reasoning, the use of wider terms that subsume narrower ones. For if you attack an individual in the name of his class or nation, you have in effect *deflected* your aim, almost like getting at him vicariously by kicking his dog. Common applications of this standard linguistic resource are found in sarcastic references to "some people," as in the awful thing that "some people" do, when *one person* present here and now is doing it. The shift from genus to species to species to genus, that Aristotle notes as a resource of metaphor, would provide deflections similar to this logical resource in the realm of imagery.

In the polemics of capitalism vs. socialism, an equivalent result can be got by widening or narrowing the scope of motivation. (See *Grammar* on "Scope and Reduction.") For instance, you can treat an element common to both as though present only in one, or an element of one as though it were common to both, or even to all mankind. Thus, though bureaucracy is present in all complex societies, the charge of bureaucracy could be popularized by the Trotskyites as a special vice of Stalinism. (Similarly, in the United States, though every business organization is bureaucratically organized, the charge is often applied only to the Ins by the Outs.) Or since both capitalism and modern socialism are based on machinery, cultural problems due to machinery per se can be attributed exclusively to the political structure that goes with it. Deflections of this sort are particularly available because all political systems have so many elements in common. Indeed, probably all the same motives are to be found in all political systems, though differently *particularized,* and in different *proportions* (and it is such particularizations and proportions that the abstractions employed in political controversy can so readily obscure).

By the same token, any reduction of a situation to an image can serve as a deflection when the image, if taken literally as a model, misrepresents important aspects of the situation itself. (Recall Bentham on "archetypation.") There were disastrous deflections in the Churchillian rhetoric that invited the peoples of the West to shape their policies in terms of "life lines," "power vacuums," and "iron curtains." The "power vacuum" was perhaps the most insidious invention of the "cold war." One could almost see an emptied place, forcibly drawing nearby movables into it, and thus sucking in the Russian armies, whether they wished it or not, unless our forces filled the void instead. And one could next imagine that, with our forces there, "Communism" would be "contained" (as though it were something that came from *without*). And when the military aid but added to the strain, as we supported reactionary governments that would otherwise have fallen by their own weight, people were invited to consider this too in terms of the "power vacuum." Such images, treated as ideas, are like cartoons taken literally. Let's at least use several, or mix them experimentally. So we propose tentatively that the international problem be discussed as the need to fill the power vacuum of the soft underbelly of the British Empire's lifeline lest it be cut by the iron curtain.

A characteristic kind of spontaneous deflection arises thus: Wherever there is control along with disorder, the *control* can be blamed for the disorder. But if the controls are relaxed and there is disorder, the blame can be laid to the *absence of controls*. Since both the controls and the relaxed controls are policies of government, it follows that government can be blamed for everything. This is a happy condition for our businessmen, whose discordant relations to one another require political controls; for they can condemn the conflicts of *politicians* who but represent the conflicting interests of *business*.

Deflection is got by a changing of the terms in which a question is considered. Such shifts in the angle of vision are precisely the way whereby new inventions, either practical or speculative, are hit upon. (For "it's good to be shifty in a new country.") A friend said: "I once saw a bird caught in a schoolroom, and fluttering in bewilderment against the ceiling. The teacher explained the bird's predicament as an instance of 'tropism.' For in obedience to some irrelevant instinct, it sought to escape by flying straight upwards whereas, had it but dipped a few inches, it could have escaped by any of the large windows, opened from the top. In behalf of his trade (he taught logic and philosophy) the teacher observed how simple it would be to help the bird escape, if we could but use a few words to modify its instincts."

Now add the use of words, and deflection as a rhetorical function enters. Out of words as liberators, it can make a new order of confinement. Where verbal inducements can be given, by drawing the lines at the wrong places words can create in effect a new level of "instincts" that keep us looking in one direction when the solution lies in another. Intellectually, words deflect by thus drawing the lines in the wrong places. Emotionally, they deflect by so distracting us that we cannot systematically ask ourselves whether the lines are drawn right (as a "color line" can deflect the terms of social criticism).

Theological doctrines were deflective, in attributing to the will of God impoverishments caused by the private appropriation of the common lands. A corresponding "scientific" deflection today is in the Geopolitician's thesis that "Imperialist rivalries are simply a matter of geography." Or deflection is implicit in the mere *selection* of "facts" (a major rhetorical resource of journalism). Emotionally, deflection can be got by introducing a stronger interest, as with the mother who, trained in liberalism, instead of saying "No" to her brat, seeks to deflect him from gratifying one wish by tempting him to gratify another. Or statesmen abide by the principle of deflection negatively when, having bothersome news to report, they release it at a time when a bigger scandal claims the headlines. Or still more negatively, here was a materialistic rhetoric to make a stubborn mule move, by deflecting him from his stubbornness: The driver's shouts and blows having no effect, a passerby stuffed a handful of gravel into the animal's mouth; and the mule became so engrossed in getting rid of it that he obeyed the driver's instructions automatically. Imaginatively, one can deflect attention by a stronger actualization. Thus, while "scrupulously" reporting both sides of a controversy, the speaker can "realize" for his audience one side much more clearly than the other. The Jesuit device for "directing the intention" (discussed in our pages on Pascal) would be a variant of "deflecting the attention." There was a superb deflection in the ways of a "friendly" businessman who, when you asked him for help as a friend, would answer severely in his role as a businessman, and when you asked him for an accounting as a businessman, would answer casually, as a friend. So you could question him for years, and never get a straight answer.

The great proliferation of laws in a liberal state allows for deflections that grant in name more freedom than there is in fact. Where it is legally permissible to revile the king, the man who shouts "Down with the king" may be imprisoned for shouting. Under a liberal constitution, the advocate of views unpopular with the authorities should take it as a maxim that he must be exceptionally correct in his conduct, if only as a rhetorical precaution. The political radical with a mistress might be tried, not for his radicalism, but for his mistress; and we might round out the symmetry by imagining him prosecuted by a conservative with a mistress (as one senatorial champion of strict racial segregation is said to be living clandestinely with a Negress).

A common deflection in the rhetoric of international relations, the shift between "ideals" and "interests," the expressing of acquisitive motives in sacrificial terms, and vice versa, was discussed previously (particularly in our pages on Bentham), and will be treated further under the head of "The Nostrum."

One common method of deflection used in parliaments is to forestall a measure not by direct attack, but by proposing a much weaker alternative ostensibly aimed at getting the same results.

And Roosevelt was making Deflection into an outright parry when, on being asked about some election returns (which were unfavorable to his party), he replied that he had been following only the returns from the battlefronts (which were favorable). And the deflection was close to simply parry when, the reporters having asked embarrassing questions about his former campaign manager, James A. Farley, who showed signs of close dealings with his political enemies, Roosevelt answered, "Oh, Jim is perfectly able to take care of himself," thus suggesting that the negotiations were dangerous to Farley rather than to Roosevelt, but that the outcome would be beneficial to them both (while at the same time there were overtones suggesting that Farley was merely looking out for himself).

Deflection can become indirection, or roundabout allusion. Thus when, in accordance with political practices during the Japanese empire, Japanese politicians aiming to brand an attack upon them as unjust, came ceremoniously to the Palace and asked after the health of the Emperor.

Deflection, along lines indicated by Bentham: Time does not permit—this is not the time—it should have been done sooner—more time is needed—we shall take that up when the time comes—the plan is so good, it is worth further study, to make it still better. One of the most skillful variants we ever suffered was at a pro-Fascist meeting at a religious school, backing the Franco regime in the name of "Hispanicism." Of course, this presenting of political and economic policies in purely "spiritualized" terms was itself a deflection. But this deflection was protected by another deflection, as an explicit request was made for comments from the audience. There was great insistence upon the desire for such comments, though it was also pointed out that they should be reserved for the last. So, whoever had reservations to make, patiently piled them up, without voicing disgruntlement, waiting for the time when it would be his turn. Then, finally, it was "discovered" that the meeting had lasted longer than planned, that "regrettably, time did not permit . . .," etc. Thus, at a time when the destruction of Spanish democracy was a matter of tense controversy,

"Hispanicism" (i.e., *Francoism*) was saluted without a single murmur of dissent.

The most perfect instance of Deflection, in fact its paradigm, is the con game. The swindlers get their intended victim (the "sucker") so intent upon efforts to swindle someone else that they deflect his attention from their designs against him. Indeed, once the mood of complicity is fully set, the victim himself acts to stifle his doubts about his cronies. The formula: hide duplicity beneath the appearances of complicity.

The con game is well described, with a crude literary flavor, in *The Professional Thief*. It is a collection of recorded interviews with a philosophic crook, annotated and interpreted by the criminologist Edwin H. Sutherland. It affords good insight into the rudiments of rhetorical deception. For many of the devices there considered involve persuasive zeal worthy of a Demosthenes. And they require mimetic and oratorical prowess (recall Demosthenes' three requirements for a great orator: "Action, action, and action!")—albeit the sheer love of the art usually leads these experts to expend their talents in mediocre plottings, leaving the management of world affairs to greatly inferior practitioners, who usually have their rhetoric done for them by ghosts and literary hacks void of conviction.

"It is impossible to beat an honest man in a confidence game," we are told by this anonymous authority. And a "professional confidence man," after reading the statement, described it as "unqualifiedly true." Another tells of "a certain business man, deacon in a church and a respectable citizen," who denied that he "had larceny in his soul," avowing that he "would not do a dishonest thing for any reason." But the swindlers thought otherwise, and they made him a "proposition." The account continues:

> The proposition was developed a little and involved depriving Jim O'Leary, who was then the biggest gambler on the South Side in Chicago, of his money. The sucker sat and thought several moments, and then said, "I have always hated gambling. I think it is ruining hundreds of people. I would be willing to go a long ways to injure the gambling business. If this proposition will assist in putting down gambling, I am willing to help. And after we get O'Leary's money can't we go down to Hot Springs and ruin some of the gamblers there?"

Here is a "confidential" letter which we once received, and which obviously abides by the rules, since it would have involved complicity in an attempt to defraud the writer's creditors. Nor should one fail to note the persuasive possibilities of a Spanish senorita, as one ingredient of the recipe:

Mexico City February 26, 1940.
Dr. Kenneth Burke.
Andover, N. J.

Dear Sir:

A Person who knows you and who has spoken very highly about you has made me trust you a very delicate matter of which depends the entire future of my dear daughter as well as my very existence.

I am in Prison, sentenced for Bankruptcy and I wish to know if you are willing to help me save a sum of $285,000.00 dollars which I have in Bank Bills inside of a secret place in a trunk that is deposited in a Customhouse in the United States. As soon as I send you some undeniable evidence, it is necessary for you to come here and pay the expenses incurred in connection with my process, so the embargo on my Suit-cases can be lifted, one of which Suit-cases contains a baggage check that was given to me on checking my trunk for North America containing the sum above said.

To compensate all your troubles, I will give you the THIRD PART OF THE SAID SUM. Fearing that this letter may not come to your hands, I will not sign my name—until I hear from you and then I will entrust you with my whole secret. For the time being, I am only signing "A".

For serious reasons which you will know later, please reply via AIRMAIL. OR WIRE. I beg you to treat this matter with the most absolute reserve and discretion. Due to the fact that I am in charge of the Prison School, I can write you like this and entirely at liberty.

I cannot receive your reply directly in this Prison, so in case you accept my proposition, you can Airmail your letter to a person of my entire trust who will deliver it to me safely and rapidly.

This is his name and address:

Manuel Gomez.
Balderas 78.
Mexico City
"A"

We admit, it was not our virtue that saved us from this plot. For several days, we lived in a mystic glow of criminality. If a car passed the house slowly, it looked suspicious. We wondered if the postman knew. We began imagining how we would spend the money. We assured ourselves it was a con game. Yet we were not released from this magic until, about two weeks later, we received an almost identical duplicate, differently phrased but using all the same details, and giving a different name and address in Mexico City. (A surprising slip-up, that almost made us lose faith in swindlers.) Even then, we found ourselves still given to fantasies, as we imagined "letting on" that we believed the story, and going to Mexico City just to watch how the various stages of the plot were unfolded, purely in the interests of science.

Complicity is very, very alluring. In a society of indifferent relationships, it is much more profoundly *social* than so many of our dealings with others. And thinking of it, we can better understand how the "Aryans" in Germany, under Hitler's chauvinistic proddings, were so readily set against the Jews. And we can see how, by such "conspiracy," the attention of the people could be deflected from the maneuvers of the cartelists, who were swindling the entire people with their racist doctrines, subjecting them by holding out the promise of subjecting Jews and others for their advantage, duping them by making them think they were accomplices in a worldwide steal.

And we think of it again, when we see how nationalistic, jingoistic thinking threatens to deflect so many of our citizens today. Indeed, in some respects, our temptation is even more ominous. For as all material interests can be translated into their corresponding "ideals," as all acquisitive aims can be shifted to the vocabulary of the sacrificial, or as children, loving violence, can have it "moralized" for them by vigilante heroes that slug in the name of virtue, so "imperialist expansion" can become "the acceptance of our responsibilities abroad."

When you get to that point, considerations of general welfare retreat behind considerations of national defense. That is, a greater percentage of the nation's efforts is shifted from economically useful goods to profits for the manufacturers of war goods. And when you reach that stage, you have the perfecting of the Hitlerite swindle. Thus the big industrialists need not face the problem of selling the people peace goods cheap. Instead, they can sell their government war goods dear. And the people's attention is deflected from this sorry state of affairs by fictions that focus their designs upon an alien object. While fearing *possible* deprivations by a *foreign* power, they close their eyes to *actual* deprivations by *domestic* powers. Through chauvinistic zeal, they are swindled in a con game; and by the expressing of material interests as ethical ideals, they are even tricked into feeling virtuous about it.

Spokesman

In the second book of Cicero's *De Oratore,* there is a section where Sulpicius and Antonius are reminiscing on an earlier oratorical combat. Sulpicius had spoken for the prosecution, Antonius for the defense.

Sulpicius is now praising Antonius for the skill by which, though he had a poor case legally, he had managed to swing the audience's sympathies for the defendant:

> When (as you told us) I had left you with a conflagration rather than a case to dispose of,—ye Gods!—what an opening you made! How nervous, how irresolute you seemed! How stammering and halting was your delivery! How you clung at the outset to the solitary excuse everyone was making for you—that you were defending your own close friend and quaestor! So, in the first place, did you prepare the way towards getting a hearing! Then, just as I was deciding that you had merely succeeded in making people think intimate relationship a possible excuse for your defending a wicked citizen,—lo and behold!—so far unsuspected by other people, but already to my own serious alarm, you began to wriggle imperceptibly into your famous defense, of no factious Norbanus, but of an incensed Roman People, whose wrath, you urged, was not wrongful, but just and well-deserved. . . . How you leavened every word with hatred, malice, and pathos! And all this not only in your speech for the defense, but also in your handing of Scaurus and the rest of my witnesses, whose evidence you rebutted by no disproof, but by fleeing for refuge to that same national outbreak.

Antonious' nationalistic shift from a defense of his client to a defense of his audience had been in itself, of course, a deflection. But within it there was a still subtler deflection. His address *to* a representative body of the Roman People was ostensibly spoken *for* the Roman People. As "spokesman" for them, he was "defending" them for feelings which he was now seeking to arouse in them.

Where there is society, there is order; where there is order, there must be some form of representation whereby a part identifies itself with a whole; and where a part represents the whole with which it is identified, there are the conditions for the Spokesman device.

If twenty men reach a decision, and elect one man to represent them in voicing that decision, he is of course their spokesman. But he is not a Spokesman in our particular meaning of the term here. For there is no *deflection* in his office, insofar as he performs the duties with which he was charged.

The Spokesman, as a rhetorical device of deflection, enters when, under the guise of speaking *for* another, we in reality speak *to* him. The Spokesman device, in this sense, is designed to *induce in* an audience an attitude which the audience is supposed to have already, and which the rhetorician is ostensibly but expressing in their behalf.

A typical method of deflection used in party politics derives from the fact that the party in power indeterminately represents both its own special interests and the interests of the country as a whole. Hence, a blow aimed at the *party* can be "resented" as though aimed at the *nation*. Thus, when the Republicans accused Franklin Roosevelt of policies that threatened to give the Communists control in the United States, he answered in his Presidential capacity as national spokesman: "When any political candidate stands up and says, solemnly, that there is danger that the Government of the United States—your Government— could be sold out to the Communists—then I say that that candidate reveals a shocking lack of trust in America. He reveals a shocking lack of faith in democracy—in the spiritual strength of our people."

The Spokesman device, in this application, clearly involves shifts in identification. Since the President is Spokesman for both his party and his country, he can seek to deflect criticism (deflection here being close to an outright parry) by choosing whichever identification serves the particular case at hand. But of course his critics can also manipulate their own variants of the device. Thus, when Roosevelt, in a bid for reelection, pointed to the successful way in which his administration had led the country in war, Governor Dewey was scandalized at the brazenness of a rival who would thus give his party credit for the mighty efforts in which our entire nation had cooperated.

This is political sparring, fairly good but not exceptional. However, there is a noble example of the device in Milton's *Areopagitica*, where Milton is saying that censorship is a dishonor to the people, in implying that they lacked the good sense to reject corrupt ideas:

> Nor is it to the common people less than a reproach; for if we were so jealous over them, as that we dare not trust them with an English pamphlet, what do we but censure them for a giddy, vicious, and ungrounded people; in such a sick and weak state of faith and discretion, as to be able to take nothing down but through the pipe of a licenser? That this is care or love of them, we cannot pretend, whenas, in those popish places where the laity are most hated and despised, the same strictness is used over them.

Milton's cause is thus quickly identified with the cause of all England, hence an attack against *his* position can be so deflected that it is an attack against the nation.

A variant of this device is habitually used by apologists of United States business interests, in their rhetorical clashes with the spokesmen for Soviet Russia. The Soviet delegates, for instance, directed their charges of "warmongering" at *special groups* in the United States. But our editors, politicians, and diplomats deflected the criticism by taking umbrage at it in behalf of the nation *as a whole*.

Similarly, during the pressure to put all parties under Communist control in Hungary (June 1947), when the Liberal party leader proposed that the elections be held under foreign supervision to "insure their integrity," the Socialist Minister of Justice became indignant in behalf of all Hungary which, he said, "could not tolerate foreign interference in her internal affairs."

Within limits, newspapers rely upon the Spokesman device (in the deflective sense), speaking *to* their readers while apparently speaking *for* them. Particularly on issues where public opinion has not yet crystallized, newspaper editors can mold opinion under the guise of voicing it. We say "within limits," since the device is not always effective. Thus, time after time, "representative" newspapers "voiced" the public's disapproval of Franklin Roosevelt, and at each election he was returned to office. Similarly, during the polemic with Russia, the newspapers were militaristic "Spokesmen" for a peace-minded public. We should also note that after Roosevelt's death, when he could no longer fight back, their representations against him became more effective.

By the Spokesman device, a minister can manage to get two sermons into one service. For besides the sermon in which he overtly exhorts his flock, there is the prayer when, ostensibly telling God how his flock feels about things, he is telling the flock how to feel. Also, of course, the Spokesman device in this application goes well with the device of "Christian vengeance," as with "non-political" prayers in behalf of persons "victimized" by rival political structures. Here, the more the speaker builds up the pity, the more he builds up the indictment. With enough of such prayers, a congregation can be quite primed for war.

In many ways, it has been noted, the representatives of dictatorships have the advantage when negotiating with the representatives of nations having a "free" press. For dictators have such complete control over the news that they can put their dealings in exactly the light they prefer. But by manipulating the Spokesman device, liberal statesmen have one big advantage denied dictatorships. They need merely assert that they cannot grant such-and-such a concession, through fear of "public pressure" at home. Since the dictatorship formally controls its press, it must assume full responsibility for its newspapers. But the liberal statesman can go to a conference well prepared for bargaining by a "troublesomely" independent press clamoring against concessions. And during the negotiations, whenever he is maneuvered into a concession that he does not want to make, he can let news of it "leak out in advance"; whereupon again a "spontaneous" and "uncontrollable" clamor back home can help strengthen his hand. This is no negligible aid, in these days of strong nationalist feeling. (If the Spokesman element is not stressed here, this device is seen to be a variant of the formula, "Our hands are tied," discussed under "Bland.")

Reversal

While it is true, as Aristotle says, that rhetoric "proves opposites," this ability is not grounded in mere linguistic trickery. An act or purpose in one situation may have a quite different meaning from the same act or purpose in another situation. An instrument used to help can by the same token be used to hinder. Rhetoricians can so readily reverse apparent meanings because real meanings are so reversible.

In his "Satire on Luxury," Diderot asks: "Where shall I go, where will I find everlasting happiness?"—and he answers: "I will go where the evils are brought to such an extreme that they will bring about a better state of things." It is the formula of "the worse the better." Another variant is a highly "dialectical" proverb we have mentioned in the past, basic to all irony: "The corruption of the best is the worst (*corruptio optimi pessima*)." One thinks of many variants: "*Homo solus, aut Deus aut daemon*"; "If winter comes, can spring be far behind?"; "*Ein Theil von jener Kraft, / Die stets das Böse will und stets das Gute schafft*"; the storm that clears the air; an easing before death; when the tale of bricks is doubled, Moses comes.

Consider how "sacred prostitution" looks, when viewed in the light of Biblical injunctions against polytheism (idol-worship). Consider how the institution of the potlatch looks, when viewed in the light of capitalist acquisition. Or how the bridegroom's servitude to the bride's family became transformed into the male purchasing of women. Or such quandaries as now beset some Congressional spokesmen for capitalism, who would uphold the system of "free enterprise" by having our Government distribute a surplus of our production only to countries unable to pay for them, while holding it treason to sell in Russia, which would pay in cash or in commodities of equal value.

Hence, there is at least plausibility to the notion that the very awfulness of atomic and bacteriological weapons makes their use less likely ("the worse the better"). The suggestion would be much more convincing if the United States had not automatically cooked many thousands of people already. Or there is the opposite possibility (*corruptio optimi pessimi*), in the thought that improved methods of psychiatry make possible a greater efficiency of demoralization.

Here is the puzzle that plagues all "revolutionary situations." Correctly or incorrectly, the cure can be said to thrive on the disease and to encourage the disease. Thus Marxism can be pictured by its opponents as causing the bad conditions that favor its spread and that it is designed to remedy. "Calls War a Spur to Religion" ran one headline—and among the reasons inducing us to call natural calamities "acts of God" may be the sudden outbursts of piety, penitence, and charity that go with them (as with the "earthquake love" vibrating for a time during the tremors and tidal wave that once beset San Francisco).

Since in successful revolutions, the outlaws become the authorities, and since corruption prepares the way for revolution, in periods of social upheaval all attempts to correlate appearance and reality must circle about the principle of "the worse the better." Reversal is in the air—and this ethical quandary is the most provoking aspect of reversal. It sets the conditions for irony, a mighty tragic irony brooding over the pitiful squabblings of our political hacks, like the deep steady hum of a great metropolis that arises from the countless disparate noises merged together.

And since liberal capitalism, Fascism, and Communism (in their relations to money and industry) have many ingredients in common, whichever of the three a man chooses to think himself a part of, he hates the other two for representing outwardly temptations he fights within. Hence, the burdens of reversal are intensified by the psychology of the Inquisition (purification by the vicarious punishment of one's own weaknesses found in alien vessels). The very attempt to treat, as mutually exclusive opposites, political systems which contain much in common adds vastly to the acerbity of polemic, in making quarrels much less clear than they seem in the light of an orator's antitheses.

At the very least, there is a wavering line between admiration and condescension, as in Sophisticate cults of crudity which, when something lacks taste, envy it its gusto. In our great confusion of innovative and "archaizing" trends are found the esthetic reflexes of reversal—often trivial on their face, but momentous in their import. The same situation, incidentally, can call forth, as a compensatory device, a rhetoric of *esthetic deflection* whereby ideas and images *politically* unsettling are felt to be in bad taste *artistically*. A poetic criterion of decorum thus serves roundabout as rhetorical protection for economic privileges. The resistance is largely justified, however, since most of the work written in behalf of a cause *is* inferior, and would be thanklessly ignored by the very posterity in behalf of which it is pleading. (At the time of Augustine, it seems, many zealous proponents of the new doctrine wanted good Christians to shun all the excellences of pagan literature. But Augustine, who was trained in pagan rhetoric, objected, holding that nothing was too good for the Faith, and accordingly that all stylistic embellishments known to Antiquity should be used to the glory of God. His position is in happy contrast with that of many contemporary Leftists who, themselves crude craftsmen, would imply that bad writing in behalf of their cause is a moral obligation, and would seem to be saying, in effect: As "thou wert" was feudal and "you were" is bourgeois, so "you was" is all that is left for the proletariat.)

What one man prescribes as a cure for evil eye, you can depend upon it, another will take for the force that lends power to evil eye. Hospitals, in being for health, come to mean disease. "Immortality" becomes the word for death. The pious monk Paphnutius converts Thais, and in the process rots in sin. Get officers of the labor union to enforce the discipline of the workers. "Protection" comes to mean the cooperation between the police and the criminal. (Similarly, at a trial in New York during Nazi rule in Germany, a witness contended that the word for support, *Unterstätgung,* should be translated, "pressure of the State.") The unruly child is given the job of maintaining order in the classroom. What goes forth as universal man returns as the specialist. What goes forth as spirit returns as matter (cf. the Church as big investor in real estate). What goes forth as freedom returns as monopoly (Plato's attack upon democracy as the step to tyranny). Attorney General Tom C. Clark, testifying before a Senate Subcommittee on Appropriations (May 1946) and discussing the legal prosecution of corporations for violating antitrust laws, said that "the payment of fines in a criminal suit is considered by many corporations as part of a fixed expense of doing business. . . . They consider the fine a license fee to continue the illegal practices." Again: by taking advantage of loopholes in the law, crooks often force the adoption of better laws. Thus financiers themselves must demand stricter government control of finance when the "unscrupulous" invade their "reputable" exploiting of such opportunities. (Thus, according to a member of the Securities and Exchange Commission, the agency to some extent has regularized controls once provided only by the "shysters" whose "roving presence struck fear in the hearts of management and finance," and thus acted as a "deterrent to excessive practices," making businessmen calculate in advance "the vulnerability of their transactions at his hands.") And criminals to a degree protect the law-abiding against repressive legislation; for the criminals make strict laws unenforceable—

and without such protest, laws might be made so strict that even the respectable would have to violate them (a neglect of which paradox enables many of the stiff-necked to love themselves inordinately).

You can't meditate long upon the nature of *sociality* without coming upon its convertibility with *guilt*. (It is the realm of interdependence, bondage, obligation, service, servitude, justification, exoneration, debit, credit, bankruptcy, and redemption.) Hence, rhetorical invitation to present imperialism as "the acceptance of responsibility" (the "white man's burden"—until, alas! someday the colored peoples, thinking similarly, as they certainly will if capitalist nationalism has its way, find that they are industrially strong enough to assume the "colored man's burden" by striving for imperialist control over the West). *Gratias Deo,* as a ritualistic bid for future favors. A company borrowing on its preferred stock, that is, borrowing on a liability (which is, in the last analysis, the equivalent of a debt). Or, since New York State banking laws are designed to "eliminate unsound and destructive competition," while U. S. antitrust laws ostensibly aim to encourage competition as a check on monopoly, spokesmen for a conference of bankers accused of collusion complained that what the State authorities advise as "cooperation" the U. S. Department of Justice condemns as "conspiracy." We suspect, but don't know for a certainty, that scarecrows inform the birds where the grain is planted; and we have heard that pickpockets find signs reading "Beware of Pickpockets" very helpful to them in their calling. For as the eye of the passerby alights on such a sign, he feels to see if his wallet is still safe; hence the thief learns where it is kept. And since all assistance is an influencing, one notes inevitably, in such projects as the European Recovery Program, the material for a rhetoric of reversal, depending upon one's feelings towards our financial adventures abroad.

Sometimes, when guilt cannot be denied, it can by reversal be turned into a defense. Thus legal representatives of banking interests have forestalled grand jury indictments by pleading that a public trial would undermine confidence in the banking structure.

And during the Sacco-Vanzetti trials, the worldwide indignation among men of goodwill at the flimsiness of the evidence seems itself to have been "conscientiously" taken as sufficient reason for condemning these men to death. For in the opinion of the enlightened public, the sovereign State of Massachusetts itself was on trial. The question of justice thus retreated behind the question of whether the citizens of Massachusetts should have faith in the legal machinery of their State. And to uphold such faith, it seemed necessary that the State of Massachusetts be pronounced innocent—which meant, of course, that the defendants were "expendable." Thus in effect the very questionableness of the trial could become an argument for approving the conduct of the judge.

Or there was reversal in the tactics of a man who, because he feared the thought of being interviewed when applying for a job, found a way whereby he could turn the tables by interviewing the interviewer. He asked very detailed questions about the nature of the work, as though to decide whether it was the sort of thing he was competent to do. Then, after careful consideration, he announced his decision: It *was* his sort of work, and he would like to take the job.

Inevitably, reversal is a major device of the cartoonist. In his *Rhetoric,* Aristotle has pointed out the rhetorical effectiveness of antithesis; in his *Poetic,* he lays equal stress upon "peripety," the kind of disclosure that dramatically changes the direction of the plot; and reversal has in it something of both. Thus, to pick a few from a vast number of *New Yorker* cartoons (where the reverse also has the piquancy of the perverse):

Caveman with club. Cavewoman whom he has slugged, has thrown over his shoulder, and is carrying away. Two other cavewomen looking on. Caption: "Well, I see she finally trapped him." . . . Prisoner sitting in patrol wagon, with air of great luxury, while police work on flat tire. . . . Dust mop being shaken from office window of vacuum cleaner company. . . . Operator in telephone exchange: "I'm sorry, sir, the Communications Building does not answer." . . . Chorus girls facing men in audience. One girl saying to the next in line-up, "The second from the left's not bad." . . . Horn peddler holding his ears while carousers blow horns lustily. . . . Patient to psychologist: "But can't you see, Dr. Friedrich, that these huge fees are only a childish attempt to build up your ego, a futile attempt to compensate for the things you *really* want?" . . . Mismated couple in expensive restaurant. Elderly gentleman to young and sexy companion: "Half of me just wants to worship you from a distance, darling, but the other half wants to take you down to Atlantic City." . . . Proud proprietor and little boy in front of store with many signs: "Closing Out . . . Moving Out . . . Must Vacate . . . Last Three Days of Sale," etc. Caption: "Some fine day, my son, all this will be yours." . . . Squad of policemen marching past fruit store. In second picture, they have passed, and fruit is gone. . . . During war, many variations of the topics of mistress eager to please servants, boss flattering his underlings, customer courting the salesman. Or, for this same period: Children with empty basket and bare table, "playing store." . . . At the time of reconversion: Picture showing as background, seen through window of office, the interior of a factory, containing a store of massive war machines. Foreground, office conference of executives, soberly inspecting tiny mechanical toy, a monkey riding a tricycle, their commodity for the next phase. (In this gentle conceit, the editors presumably did not foresee how a properly coached "crisis psychology" would be able to keep many of such plants busy on war goods despite the cessation of fighting.) . . . Grown-up attitudes or remarks of children. . . . Sophisticated statements by savages. . . . A sheep putting itself to sleep by counting people jumping over a fence.

Reversal fits particularly well in a cartoon strip telling a story. Thus, first picture: man meets woman who is taking dog for walk. In transitional pictures, they become acquainted, and marry. Last picture: man taking dog for walk. . . . Variant in the Mexican theme: Man carrying bundle—meets woman—courtship, etc.—last picture: woman carrying bundle. . . . Caveman and woman in cave—evolution through ancient, medieval, and modern times—newspaper announcement of war—last picture: couple with gas masks in cave. . . . On topic of meat scarcity during war: Diner in restaurant, starts to eat steak, notes sign, "Watch your hat and coat," turns to see if his are safe; when he turns back, his steak is gone. . . . On help shortage during war: conference of bankers, in various "top management" poses. Last picture: after hours, still with big-money cigars in their mouths, executives on knees scrubbing floor.

Often, where a single cartoon is built about the exaggerating of a before-after contrast, the humorous effect can be heightened by a deliberate imbalance in the design. Thus: Students being graduated from a Hollywood school of dramatics. In the center, a professor is handing out testimonials of graduation. As the line of students files past him from left to right, he hands each in turn a diploma and dark glasses. Hence, the pale-eyed on one side are outweighed by the saliently goggle-eyed on the other—and the comic idea itself supplies the psychological factor that rectifies the formal violation of symmetry. Or again, as burlesque of the Adler "you can be taller than she is" slogan: Two doors, side by side, but ill-matched, a short one marked "In," a tall one "Out." (This aspect of cartoons, whereby the perception of a comic idea can correct a formal imbalance, but where the idea itself is enhanced by the imbalance, may also lie at the basis of grotesque art, where no laughter is intended but where psychologistic motives coexist with breaks in symmetry. Consider the discordancy in Peter Blume's "The Eternal City," for instance, a picture which, by our interpretation, contains within itself a "before," an "after," and a transition between them, the succession being "telescoped" into a pictorial simultaneity. An absurd equivalent would be in the story of two models, one male, one female, posing in the nude for a picture of Pan and nymph. The nymph refused to pose at the same time as Pan, so the artist arranged them to appear at different hours. But, in the final summing up, lo! there they are on the canvas, together in mystic oneness.)

Behind arguments over policy there are different philosophies. But in the haste of the Scramble, rival orators cannot be expected to hunt down all the philosophic implications behind their positions. The War of Words is largely a hit-and-run affair. Hence, since opposed philosophies finally lead to opposed attitudes on a given subject, and since an attitude may be expressed by a gesture or a tone of voice, often the whole unspeakable complexity of differences, say, between a Catholic terminology of motives and a Marxist one must be reduced in battle to little more than a Benthamite choice of "censorial appellatives," a Reversal of Tone whereby one speaker mentions in a "eulogistic" accent what the other mentions "dyslogistically," with perhaps whatever fragment of imagery or idea serves most readily as sanction for the choice.

Such Reversible Tonalities can readily obscure the situations underlying a rhetorical combat. Thus, following the United States' "victory" in the Italian elections of April 1948, there was a considerable sobering up. All the appeals to nationalist prejudice against the Yugoslavs, plus the threat to withhold relief funds if the Communists won, plus a campaign fund of at least four million dollars to subsidize the Catholic political faction—it began to become apparent that we were pouring a great deal into Italy for the privilege of being able to pour in a great deal more, until either our people protested because we were giving too much, or the Italian people protested because we were giving too little. We won the right to continue supporting a political party that must go on needing support. Its very reason for existence in Italy is to uphold the faulty system of land ownership and the faulty control of industry that will drastically help make Italy unable to support itself. The more closely you look at that situation, the more you discern the ironies of the Inside Out, Upside Down, and Backwards (except, of course, insofar as Italy can be made into a military base to bear the brunt of possible war—while, as we shall consider when reviewing the Rhetorical Situation, losses to our *nation* as a whole may mean sizable gains to a selected group of our *nationals*).

Our main purpose at the moment is to ask that, if only as a mental exercise, one try to feel at home in thoughts of Reversal. If you were going on a trip, think of what you would write to a friend whom you would persuade against his will to accompany you. If, on the other hand, the same friend wanted to accompany you but could not, think of what you might write under those conditions. Then recall that in both these letters you might be quite sincere. Men are not worried that a door is used for both entry and exit, that a ladder takes them both up and down. Yet they want human institutions to be like either gods or devils, either entries or exits, either up or down; and they feel demoralized when denied this preposterous certainty.

Here the conditions of their demoralization are in the oversimple cult of certainty itself. They should not permit themselves to have such dingy gods in the first place. The proper protection against demoralization of this sort is not in an attempt to rigidify in terms of one rhetoric. Rather, the only protection worthy of human freedom is in the systematic study of rhetoric itself, until one can approach rhetoric from both without and within. When we are beset by a "crisis psychology" deliberately engineered by political and journalistic hacks, then as a sheer intellectual and imaginative enterprise we might try picturing for ourselves how the day's news *could be* presented in the interests of an *exactly opposite kind of goading* (without either presentation necessarily being wholly a lie). And in such tentative thoughts of reversal, we should lay the groundwork for being something more than a mere resultant of propagandist pressures.

By systematically contemplating the lore of reversal, we have an exercise for "limbering up." For we must remember that the rhetorician is doing all in his power to crystallize us. We would be free. But he would hold down a job, and his job, as a master of persuasion, is to restrict our freedom. Hence, at the very least, we should make his work hard for him. And by exercising (somewhat in the spirit of De Gourmont) an aptitude for Reversal, however tentatively, we set the proper conditions.

A friend said, of his fox terrier: "He has but one sorrow. Every time he sneezes, he bumps his nose on the floor. Apparently it has never occurred to him that one might sneeze with less drastic results. He probably just takes it for granted that a dog-sneeze by its very nature means a bump on the nose, and that it's just his hard luck to sneeze often." And isn't that how it can be with all of us, when the war-scare rhetoric of an officialdom, with the help of radio and press, has long been at work on the public? Don't we just come to take it for granted that when we would sneeze away the obstructions of our economy, we must bump the nose on the floor? Or, translating the example to present conditions in the United States, are not people brought by propaganda to take it for granted that the only way of promoting international amity is by war-minded squanderings that require inflation, conscription, and shortages of peace goods? While having the greatest capacity for peacetime production in all history, we are goaded to believe that we can sneeze away the obstructions to peace and plenty only by bumping our noses hard against scarcity and war.

Say the Opposite

Reversal being so attractive psychologically and formally (in the appeal of antithesis) and being grounded, at critical moments, in extra-verbal realities, it invites to the rhetorical device of Saying the Opposite. For every hold, a counterhold; for every thrust, a parry—but to Say the Opposite in the sense we mean here is more than that, it gives to defense a positive assertiveness. And whereas there is a certain smiling or smirking or sneering ambiguity in ideal Blandness, to Say the Opposite is to be, if not really right, then at least forthright, outright, and downright in appearance. Blandness can admit an ingredient of irony. But though the device of Saying the Opposite may make the analyst feel ironic, its stylistic nature is to go straight at the target, while conveying no other motives but the desire to get there. Yet many examples do seem on the edge of Blandness. The distinction cannot be kept clear. And if the reader finds it easier, he can think of it as a remote variant of Blandness, got by stress upon an element of Reversal.

Current advertisements for tobacco could serve as the paradigm. Does all tobacco irritate the throat? Then recommend your brand as a throat ease. The Federal Trade Commission may get a court order requiring you to "cease and desist" from saying this in so many words. If so you need but introduce ambiguities into your statement. And your readers, blunted by sales talks, can be expected to miss the qualifications which the commission required you to insert. You can deflect the critical attention still further by reference to statistics and scientific tests. But it all adds up to the same thing in the end: "business ethics" whereby a throat irritant is sold as a throat easement, with the glad tidings spread "freely" by press and radio throughout the nation.

Blandness requires complexity; its simplicity is shrewd. But with this device the artificer can be as simple as he seems. You need merely develop an utterance thus: Are you talking about an A? Then say it's a non-A.

In line with this principle, an old codger, preparing to speak ill of a neighbor, explained: "I don't believe in saying anything against a neighbor. And I aint a-going to say anything against my neighbors. All I want to say is this: I know Joe Quade, I knew his father, and I knew his grandfather. And anytime you do business with that little p***pot, look out."

Would a government official delay a report for sixty days? Let him issue an order *demanding* that the report be submitted in *not less than* sixty days. Would you call for laws permitting businessmen to *keep prices up* by making price agreements? Then let the press be filled with articles insisting businessmen be permitted to *lower* prices by making price agreements. (The procedure is usually obscured by the fact that the demand for such agreements arises when prices, having gone too high, are threatening to topple of their own accord. Hence, great jubilation can be made over the possibility of agreements that would lower them ten percent, whereas without the agreements they might be in danger of falling three times as much.) Similarly, the New York milk distributors asked for the right to increase the price of milk, on the grounds that it would keep the price down (since a refusal to grant the increase would "starve" the industry, thereby causing "much higher increases to the consumer later"). And the history of government lawsuits against business combines acting in restraint of trade is one long list of pleas by defense lawyers designed to show, by a variety of legalistic squirmings, how the combine promoted free trade and the price gouges made the product cheap. Only too often the pleas were not expected to convince, but were designed to give the acquiescent court a pretext for proclaiming itself convinced (as a seducer, who despised rape, and took delight only in voluntary yielding, might nonetheless be gentleman enough to threaten just enough force to give the fortress a pretext for surrender).

When the Leftists were advancing in Manchuria (after several days of stories announcing Nationalist advances in the same area), newsmen played up the places that the Communists would probably *not* be able to take. The *advance* could thus "honestly" be presented as an *inability to advance* (a trivial matter in itself, since nothing is more futile than a battle won on paper when it is lost in reality—but more important in this instance because our citizens' misunderstanding of the situation in China keeps them from protesting against United States adventures there).

A vigorous variant is the *Tu Quoque* rejoinder: "The charge you make against *me* applies perfectly to *you*." The pattern is symmetrical when two opponents accuse each other of mud-slinging.

"Frankly," he said. And his confidant asked himself: "Just what is he going to conceal now?" . . . Or similarly, Josephine (to Joseph, earnestly): "You *must* go along. I was counting on it. I'll have so much better time if you go too. Promise you will go. Don't be stubborn." Joseph (to himself): "Why in the devil doesn't she want me to go?"

In the rhetoric of personal outwittings, where one would work persuasively upon oneself as audience, the Saying of the Opposite necessarily takes another form. For when one is speaker and audience both, the ways of persuasion will not be exactly like those prevailing when speaker and audience are distinct. Devices of magical humility enter at this point, attempts to court success by the modest confession of misgivings, to coax victory by admitting strong fears of defeat (a twisted variant of "homeopathic magic"). And so it was with the earnest fellow who, when middle-aged, deliberately cackled like an old man, in the hopes that he might be better able, in old age, to avoid cackling like an old man. The Saying of Opposites, directed outwardly, begins with such devices as the confessing of self-dissatisfaction to elicit praise. But the man on his own is happier with these forms than is the representative of some corporate entity. Thus, a politician individually modest must boast in behalf of his nation. And businesses must out-clamor one another. (As for agitation that gets federal benefits for private corporations, the reader can decide for himself by what mixture of modesty and boasting this result is best accomplished, in accordance with the solemn rhetorical principle that "the squeaking wheel gets the grease.")

One way in which the device overlaps upon Blandness is when, instead of saying the opposite, it *implies* the opposite. Thus: Our hero thinks he has done a good act. He goes to his friend, all primed to receive approval. But his friend is a device-user, and exclaims vehemently: "I told them. I silenced them. I said you were quite right to do what you did. And they couldn't answer me." Our hero found it peculiarly hard to boast, when he was thus being defended, and hard to defend himself, when he was thus being forgiven.

Sometimes the cult of the counterhold can become a game. Thus, one polemicist objected to an organization "which proceeds by deciding what it thinks Russia wants and advocating the opposite." He said: "I find this new tyranny by a foreign power unbearable and un-American." (Turning a slogan against the sloganizer.)

Here are instances of hold and counterhold, noted in recent ideological sparring: When the Communists assumed power in Czechoslovakia, spokesmen for "the West" were doubly startled because, as the

Reds pointed out, the shift was contrived without disorder, and with many fewer casualties than on a "normal" Fourth of July celebration in the United States. But Masaryk's suicide gave foreign enemies of the new regime a very persuasive argument. Or so it seemed until the Communist Minister Gottwald's speech at the public funeral revealed an equally persuasive counterhold, in the mention of the many telegrams Masaryk had received from former friends abroad, reproaching him for his decision to collaborate with the new Government. Thus it was said to have been Masaryk's own Western friends who had destroyed his peace of mind; and Gottwald could vow his regime to avenge the victim's fatal anguish.

As for the coup itself, the fact that the union of Communists and Left-wing Socialists made a Parliamentary majority could have been embarrassing; but since the Communists without their allies were a minority, the stress could be placed upon that aspect of the case. As for the fact that the change had been accomplished without bloodshed, this could be taken as crowning evidence that the move had been doubly sinister.

We need not attempt to decide matters of justice here. Obviously, the issue is too controversial for that. For present purposes we need only note the rhetorical reversals. And in particular we should note again the use of reversal by *tonality:* as in this case the polemic effect was got by taking the tonalities that usually go with bloodshed and applying them to the absence of bloodshed. Similarly, when discussing "the difference between the Soviet system and others," Churchill once said that the Marxists "do not have to hire their agents in the ordinary manner. In the Communist sect it is a matter of religion to sacrifice one's native land for the sake of the Communist Utopia." Obviously, the same point about the zeal of the Marxists could readily be given the exactly opposite tonality, for instance in contrast with regimes which can hold allies abroad only by fantastically enormous monetary bribes. Indeed Churchill might well have arrived at his move by reversing the tonalities of opponents who had been exploiting this opposite emphasis.

Saying the Opposite often leads into reversals whereby effect is treated as cause. (The fallacy of Non Causa pro Causa is more general, treating any non-causal element as causal.) Here could be included such standard practices as when imperialists rule by fomenting faction, and use the faction as justification for their rule. Or depriving Negroes of opportunities for education, and then using their ignorance as evidence that they don't deserve to be educated.

The Spokesman device can sometimes be worked into the device of Saying the Opposite. Thus, if a people did not want war, but their Spokesmen wanted war, the Spokesmen could prepare a warlike situation in the name of peace, confident that, once that situation was ripe, the people "of their own volition" would answer the call to war, maybe even clamor for war.

Spiritualization (the Nostrum)

Of all opposites, all reversals, rhetorically the most resonant, characteristic, and far-reaching is polemic translating back and forth between materialist and idealist terms for motives.

Are things disunited in the "body"? Then unite them "in spirit." Would a nation extend its physical dominion? Let it talk of spreading its "ideals." Would you gloss over the conflicts of private ownership? Then talk of patriotism. Do you encounter contradictions? Call them "balances." Is an organization in disarray? Talk of its overall "purpose." Are there struggles over means? Celebrate agreement on "ends." Would you sanction expedients? Speak of the corresponding principles. Praise conditions in the name of "freedom" (the unconditioned). Spiritualize nature as the signature of God. Sanction the manifest (the incarnate) in terms of the invisible and intangible (the divine).

We discuss spiritualization here, not in the hopes of saying anything new about it, but because it is so prevalent. Also, there may be profit in reviewing its range of variants. There are more words for Spirit in an old language than in a young one. Yet you need only give a person or a place a name, and you have conjured up a spirit. A young, realistic language shows constant awareness of spirit's emergence. An old language is so full of it that even its attempts at materialism are fraught with idealism.

We call spiritualization the Nostrum because, where *mine* and *thine* (the *meum* and the *tuum*) are distinct, they must be spiritually merged in an idea of "ours" (the *nostrum*).

Thus consider St. John Chrysostom, on "Mine and Thine," in his sermon on Christian marriage (a commentary on St. Paul's Epistle to the Ephesians, written towards the end of the fourth century).

Admonishing the husband against the wife's naïve respect for wealth, Chrysostom explains that, though the husband corresponds to the head, and the wife corresponds to the body, not even the husband can enjoy marriage "if he lives with his wife as with a slave." The solution is in banning all talk of "my own," a "cursed" and "unholy" expression introduced by the devil:

> Above all, banish this notion of "mine" and "thine" from her soul. If she says the word "mine," say to her, "What things do you call yours? For, in truth, I know not; I have nothing of my own. How then do you speak of 'mine' when all things are yours?"
>
> Freely grant her the word. Do you not see that such is our practice with children? When, while we are holding anything, a child snatches it and wishes again to get hold of the other thing, we allow it, and say, "Yes, and this is yours, and that is yours."
>
> Let us do the same with a wife too; for her temper is more or less like a child's; and if she says "mine," say "But everything is yours, and I am yours."

This is not flattery, the Saint explains, because in flattery "a man does an unworthy act for an evil object." On the contrary, it is "exceeding wisdom," the "highest philosophy," for the Christian husband to keep peace by saying, "Even *I* am yours, my dear child."

> By saying these things, you will be setting her at rest, you will have quenched the fire, you will have shamed the devil, you will have made her more your slave than one bought with money. With this language you will have bound her as with a spell. Thus, in your own words, teach her never to speak of "mine and thine."

Taken in the most strictly literal sense, the writer seems to contradict himself. He has not banished "mine" and "thine" (the *meum* and the *tuum*). For the husband is admonished to let the wife call hers all that is his. The two are merged, being dissolved into a larger whole. For if husband and wife "are no longer two, but are become one flesh," if "both have become one person, one living creature," then would not the word for such possessions held in common be "ours"?

Hence our formula: When "mine" and "thine" (the *meum* and the *tuum*) are spiritually merged, the result is "ours" (the *nostrum*).

Particularly during periods of federal price control, there develops a practice of "tie-in sales" whereby wholesalers will fill a retailer's orders for popular brands of goods only on condition that he also buy some unwanted, unpopular brands at the same time. Much liquor distribution was done by "tie-in sales" during the war. "Block booking" is of a similar nature, in the distribution of motion pictures, as the proprietor of a theater must accept pictures he does not want in order to get the ones he does want. These practices are, as it were, visible models of this spiritualizing nostrum, the idealism that gives you one thing only if you will take something else along with it. A more drastic analogy would be the "bait and switch" device, where a good bargain is featured to attract customers, but once they are in the store "the salesmen endeavor to sell them much higher-priced articles on which a bigger margin of profit is made." (Better Business Bureau of New York City. Cited *NYT*, 4/6/47.) Tie-in sales and "block booking" would seem to illustrate the way in which "interests" are involved in "ideals" when a nation makes international arrangements that promote its own prosperity through promoting stability in general. But in our dealings with the rulers of Iran, who manage to maintain their rule solely by keeping the people ignorant and impoverished as a matter of public policy, when we were assured that the purpose of our diplomacy there was "to maintain the ideals of Western democracy," that spiritualization of the scent of oil seemed more like "bait and switch."

Cf. the Spanish proverb: "A friar who asks for God's sake, asks for two." The material aid for the friar has thus been spiritualized (though the proverb is, of course, ironically suggesting that the nostrum be translated back into material reference again).

The principle of *cui prodest* (the question, "Whom does it profit?" when trying to decide who is guilty of a crime) is also the principle (along Bentham's utilitarian lines) for materialistically debunking all nostrums (spiritualizations, idealizations, "eulogistic appellatives," and the like).

Deprive politics of the Nostrum, and imperialist unction would be impossible. But unfortunately, many wholesome forms of political cohesion would likewise be impossible. There are good Nostrums and bad, just as cooperation may be for peace or for malice and the lie.

As regards the justification for "spiritualizing": Quite as individual beings (division) can all be treated as participants in a common ground (merger), so there are no cases without *some* good arguments for the nostrum (we are here fully in the rhetoric that "proves opposites"). An end being ideal, the means must have a material nature of their own, over and above their nature as means used for any particular end; hence to that extent means must be "impure"; and this "impurity" can be "spiritualized" by putting still greater stress upon the purity of the end. Otherwise put: organize any plan, institutionalize any idea, bureaucratize any imagined possibility by translating it into its corresponding material embodiment, and you have a residue that is alien to the originating purpose. This residue, this "unintended by-product" (a kind of "materialistic excrement") will be a body of "conditions" which one can re-spiritualize either by reading the original purpose back into them or by "prophetically" endowing them with a new character, or essence, calling for a new correspondingly kind of act and purpose. In brief, one can treat them as a motivational ground, the nature of which inspires mankind with new aspirations. And these in turn are nostrums, insofar as they inspirit, and lead men to "breathe together" in "conspiracies" of varying scope and public benefit.

Our purpose at present is not to offer canons for deciding when a given case of spiritualization has the preponderant number of arguments in its favor. (If you had a set of perfectly correct canons, you would still need a further lore, such as we intend to consider in "The Rhetorical Situation," to decide how the canons applied to a given case.) Our purpose at present is to review the entire subject of "spiritualization," and to consider the wide range of utterances that could be treated as variants of this rhetorical device. We are not trying to sanction or debunk spiritualization *per se;* we are trying to "appreciate" how much spiritualization goes on, even in terminologies that on their face are wholly materialistic. Whenever you get to the "character," the "essence," the "core," the "substance," the "principle" of a situation, whenever to talk of "what it all boils down to," or give it a "title," you are on the spiritualizing side. The nature of your summary is implicitly a plea for acts and attitudes of a corresponding nature.

As the logical positivist Rudolph Carnap has pointed out, many expressions that look like statements of fact are really commands. Thus with a creed, "There is only one race of superior men, say the Hottentots, and this race alone is worthy of ruling all other races," to get what is really going on here, we should change the sentence from the indicative mood to the imperative, making it read, "Members of the race of Hottentots! Unite and battle to dominate the other races!"

Repeatedly, through this route, a rhetorical ingredient is smuggled into writing that pretends to be purely scientific. For in every statement of conditions, there are directives more or less clearly implied. Whenever a reporter describes a scene, insofar as we believe him, we are inclined towards attitudes and acts in keeping with his description. Hence any statement as to how things are, ranging in scope from a news dispatch to metaphysical theories on the nature of God and the Absolute, function somewhat as *inducement.* A belief that a certain state of affairs prevails can lead to an act or attitude in keeping with it. The scenic description or report thus had a certain essence or spirit that served rhetorically to induce an act or attitude of corresponding spirit. This is why we believe that even the most positivistic of terminologies possesses a measure of rhetoric. (One might further note, in the Carnap citation, the rhetorical effect got by incongruously selecting a race of near-Pygmies as the example of world conquerors.)

A variant of spiritualization seems to be implicit in the relations between pairs of the five terms: act, scene, agent, agency, purpose (relations discussed as "ratios" in the *Grammar*). For instance, a purpose-agency (means-ends) ratio would seem to be involved in the treatment of an organization (agency, means) as imbued with the spirit of the purpose (end) for which it was founded. Or to say that a situation (scene) will lead to a kind of human behavior in keeping with it (a "scene-act ratio") would amount to saying that the nature of the act is analogously present in the nature of the scene. Or otherwise put: the act is in the scene potentially, substantially, implicitly, or in principle. Or reverting to Carnap's example: The scenic statement is a disguised scene-act ratio; for it attributes to the scene a certain spirit or character for the purpose of evoking an act of kindred substance.

During our imperialist expansion across the continent, when the land of many Indian nations was seized and occupied, "manifest destiny" and the "white man's burden" were slogans whereby formulas apparently *substantive* were actually in the imperative mood, thus expressing in terms of universal or ethical *ground* what was but the *inspiriting* to an act. Similarly, the geopoliticians' notion of *Lebensraum* was a command to think in terms of nationalist expansion through foreign dominion. (This may explain why prophets of an "American Century" would take up where Nazi geopolitics left off, while looking for churchly allies to aid in the inspiriting.)

A close counterpart to the rhetorical shift between spirit and body is the change of scope that goes with changes in the "level of abstraction." (See Karl Mannheim, *Ideology and Utopia*, 248–250.) In imputing motives, for instance, one can so generalize that "we are all in the same boat" (as with the doctrine of "original sin"); or one can specify and particularize. Thus the concept of "ideology" has been generalized to the point where Marxism too would fall under that head, whereas Marx himself used it so specifically that it would apply only to his opponents. And Mannheim gives this example of Marxism's refusal to generalize as broadly as the "sociology of knowledge" would require:

> One is not even allowed to raise the question whether "impersonalization" (*Verdinglichung*), as elaborated by Marx and Lukács, is a more or less general phenomenon of consciousness, or whether capitalistic impersonalization is merely one particular form of it.

In this particular case, Marxism seems to have lowered the level of generalization (or abstraction) used by Hegel. Hegel treated such processes as universal, as with the organization (*Vermittlung,* mediation) whereby ideas are given body, like a God incarnate. Marx was always working against this idealistic tendency, which Mannheim calls the "flight into the highest realms of abstraction and formalization," and which may, "as Marxism has rightly emphasized, lead to an obscuring of the concrete situation and its unique character."

Spiritualization (in this case, generalization, or high abstraction) can be used to obstruct choice (as the attempt to reject one policy on the grounds that it is more provocative of war than another might be confused by the broad assertion that war is inevitable, since "there always have been wars and always will be"). On the other hand, such generalized statements can have a "whom the shoe fits" quality, the shoe being big enough to fit any foot, but the spokesman pointing to one particular wearer. "Disinterestedness" can operate to this same end, if one can choose the occasions on which to be "disinterested," by being "above the battle" only when the other man's ox is gored (or by being willing to deliberate, when delay favors your side).

Remotely classifiable under the head of spiritualization would be the liberal neutralizing of factionally censorial terms. For instance, everywhere that Marxism finds an "inner contradiction" in capitalism, liberal apologetics (or "disinterested study" in the same mode) can find rather a "recurrent problem," solved more or less felicitously by compromise and reforms. Or "contradictions" can be treated as "mutual checks and balances," the rivalry of competing interests being said to reach an unstable but adequate adjustment of the competitors to one another through freedom of exchange in goods and ideas. The "contradiction" between high profits and low wages is seen merely as a point at which bargaining is called for, with unemployment insurance and governmental distribution of profits through taxes and public services correcting to a degree the inequalities between profits and wages. And the various regional discordancies of interest, or conflicts between city and country, or between the many occupational groups, can be considered as mutually corrective of one another, within limits (since each group must align itself with partially antagonistic groups, in parliamentary blocs, to get some elements of its program by sacrificing others). Such a "neutral" view of capitalist action, as indeterminately competitive and cooperative, could be called a "spiritualization," as contrasted with the

Marxist interpretation of the same motives, because it supplies a comparatively "good explanation" for what Marxism would consider dyslogistically, as contradictions inherent in capitalism and leading not merely to instability but to inevitable collapse of the system. (Indeed, underlying the capitalist version of the free market there is a quite Pauline pattern of thought: the universal "God-principle" here would be the notion of competitive-cooperation in its widest dialectical sense, to describe the form of human relations in general. And capitalism would be the "incarnating" of this universal motive in terms of specific institutional conditions that retain the ironic spirit of the original dialectic ambiguity whereby one can never clearly say when mutually beneficial cooperation ends and downright antagonism begins.)

Since the era of the New Deal, the economic factors in unemployment are generally recognized. Yet it is relevant to remember that, at a time when even mild unemployment insurance was being fought, the press favored nostrums built upon the thesis that "unemployment is a spiritual and educational problem," not an "economic" one. (We are quoting a past pronouncement by Roger Babson.) This particular proposition is gone. The Congressional enactments that it was designed to prevent have been passed, and have become a traditional aspect of our culture. But the animus behind it will go on forever, the rhetorical device of deflection by spiritualization, as when the National Association of Manufacturers proclaimed, "We are not for freedom from this or freedom from that—but for *freedom in itself.*" That is: Let us talk about freedom in the absolute, and forget about the *conditions* of freedom.

People are so prone to Spiritualization that they readily mistake the promise for the reality. Thus, when an editorial said that "we need a positive reaffirmation of what life is and can be. We need a bright new sense of its glory and significance," a reader wrote in, enthusiastically, to say that these sentences "have helped me tremendously to orientate my mind and spirit." Whereas he had been "giving a 'negative response' to the news," he testified that this editorial "has done me good." And he concluded, "I shall be happier today." The editorial, you will note, had said *what we need.* The reader presumably felt that he was *getting it* (as though hunger were gratified by an editorial saying, "What we need is food").

Spirit, as allied with purpose, has no difficulty at all in solving contradictions. For the contradictions exist only in the realm of conditions. Thus, political promises are vibrant with Spirit. And they are most vibrant when they have in them an idea or image that merges antitheses.

"Our conservative aim," said Churchill (*NYT,* 10/6/46), "is to build a property-owning democracy, both independent and interdependent." Carried into the realm of conditions, this would mean a host of choices. Is the property-owner's "independence," for instance, to mean that he can buy and sell as he chooses, that he can import luxuries when many lack necessities, as with the merchants profiteering on scarcity in Greece? Or at that point should considerations of "interdependence" intervene? Obviously, in terms of conditions, Churchill's happy coexistence of these differences would require an either-or. But in Spirit, in principle, it can be stated as a both-and. (Indeed, generalize it sufficiently, and you come upon the universal and inevitable dialectic formula whereby even the laxest government or the severest tyranny involves both independent and interdependent trends.)

Recall the previously mentioned "Congress" in behalf of "Hispanicism." The orator had presented matters thus: After discussing the troublesome *conditions* that beset democracy, communism, and German and Italian Fascism, he turned to the *promises* and *ideals* (pure spirit) of Hispanicism. Then, having listed these promises and ideals, he concluded: Now, in the light of these *accomplishments* . . . etc. The same rhetorical effect was amplified by a heavy pageantry of religious emblems, national flags, church vestments, and police and military uniforms. Here was a whole museum full of spirit made manifest, as priestly flags in Tibet, flown to ward off unseen evil powers, thereby "reveal" their presence.

The Spirituality of promises has its counterpart in the Spirituality of fears. Thus a speaker before the Association of National Advertisers (*NYT,* 10/2/46), deciding that this is no time for complacency, "emphasized that copy should drive home the consequences of abandonment of traditional American practices rather than concentrating on benefits derived from their retention."

Obviously (we are here commenting, not reporting) if you lay the stress upon the *positive attainments* of an economy (that is, upon the respects in which the "promises of American life" have been *fulfilled*), your argument is good only so long as those promises *are* being fulfilled. But if the people are subjected to high taxation, high prices, and scarcity of the commodities that are identified with the American "higher standard of living," an argument so clearly capable of being tested by reference to material conditions becomes not merely weak, but a downright embarrassment. But by substituting a negative, fear-breeding psychology for the promissory, hope-breeding one, you automatically escape such problems. By building up the fear of a situation that does not exist, you enable apologists of the actual to get the advantages otherwise reserved solely for prophets of an ideal future.

Later, under the Truman administration, one saw how perfectly the requirements of this formula could be met by the systematic goading of the people to fear of "alien ideologies."

"Spirit" being "free," spiritualization becomes a typical resource of liberalism in its contests with Marxist materialism. Thus, during the debates (in the U.N. Council) on control of the atomic bomb, the Russian delegate was always attempting to specify the *conditions* of control, while the United States was eager to establish rather the *principle* of control, along with an international body to carry out these principles. As the Soviet delegate Gromyko pointed out, by such an arrangement, whoever controlled the majority of the control agency could then decide on the exact conditions of control and inspection. And on the basis of finaglings on other issues, it was likely to be "a majority on whose benevolent attitude toward the Soviet Union the Soviet people cannot count." Hence, again and again, from the founding of the organization, Soviet delegates have been pressing for agreements in terms of very specific conditions, while Britain and the United States are in favor of more liberal arrangements. Declarations about human rights, for instance, were much more "spiritual" when coming from the liberal side—and by avoiding strict definition of such rights in terms of conditions, they would make it easier for nations in control of the U.N. majority to censure the minority nations for violating their solemn international pledges. For if the pledges were stated vaguely enough (as "spiritualization" would enable them to be) then the majority could later decide, "on the merits of the case," just exactly what these pledges had meant, as translated into terms of specific situations.

However, according to Albion Ross (*NYT,* 6/8/48) the Communists also know how to spiritualize, when there is a rhetorical gain in doing so. Thus, in proposing political grounds for Eduard Benes' resignation as the President of Czechoslovakia, the Ross article from Prague says:

> The first and most important reason is that it is a vague document that must be implemented by some fifty laws from the new Parliament. The meaning of a whole series of general clauses will first be made clear by this implementation. It is said that this would mean that the President, in signing the Constitution, would have given his approval to a great variety of things without being able to determine in advance what they really were.

During negotiations over the establishment of the "Western Union" in Europe, Spirit long stood our headline writers in good stead. For all the time the organization was being delayed, they could exult in enthusiastic stories about the formation of a "nucleus" and the adopting of "principles," while in actuality the British were deliberately killing attempts to specify "conditions" (not through any love of the diabolic but because they could not have specified the conditions of an economic union with France and Benelux without thereby violating the conditions of their arrangements with nations of the British Commonwealth). Presumably it was felt that, whereas too great stress upon *conditions* would have made the obstacles to economic union only too apparent, great rejoicing about the Spirit of union would suffice for getting Congressional appropriations for armaments to be supplied by U.S. manufacturers.

In Red Rhetoric, particularly during the literary battles of the Thirties, the Nostrum often came in handy as a means of amplification. For whereas, in much late liberalism, critics had been reduced to treating of judgments as personal aberrations or idiosyncrasies, the Leftist became spokesman for decisions established by no less an authority than Universal Necessity. Thus a private competition between rival operators could readily be translated to the realm of purely public motives. "My Likes and Dislikes" retreated behind "The Verdict of Dialectical Materialism," the critic speaking not merely to his reader but for his reader, and for his class, and for the voiceless Logic of Nature and History.

The transformation of special interests into corresponding terms of ideals is in effect the expressing of private ownership in terms of universal ownership. It is a variant of the shift between merger and division that we considered when on the subject of Deflection and the Spokesman. The ideal is "everybody's," the interest it sanctions is somebody's to the exclusion of somebody else. There is a Spanish proverb: "When two friends have the same purse, one sings and the other weeps." We can think of "ideals" as the "spirit" of the purse owned jointly while "interests" are the arrangements whereby the nostrum is split materialistically into an eighty percent *meum* (singing) and a twenty percent *tuum* (weeping in exasperation or idealistic confusion).

Ideals and interests coincide (being *consistently* related) when a policy that would benefit society in general also brings special benefit to some individual or group. For instance, special rewards to inventor and manufacturer for some product beneficial to mankind generally.

There are two ways in which ideals and interests can be *indifferently* related. First, one may be in the position of a judge who stands to benefit more by delivering a correct judgment than by favoring either faction of a controversy. Second, one may be completely unconcerned about the controversy. Fluctuating somewhere between these two kinds of "disinterestedness," there is the "high idealism" of signing petitions in behalf of better conditions abroad, the farther off the better. Thus similarly, officials might "idealistically" clamor for better elections in a foreign country, while remaining silent about systematic disenfranchisement of domestic voters. Usually, idealism of this sort is not *activated* unless some influential group has a special interest that would be favored by the triumph of the universal ideal abroad and/or disfavored by its triumph at home.

Ideals and interests may also be *antithetically* related, as were "justice" to demand that *our* ox be gored, and we were to uphold the judgment sacrificially by surrendering our ox without protest. Here is willingness to sacrifice one's special interests in favor of the common interests (as backed by a corresponding ideal). Agamemnon's relinquishment of Iphigenia or Abraham's readiness to offer up Isaac are the prototype. Priestly vows fall under this head, a disastrous one when the sacrificial nature of such vows comes to provide resonance and persuasiveness for purely acquisitive ambitions ("religion as an instrument of politics").

Antithetical relations between ideals and interests may be avoided by choosing instead an alternative ideal with which the interest can be *consistently* related. This can be done deliberately, or it can draw upon motives in the "unconscious," as one might "sacrifice" his chances of marriage through a hidden dislike of heterosexual union. Such considerations are a typical modern preoccupation, making for a "psychologistic" reading of the old heroic myths, as were the novelist to offer an infanticidal motive to explain a father's acquiescence in a "tribal" command that he sacrifice a child. Here would figure such motives as, in our project, belong best under Symbolic. They involve somewhat Spinozistic concerns whereby will and necessity become one, as in a being that *must will* to be the sort of being it is. For instance, if a man equated monetary power with physical prowess, and was himself physically slight, he might persist in financially disadvantageous choices, for his destiny would thereby be kept "consistent with" his physique, rhetorical considerations thus retreating behind the "poetic" of a uniformly developed character.

When a utilitarian policy is to be motivated on idealistic grounds, you could present the case thus:

(1)   Such-and-such are the *material* motives for this policy.

(2)   These material motives happen to fit with (or can be shown to fit with) such-and-such *ideals*.

As so stated, the appeal to ideals is justified.

We have spoken of the shifty gentleman who, when questioned as a friend, answered as a businessman, and when questioned as a businessman, answered as a friend. That is the design for a "dialectic of idealism and materialism," or for a rhetoric of deflection got by the shuttling between two orders of terms, one "worldly," one "spiritual." The position of the Church as *bridge* between the timeless and the temporal is the perfect paradigm of "spiritualization." Whenever the *secular* power of a Church is attacked, its spokesmen can deflect by reaffirming the Church's purely *spiritual* function. Yet obviously, its spiritual function is attested by its influence upon *practical* affairs. Hence, "spirituality," in affecting political decisions, becomes a sanction for profane purposes. And here arises the opportunity for the rhetoric of spirit, or use of religion as an instrument of politics in the Machiavellian sense.

However, in the modern world, where so many of our attitudes are formed by the press and radio rather than by the clergy, spiritualization as a rhetorical device must rely for its maximum effect upon spokesmen wholly secular and journalistic. They admit to fallibility in the interpretation of spiritual utterances, but it is their business to apply such utterances for use in political controversy. This combination of Spiritual Counsel and Secular Spokesman is needed, to make the device of Spiritualization most effective under modern conditions. Otherwise, it becomes but the kind of deflection we find when *economic* interests are translated into corresponding *esthetic* values (a quietly and permanently pervasive influence, but without the sharp pointing-up needed for urgent political controversy).

A truly spiritual statement should not, could not, and would not descend to the level of everyday political hagglings. For a spiritual statement must retain its relevance throughout the ages, whereas political programs come and go, and sometimes the slain snake that lives until sundown outlasts the decisions of a political faction. Hence a normally spiritualized utterance is so worded that it does not apply to any one particular situation in time. And though the Grand Apex of the Only Church of Ancient Madagascar, if his words were spiritualized as befits his office, might have made pronouncements that were, in their day, interpreted by Lesser Spokesmen as *attacks upon* the rising political faction of Loathesomites; yet later, if the Loathesomites came to power, those same pronouncements could be repeated as a doctrine that *supported* Loathesomite rule.

Thus, journalistic Spokesmen repeatedly take liberties with pronouncements of the Roman Pontiff, giving them *timeserving applications which are never to be found in the spiritual statements themselves.* The Pontiff will inveigh against secularism, or modernism, or injustice, or threats to peace, in sum, against lapses from virtues that are found to varying degrees at all times and in all places. But the journalistic Spokesman assures us in headlines: "See, he means not us, but them." It is the Spokesmen that point up such timeless statements for use in time-serving political hagglings, quite as spokesmen for either side in a nationalist war can use the words of Universal Spirit as evidence that their cause is the righteous one.

For instance, during one period of political tension in Italy, our press repeatedly gave the impression that the Pope was involved in electioneering on about the level of the Chairman of a political party in the United States. The paradigm for such headlines might well have been: "Holy Father endorses Jim Bloop for President." For instance, the *Christian Science Monitor* of May 10, 1945, printed a story by a staff correspondent: "Vatican Says Italians' Duty Is to Vote Against Communists." The writer says, "Although this is not the first time the Vatican has indicated to Italians how to vote, it is doubtful if it has done so in such a vigorous manner in many years." Again: "In simple terms the 17-Cardinal Congregation, headed by Pope Pius XII himself, has just told Italians to vote against the Communist-dominated People's Bloc. It justified this action on the grounds that a victory of the Communists and their left wing Socialist comrades would basically endanger the Roman Catholic Church in Italy." The Congregation warned that Catholics "must vote for those parties actively opposing the Communist concept." And so on. Yet it is notable that *not one sentence from the statement itself is directly quoted.*

However, there is also an Associated Press dispatch, printed under the same headline. It *does* quote. Thus:

> Pope Pius XII, in an annual address to the Rome clergy, told them it is their right and duty to impress upon Roman Catholics "the extraordinary importance" of Italy's election April 18.
>
> This is considered the Pontiff's reply to Communist charges that the church is intervening in politics.
>
> The Pope's speech March 10 placed his prestige squarely behind the efforts of Italy's cardinals, bishops, and priests to mobilize Roman Catholic votes to defeat the leftists.

Here finally we get a direct citation. The words are: "the extraordinary importance." We are told that *this is considered* to be such-and-such, that the Pope "placed his prestige" behind certain temporal efforts. But there is no direct quotation of any statement by the Pope saying, as the headline says, it is the Italians' duty to vote against the Communists in a particular election. Spokesmen, in this case presumably Protestant spokesmen, supply the temporal pointing for statements in themselves much too universal for such local campaigning. Only the spokesmen suggest that the Church's interests are like those of a ward boss in Jersey City.

It is not our purpose here to review the press. Our treatment of such rhetoric belongs in another chapter. But we might briefly list some other examples that we have noted. Thus, the *New York Times* of August 2, 1947, prints a dispatch announcing that "Pope Pius today praised democratic government and condemned totalitarianism." The report quotes a couple of paragraphs from the Pope's address. Yet in it *no mention is made of either totalitarian or democratic government.* (Obviously, if the Pontiff were electioneering thus, attacking totalitarianism and praising democracy, what of Franco Spain, with whom the Church is on good terms?) Actually, the Pope spoke against the temptation of ambitious men "to exploit the common people for the benefit of one individual or group," and referred to "Nero's despotism," remarks that could apply quite well to any oppressive monopoly in the United States; and he made a definition of "just government" that any Leftist could subscribe to. Yet, we are informed: "It was clear to some of those present at the private audience in Castel Gondolfo that the Pontiff was referring to the Government in the United States as contrasted with the Government in Russia." So the story is headlined: "Pope Praises Democracy," and presumably it is so filed in the NYT *Index.* But though you can find it in the headlines, and probably in the index, you will not find it in direct quotations from the article itself. It may have been "clear to some of those present" (evidently not even clear to all those present?) that the Pontiff was putting out such a statement as might be issued by the Republican National Committee. But it wasn't clear enough for the reviewer to be able to show it to you in the words themselves. It was clear only in *his* words, and in those of the headline writer.

One of the most remarkable cases on record surely is to be found in the *New York Times* of June 3, 1947. The official English translation of a speech by the Pontiff to the Cardinal is printed in full. Its subheads are: "Security; Prosperity; Liberty; Youth; The Family; Fear

Not; Peace; Love." The accompanying story by Camille M. Cianfarra is headlined thus:

POPE WARNS WORLD

OF TYRANNY, WAR

Scores Lack of Progress in

Peacemaking—Imputes

Blame to Russia

And the subhead "Security" in the Papal address has a corresponding subhead in the news story: "Emphasizes Insecurity."

As for the blame "imputed" to Russia: There are references to "false prophets" who propagate "anti-Christian and atheistic concepts of the world and of the state." These could apply equally well to many modern scientific naturalists in capitalist countries, including of course some founders of the U.S. Constitution. And the references to "exploiters of class warfare" who ensnare the people "by telling them that Christian faith and the Catholic Church are not their ally, but their enemy," remind us that even today a patriarch of the Greek Catholic Church in Russia could subscribe to this position fully. The *headline writer* "imputes blame to Russia." The Pontiff did *not*.

Or again, the Pontiff delivers an address against "anticlericalism" (reported *NYT*, 12/23/46). Such spiritual stand is in the leader of a Church perfectly understandable—and it would, of course, apply to wide areas of the non-Communist public in all Western nations. But the headlines on Arnaldo Cortesi's story announce that the talk is to be taken as a "stern warning to communism." The Pope speaks out against "the wicked negators of God, the profaners of the divine Church, the idolaters of the senses"; he mentions opposite camps, for Christ and against Christ, for Church and against Church; and at the end he pronounces an apostolic blessing, not only upon the faithful, but also upon "all those who fight and vilify religion." As thus spiritually couched, the remarks could have been relevantly uttered in any year since the Church was founded. And only in the headlines of the accompanying news story by Arnaldo Cortesi are we informed that the talk is to be taken as a "stern warning to communism."

Or again, in the *New York Herald-Tribune* (2/21/46), we are told of a Papal statement against modern imperialism. Now, the charges of imperialism carry far. Britain is an Empire. Many seem to discern imperialistic tendencies in our own foreign policy, expansionistic commercial aims that some of our Latin American neighbors call "economic imperialism." Yet the Spokesman in the headlines assures us that these are "Criticisms Viewed as Aimed at Russia." The journalistic time-servers must supply this interpretation. It is not to be established by direct quotation from the spiritual statement itself.

Letting the various persuasions comment upon one another and without ourselves intervening, we might briefly review these news items of June 1947:

A Metropolitan of the Greek Orthodox Church in the United States (as reported *NYT, 6/6/47*) declared that "the attitude of the Russian Orthodox Church in America toward its mother church should not be suspected by Catholics in America because they are in a somewhat similar position in regard to the Pope and the Church of Rome." But a writer in a Jesuit periodical, reported in the same news story, said that the Soviet government's more lenient attitude towards the Orthodox Church was due to the "servility" of the Church:

> During the war, the church gave its complete support to the Government and by its propaganda strengthened the Russians' will to fight. To please the Soviet Government representatives of the church have given up the foremost command of Christianity, to love your enemy. Such is the servility of the church in a godless regime.
>
> Furthermore, the Soviet Government makes use of the church as an instrument to reach its goals in foreign policy. In fact, the Russian Orthodox Church, which has good relations with the Anglican Church, did much to facilitate the alliance between Britain and Russia. In this way it supports the imperialistic dreams of Moscow's foreign policy.

Similarly, when the Catholic Church proposed to enlarge the College of Cardinals by elevating bishops from nineteen different nations, Moscow attributed the move to political motives. But the hierarchy replied that Moscow could not distinguish between religion and politics. And then, as though to show how the two realms could be distinguished, Archbishop Spellman went to Rome, accompanied by the former Chairman of the Democratic Party, James A. Farley.

Thoroughly outwitted in spirit, Moscow did work out a kind of rejoinder in the realm of lowly matter, however. It delayed the departure of the Hungarian primate, Joseph Cardinal Mindszenty. By this delay, and by the public demonstrations accompanying it, Moscow did all it could to bring out the fact that the Consistory was elevating a strong opponent of the Hungarian land reforms by which large estates were being distributed among landless Catholic peasants.

Occasionally, when the Protestants are not helping to build up the picture of the Pope as an endorser of political candidates, they apologetically observe that there is nothing contrary to Catholic doctrine in resisting the *temporal* policies of the Church, and that even good Catholics can do so without excommunication. Thus, the *Christian Century* (as reported in the *New York Sun,* 6/20/47) stated editorially:

> Even a Roman Catholic layman is within his rights if he opposes the use of public money for the maintenance of Catholic schools or for transporting pupils to them. If he does so he will doubtless be subjected to strong pressure to make him change his mind or keep silent, but he will not be attacking the church. Protestants have the same right. There will not be any "crusade against the Roman Catholic Church" unless its leaders, like Cardinal Spellman, go on denouncing as anti-Catholic "bigotry" and "bias" every criticism of Catholic procedure or every word of opposition to Catholic demands for special privileges.

So much for the rhetoric of spiritualization (which we also considered earlier when discussing the Marxist concern with "mystification"). We should also note how the rhetoric of spirit is grounded in a poetic factor. Thus, since an image stands for both an object and an idea, the idea has more components than belong literally to the object. To this extent, the image represents something unattainable to the bodily senses: it is thus "spiritual," the "clothes" that symbolize principles of order not physically present in them as mere things, but there only insofar as these things are "fetishes" ("ideas" as well as "objects").

Mounting, considered as act or image, may combine ideas of mounting in the sexual sense with ideas of improved social status ("climbing") and of moral betterment. Yet even if you hypothetically omitted the third, an idea that combined sexual mounting with social climbing would contain motives beyond the powers of bodily sensation alone to encompass. The ingredient of social hierarchy would "inspirit" the sexuality, and the sexual motive would "inspirit" the social edification. A young girl, about to be graduated from grammar school, walking down the road carrying flowers, and singing a *bridal* song: Surely, we thought as we heard her, that could be a tangle of motives sufficient to "spiritualize" a lifetime. If leaving school means getting married, then someday doubtless getting married will mean leaving school. As she walks down the aisle in her bridal train, perhaps, "disrelated" thoughts of that day on the road will occur to her. And the idea of marriage will also probably contain notions of education as a hierarchic promise (unformulated thoughts that education improves one as a property for sale, mixed with vague notions that graduation is a transcending, in the words of the Negro spiritual, "one rung higher").

The Rhetoric of order is thus grounded in a Poetic, or Symbolic of order (Poetic in our scheme being, we repeat, a special case of Symbolic, the Symbolic realm of life in general confined to the realm of formal expression). There are many rhetorical motives for both its use and its misuse, but it has reasons for existence regardless of these. The religionist will derive them from the nature of God as Spirit. For our purposes, at the very least, they are seen to be grounded in the "transcending" nature of language itself whereby, quite as a word transcends the thing it names, so words implant in things the order of human spirit. Such spiritualization derives mostly from the relation the language bears to the prevailing structure of social advantage (a relation that can suggest the forms for a celestial duplicating of the mundane order). But it can also be reduced even to the level of pure pun. For the pun, when basic, always reveals spirit. Imagine a hypothetical language in which the word for "man" happened to be "zoof," and the word for, say, "tree" happened to be "soove." In such a language, there would be more of a tree-ness in man and of man-ness in tree than there would be in an order typical of English. Each, that is, would be more strongly "spiritualized" by the other.

Making the Connection

"In a melon patch," says a Chinese proverb, "don't adjust your shoe; under a plum tree, don't adjust your cap." Doubtless because people might assume a sinister connection, an ulterior motive. They would put two and two together, whether you had or not. People *will* make connections. Hence the Hebrew proverb: "He that hath one of his family hanged may not say to his neighbor, hang up this fish"—or the Spanish variant: "Don't speak of rope in the house of a hanged man."

When our news gatherers broadcast from countries subject to strict censorship, they often seem to be mutely inviting us to put two and two together, by the order in which they take up "disrelated" topics. Thus, during the Nazi occupation of Czechoslovakia, a U.S. reporter broadcasting from Berlin first told of Nazi propaganda condemning the British in India, and then turned to the "disrelated" subject of Czechoslovakia. We asked ourselves whether there may have been a sly, uncensorable hint in this mere sequence of topics. And we believed that at least sometimes a news sequence may be deliberately planned, when reading (in *New Republic*, 3/29/48) of a former newsroom manager who had resigned from radio station KMPC in Los Angeles. He made a sworn statement that the owner of the station had told him "always to follow any story about Communists with a story, derogatory, about any member of the Roosevelt family."

Or a waiter invites us to get the connection when, presenting a bill, he expresses his thanks with warm emphasis (whereat the customer uneasily calculates what size tip would be proportionate to such fervor).

New Yorker cartoon of an overweaningly complacent motorist to whom a policeman is about to present a ticket for a traffic violation. Caption: "Downs is the name—'D' as in Dewey, 'O' as in O'Dwyer, 'W' as in Wallander, 'N' as in Magistrate Norris, 'S' as in Lieutenant Sullivan."

The mother telling her child to be quiet, when obviously the neighbor's children are making the noise. (It takes a quiet child years to get the point of that one. He just thinks that he is the victim of injustice.)

The device of putting two and two together by saying the word at the appropriate moment is regularly used to good comic effect in the radio show "Duffy's Tavern." Once on each program events are so arranged that, just as Archie is on the subject of stupidity, the fantastically stupid Finnegan enters, speaking in the abysmal tonalities that are the mark of his role. The effect is also got by a reverse application of the same device, if Finnegan enters just when Archie is on the subject of intelligence.

In form, the device of saying the word is as though one distinct and significant expression were to flash out suddenly from a context of unintelligible mumbling, thus:

mumble mumble mumble mumble THE WORD

mumble mumble mumble.

Indeed, a comedian might use the device in exactly this way, talking to himself aimlessly and absent-mindedly, and then of a sudden blurting out the one remark which, as placed in the context of the plot, was the all-revealing disclosure. One can imagine the others looking at him in astonishment while he, having said the word, returns to mumbling aimlessly and absent-mindedly.

An Ovid-minded friend said: "I guess it isn't very important. But when my dearly beloved is at table, and I suspect that she may be meaningfully answering the touch of the next man's foot, I do wish her conversation were not suddenly ablaze with expressions like 'pushing ahead,' 'step on it,' 'contact,' and 'secret pressure.'"

Many people are so ready to make the connections that, should you bring them a gift, without thinking they wait to see for what it is an advance payment. Thus, a friend said: "I gave some tennis balls to the children playing in front of our apartment. They took the balls without a word, and stood looking at me, until in embarrassment I left. A bit later, they rang the bell; and when I answered, they thanked me for the tennis balls. And from what they said, I gathered that they had been waiting to find out what I was going to ask of them." They took it for granted that this was not a mere gratuity, but a *quid pro quo*.

And this expectation prepares for the effectiveness of the Said Word and the Word Pointedly Left Unsaid (as in office conferences, if the head of the credit department offers suggestions for improving the sales department, these soon call forth, "without connection," proposals by the head of the sales department for improving the credit department—until each department learns to leave the others alone, in order that it may be left alone, and the entire bureaucratic structure rigidifies towards death, unless jolted into quickness again by forces encroaching upon it from without).

These devices partake of blandness, since they can be so innocent. Nothing is more spontaneous than the changing of a subject from something unpleasant to something pleasant. Yet, out of such Edenic simplicity there may come the rhetorical fall, when a subject is deliberately changed as a way of calling attention to the fact that it is unpleasant. Nothing is more spontaneous than the unconscious give-away of associated ideas, as when a reference to Mr. Blane brings up an "innocent" reference to Miss Pettengill, who is suspected of having guilty relations with him. Yet out of it can arise the rhetorically pointed association, as when the speaker deliberately suggests the relation by pointedly shifting from one to the other. Or the conversation is about liars—and someone asks, in a *non sequitur* that is anything but a *non sequitur,* "and by the way, where is Joe McQuade these days?"

The device, in its simplicity, retreats into such blunders as Freud would include under "the psychopathology of everyday life." Heaven only knows what was eating at that compositor of the *Christian Science Monitor* (1/16/48) who referred to self-help among the European countries as "self-whip programs." And we recall how, during the Hoover depression, another James Joyce among the typographers sent forth a report prophesying "prosperfidy." On the radio we heard a speaker who, intending to honor a dead politician by reference to his "gifts," by *lapsus linguae* spoke instead of his "guilt." And during the height of the "get tough" policy, our own typewriter startled us by writing "Hate Department" for "State Department." Similarly, at a time when many influential groups in the United States wanted our armies to be kept in various "trouble spots" throughout the world, to help maintain the *status quo* by protecting unpopular governments from the forces pressing for reform, we heard an Under-Secretary of War plead, on a radio program, for an extension of the draft. He meant to say, in politically neutral terms, that we needed a large number of men to close down properly the various establishments abroad we had set up during the war. "The army," he said, "must clean up the thousands of the leftovers of the war." But he stumbled on the word "leftovers," so that his statement ran: "The army must clean up the thousands of the Left [stumble, pause]—overs of the war." One can think of many examples, made deliberately for comic effect. Or there are subtler cases. Somewhere in Gertrude Stein, for instance, there is a passage that dwells hauntingly upon the thought, "The chicken is a dirty bird, a dirty word, a dirty third." Surely its great power and profundity are to be found in its earnest striving to all-but-say the rhyme it leaves unsaid, yet comes so drastically near to saying in the syllable, "third."

A friend said: "In sending letters of congratulation to people with whom I was well acquainted, I often inclined to prefer slang, writing not 'congratulations' but 'congrats.' One time it so happened that 'congrats' had to be divided, with the first syllable at the end of one line and the second syllable at the beginning of the next. To my surprise and enlightenment, I found myself so dividing the letters that the second line read: 'rats on your good luck.' Since then I have gone back to using the full word; but I often receive letters that have the slang term; and anyhow, even in the formal expression, there's still one rat left."

In this area, rhetorical and poetic motives cross bewilderingly. Thus a friend said: "I had been shouting in an argument; and my opponent, if only by contrast, was put in the role of 'gentleman.' At one point in the argument, to illustrate his meaning he referred to the word 'bark.' He was supposedly using it in the sense of a tree's bark, not in the sense that would apply to my alcoholic yaps. But I now take it that both meanings were there. He was looking for a term that would illustrate the situation he had in mind. But what was the situation he had in mind? It had two important elements: (1) The point he was making in the argument, calling for a reference to the bark of a tree as illustration; (2) his resentment at the shouting. The double meaning of 'bark' brought both motivations into a single syllable—but probably he did not realize its full relevance as a saying of the Word until he heard himself use it."

Or a hostess, when a guest was overloud, suddenly began telling a story in tones barely audible, and then interrupted herself in vexation, exclaiming: "But I am being too loud."

In the second of these instances, we have surely moved beyond the regions of sheer simplicity. Yet, the effectiveness resides in the fact that we are always hovering on a borderline, always in the virtual region of simplicity. We drop back into the pure condition, along with rhetorical overtones, potentialities, when Primus, who suspects that Secundus wants something for nothing, suddenly to his surprise hears himself saying to Secundus: "Tertius is always expecting something for nothing." Primus realizes the aptness of his remark; he is glad he has said it, and he glances furtively at Secundus to see whether it has taken effect. Yet, had he thought of this device in advance, he would have gone out of his road to avoid using it.

Consider even a usage so low in the scale of social combat as a pointed reference to bad neighbors in general for suggesting (on a "Whom the shoe fits" basis) that some particular neighbor is meant. This raw device is rooted in a principle of classification essential to both philosophy and art: the propriety of surrounding a given theme with details in keeping, as with the scene-act and scene-agent ratios discussed in our *Grammar,* or as the lover will talk of love in general when leading to talk of his particular love. (We have seen previously how in print such specific pointing of a generalization may be contrived through the Spokesman device. In conversation, where the situation itself delimits the universe of discourse, it can be more easily done by a mere glance, or gesture, or tonality.)

Let us say that something has an element very unfavorable to you. It also has a neutral, or slightly favorable aspect. The artificer recommends it to you for the neutral or slightly favorable aspect, leaving it for you to discover the sharp relevance of the unmentioned. This would be the pointedly unsaid. Yet the device can originate in Edenic simplicity. Thus, a literary friend said:

> A man I met wanted to see something I had written. He had told me quite a lot about himself, and we were on quite amicable terms. For some reason, I decided to show him, not anything I had written recently, but an essay I had written 25 years ago, and a reprint of which I had recently received. After he returned it, with an attitude of constraint that would not have been justified had he merely found it uninteresting, I read through it again myself. And I

discovered that it contained a long passage easily capable of interpretation as an obliquely but pointedly unfavorable allusion to a situation much like his own.

I had not remembered this part of the essay. If I had, I would have selected something else to show him, since I had no desire to insult him. Yet, had I completely forgot? Didn't that forgotten element really figure among the motives that made me select that particular essay for that particular person?

I do not mean that I was motivated by "unconscious malice." The motive rather would be "uncriticized relevance."

That is, my vague memory of the article correctly suggested to me the thought that it was particularly relevant to this reader. But the memory was too vague to specify just what kind of relevance the article had. In general, it was relevant; specifically, it was unpleasantly relevant. As regards social relations, the specific differentiation was the more important. But as regards the methods of classification, the Edenically simple sense of relevance in general was primary, as it should have been.

The saying of the word, in words themselves, or in deeds that speak for themselves, is so effective because it is so imperious, so ever on the alert to break through, however unwanted it may be by the artificer who may himself be in its power, as a medium communicating from the world of spirit. Thus, a friend said: "My neighbor and I had once been quite intimate, and then for several years we were kept apart by a quarrel over property. One day, in a casual conversation, we attempted to patch things up. But I saw that the situation was hopeless when I realized that, while making affable remarks, he had kept spitting, and I, amid smiles, had continually reverted to the subject of exterminating rats."

As for Truman's notorious slip of the tongue at the Jackson Day dinner where, instead of Franklin Delano Roosevelt, he listed Theodore Roosevelt along with Jefferson, Jackson, and Wilson as great men of the Democratic Party's illustrious past, a friend said: "Whether spontaneous or deliberate, it showed how far things had gone in the few months since his death, when his very name could not even be pronounced without constraint among representative members of his own party. Yet there was much propriety in the evasion, since the resonant name of Franklin Delano Roosevelt, uttered by a tin horn like Truman, would be like a grand operatic aria sung through a comb."

Returning to the realm of the wholly rhetorical: In diplomatic sparring, when British and United States army men were known to be conferring on plans for possible joint action against Russia, Montgomery sought to neutralize the significance of the conferences by proposing that British and Soviet military academies exchange student officers.

But, according to the official Russian news agency, Tass, Stalin rejected the proposal on the grounds that such measures in peacetime "might be interpreted as preparation for war." The agency explained:

> Stalin noted . . . that various press organs denounced Britain and the United States as preparing for war by practicing an exchange of officers and a standardization of training and armaments.
> The Soviet Union would not like also to become an object of denunciation, which would be the case had the Soviet Union also adopted such a path for better or worse.

Thus, the British made the offer to suggest that close military cooperation between Britain and the United States had no sinister implications, since they also offered an exchange of military personnel with Russia. But Russia, in rejecting it, contrived to point up the very connections which the proposal had been designed to obscure.

As for cases where the word can be left pointedly unsaid, since the situation speaks for itself, there is the incident of the husband who, having lost a week's salary at the races, told his wife the money had been stolen. They arranged that, to economize the next week, he would carry his lunch instead of eating at a restaurant. When he bit into the first sandwich she had packed for him, he found it filled with cancelled race tickets which she had found in his pockets. The sandwich spoke for itself.

Or the making of connections by "letting a situation speak for itself" can be used for intentional misrepresentation, thus: Preen would complain to a workman of his work, yet would deflect the man's resentment from himself. Prone chances by. Preen talks to Prone confidentially, in full view of the workman, but out of earshot, occasionally pointing to the scene of operations. After Prone has left, Preen goes to the workman and states his objections in one-two-three order, as though repeating a lesson he had been taught. The device is still more effective if Prone is to some extent a rival operator of the workman criticized. Preen tells no lie; he merely so stages the situation that the other man, being invited to "get the connection" for himself, accepts the criticism from Preen while hating Prone. Mildly, this is a device of stagecraft used by so great a master of the art as Iago.

Yet there are also variants that can be used in the cause of amity. Thus, Preen has done something which he knows will irritate Prone greatly. So he asks Prone to do him a certain favor (the favor to be done at a time *after* Prone is due to get the irritating information). Prone promises, and later is informed. If he then refuses to do Preen the favor, he will be going back on his promise. But if he does carry out the promise, he will be implying that Preen has been forgiven. (Prone may be even grateful for the scheming, which makes it easier for him to let bygones be bygones, whereas otherwise he might have had to maintain several days of burdensome sullenness.)

The pointedly unsaid can be effectively sharpened by narrowing the universe of discourse to two themes, and then mentioning only one in such a way that the hearer immediately asks himself, "What about the other?" Thus, in sparring between two lady novelists, one said to her colleague, who was also a mother of three children: "Three children and three books—and what excellent children!"

Or, as Gertrude Stein formulates the same principle in *The Making of Americans*:

> Another one once was always certain that some one who one time told him that he would sometime later be successful in teaching meant it that he would not be successful in painting and that this was because that one was jealous of this one although that one had just met this one.

Or there is this variant, involving ironic reversal, by a friend who said: "When my son was barely able to toddle, I got a little harness for him, and would take him for walks in the park. But I found that the women who were walking their dogs made no distinction between their dogs and my boy. One gracious lady came bouncing up, following the lead of a detestable poodle that was straining at his leash in eagerness to lick the child's face. Each time I pulled away, she would move closer, assuring me that the dog would not hurt him, but merely wanted to give him an affectionate kiss. I said: 'Madame, I am afraid that if the dog licked the baby's face, the baby might give him worms.'"

Another variant: Author Prone has just spoken, and has received his measure of applause. Author Preen, a "rival operator" to whom that applause was as the venom of a cobra, arises to speak next. He begins: "I would like first to pay tribute to the only significant writer of our day. I hardly need say whom I mean—Mr. Zanzibar Bezant." Now, it might seem at first sight that Preen had hurt himself in the effect to get Prone, like the man of the dirty joke who sought to contract a vile disease so that, roundabout, the priest would get it, "and he's the one I'm after." But look again, and you will note that in this generous tribute to Bezant, whereas it so stoutly attacks Prone by implication, Preen himself is spared. So far as his own reputation is concerned, he has but taken the role of a speaker fittingly modest about his own accomplish-ments. Indeed, his "modesty" even makes the device a secularized vari-ant of Christian vengeance, combined with the device of speaking in such a narrowed universe of discourse that his attack is directed at the speaker who had just preceded him.

Here is the commonest application of the form, as used for minor misrepresentation: "Ethel and I were talking the matter over, and I think that you should . . ." etc., where the implication is that both Ethel and the speaker had arrived at the decision, whereas literally there is only mention of a previous talk with Ethel, with the author invited to infer that the speaker is spokesman for them both.

But we know of one instance where the artificer was ingenious and imaginative enough to establish a misrepresentation in full view of the victim, and to his complete knowledge. Thus, a friend said:

Once I worked as a private secretary for a brilliant, erratic, and somewhat imperious man whose temperament had unsettled his digestion, so that he was on a strict diet. He had his kinds of generosity, but he also had his kinds of meanness; and for one thing, since I took my meals with him, he showed that he very definitely had no intention of watching me dine well while he systematically starved. It was not the cost he minded; he was quite well-to-do; but he could not tolerate the idea of watching his secretary eat steak while he picked disconsolately at his little dishes of strained vegetables. So he explained that he was asking me to share his diet because his chef was stay-ing under protest, and would resent being asked to prepare two different kinds of menu. So I resigned myself, simply taking it as a regrettable but inevitable aspect of the job. Yet I doubt whether even he himself believed his fiction; for it was a rambling old house, so arranged that I had to cross the kitchen on the way from my bedroom to the dining room—and when going to the little dishes of mashed, strained carrots, and the like, I would pass through an incense of broiling meats, which the chef was preparing for him-self and his Negro helper.

Finally, though I said nothing about it, I was so obviously disconsolate as I passed these succulent masterpieces that the chef himself came to my employer and asked if he might serve me the same meals as he prepared for himself and his helper. Naturally, my employer had to agree, since I was present when the suggestion was made. So the next meal was a miracle for me, though my employer tried to make me feel like a caged beast being watched by visitors at a zoo.

But he had resources. He had no intention of letting me get away with that. And he worked quickly. Of a sudden he began to complain about his strained green beans. They had not been properly prepared. So he asked me if I knew how such beans were prepared. I said I assumed that they were pressed through a narrow-meshed sieve, so that the coarser parts of the pod, along with the strings were left in the sieve and discarded. He got me to repeat all this. I felt like an ass, for this wasn't very complicated lore; and though he usually knew little about such matters, I could not imagine why he seemed to be getting such enlightenment from my description. He hung eagerly on every word, and repeated each step as though I were telling him of some exceptional culinary trick such as cooks have who lock the door when mixing a special sauce. After I had finished, he rang for the chef. And when the chef came, he said: "These beans are not prepared properly. They are too coarse. Now Mr.—[pointing to me] says that they must be strained through a sieve in such a way . . ." etc. The chef gave me one withering look—and I knew that I had had my last piece of steak under his dominion.

But skill in non-committally inviting the hearer to put two and two together can invite to vandalism, as in a planned Failure to Make the Connection. Thus, of a woman who was adept at sly allusions, enriching her gossip with veiled but pointed suggestiveness: a friend, while relishing her stories, could not resist being deliberately obtuse, and asking for further clarifications until this art of innuendo was robbed of all finesse, spice, and protectiveness.

There is at least one other way in which the arts of allusion can be crippled. Thus, we once heard of a man in Russia who, while somewhat hostile to the régime, never uttered one single world of protest. He would merely select passages from earlier literature, written under the Czars, passages which, if read as *double-entendres,* might be interpreted as arch comments on the contemporary rulers. Never an outright word of protest would he utter, not he. He would merely select classic passages having allusive possibilities, and he would say non-committally, "Read that," nothing more. Yet people quite often got the connection. It was a perfect device, quite impregnable. Then one day his friends began asking, "Where is Ivan?"

Many cases of saying the word are based on the principle that there is no negative in imagery. Hence, an idea can be suggested as well by warning against it as by pleading for it, or by a question as by an assertion or a command. Thus: Primus owes Secundus money, and Secundus would remind him of the debt, yet suffers from a certain financial prudency. So he asks Primus eagerly: "I don't owe you anything, do I? Are we all settled up?" He has said the word.

Perhaps the most terrifyingly gorgeous example of the Say the Word device, through imagery plus a negative that the imagery itself sweeps away, is in Act III, Scene III, of *Othello.* Here Iago leads Othello by delicate gradation from the first faint flicker of uneasiness (which Iago slowly intensifies by his non-committal mutterings, vague questions, and an apparently embarrassed repetition of Othello's own words) to strong jealousy. (Iago sums it up for Othello and for us by his apparent admonition, "O! beware, my lord, of jealousy"; and later he makes it almost unbearably vivid by a ruttish or "riggish" imagery which, while *logically* making no direct charges against Desdemona, charges her *psychologically:* "Were they as prime as goats, as hot as monkeys, / As salt as wolves in pride". . . .) And so, at the end, after the talk of killing Cassio, Iago completes the symmetry of his pattern by suggesting the murder of Desdemona in apparently warning against it: "But let her live"— whereupon Othello shouts:

> Damn her, lewd minx! O, damn her!
> Come, go with me apart; I will withdraw
> To furnish me with some swift means of death
> For the fair devil.

In sum, we have here considered: Putting Two and Two Together, or Making the Connections; Saying the Word; the Relevant Association; the Pointedly Unsaid (particularly by narrowing the universe of discourse and then omitting what cries to be mentioned); the *Quid pro Quo;* Letting the Situation Speak for Itself; the Imagistic Inundating of the Negative.

Say Anything

To say the Word, to Say the Opposite, to leave Pointedly Unsaid—the pattern is completed in the artificer's willingness to Say Anything. Nothing in this world being the perfect means for all purposes, there are legitimate grounds for an objection of some sort. Further, there are many objections which, though not much good in a formal argument, do well for hit-and-run purposes, particularly in cases where the opposition is at a disadvantage in answering, as with nationalist polemics for home consumption. Here the device of Say Anything comes into its own. And without it, our newspapers would be much briefer.

A fan is not handy for driving nails, water makes a poor ceiling, there are many things better than wood for quenching thirst. Particularly if it is your business to promote international ill will, as with so much journalistic comment today, you will never leave such wisdom out of your sight. If he's here, he's not there; if it's five, it's not ten; the rider is not walking; the walker is not riding; the blank verse is regrettably not in rhymed couplets; the prose novel is regrettably not a poetic drama.

Hence, at all such points, where there is the ill will, the device of Saying Anything, the mainstay of the Word Racket, can be the way.

To avoid arguments over facts, let us use a hypothetical example. Let us imagine a rhetorical project for the systematic encouragement of bad relations between the populace of Perfectland and a distant nation we shall call the Loathesomites. And let us further imagine that you, princely reader, are in a position to guide the rhetorical policies of Perfectland. How would you go about it to Say Anything in behalf of bad international relations? In the spirit of a New Machiavelli, you might proceed thus:

First, as regards conferences. Let us suppose that a "global" body called the Disunited Nations is to be established. And the charter is being drawn up. You naturally want to make sure that relations with the Loathesomites begin on as outrageous a basis as possible. So, when the Loathesomites make a proposal with which you do not agree, you rage against their "uncooperativeness," you say that they are trying to wreck the conference, and you announce rumors that they are planning to withdraw. If they ask for five, as a standard bargaining procedure in the hopes of settling for three, you bewail their unbridled arrogance. When, later, they agree to a compromise, you announce exultantly that the Loathesomites have suffered a humiliating defeat. If both Perfectland and the Loathesomites wanted a power of veto, but the Loathesomites later were compelled to use it in ways that interfered with the schemes of Perfectland, then you let the people of Perfectland think that the veto is an exclusively Loathesomite invention. And when this fiction has been used for all it is worth, next decide how the veto might be limited just enough, but no more, for your benefit, and start clamoring for that. Insist upon maximum publicity for delicate international dealings; extol it as the very flower of democratic procedure; but when the Loathesomites present their case at meetings of the Disunited Nations, regret that they are using the organization as a mere "sounding board for world propaganda." And interlard rumors of their plans to walk out with demands that they be thrown out. In brief, Say Anything in behalf of worldwide malice.

Whenever they make a concession, greet it by announcing that they show signs of weakness. Or warn that it is a mere ruse for lulling Perfectos into a false security. In any case, Say Anything that will prevent it from being seen as a reasonable move in exchange. Clamor that only by yielding on all important points (which you call your "principles") can they give trustworthy evidence of their good intentions. And to round out the pattern, Say Anything calculated to establish the assumption that they can attest their genuine love of peace only by letting you set up your guns along their borders.

Or if hundreds of thousands of acres of Loathesomite territory had been devastated by war, while Perfectland, beyond the reach of the enemy, had built up a mighty industrial plant that was completely intact at the close of hostilities, gloat that the "standard of living" is lower among the Loathesomites who suffered the fantastic devastation. Contrast their condition with the enrichment of Perfectland. Attribute the difference to the nature of Loathesomite political institutions alone. Set up a "Voice" that carries this generous message throughout the world. And see to it that the Loathesomites are made to suffer as long and as drastically as possible from the ravages of a war in which Perfectland was supposedly their ally.

Get Perfectland officials to outdo themselves in statements inimical to the Loathesomites. Then, for the crowning effect, have them explain that diplomatic embarrassments will not let them divulge information still more damaging. (*Quae latent meliora putat.*) In brief, make the indictment as strong as verbal misrepresentation can make it, then make it still stronger by demurely desisting from any further representation at all. For rounding out the effect, "leak" ominous rumors to the news agencies, which freely distribute it as "inside information," got from "reliable sources."

If the Loathesomites had for years called for arms reduction, while strong elements in Perfectland had helped build up the bellicose nation of Geopolitia whose rulers promised to destroy the Loathesomites, and if then the Loathesomites contrived to delay the Geopolitian invasion of their country, let the morally delicate of Perfectland be aghast at such Loathesomite treachery. Next suppose that, after the war, the Perfectlanders possess a fantastic New Weapon; and they are assured that they can threaten the Loathesomites with it. But in time people realize that the Weapon is not completely satisfactory, since the armies of the Loathesomites might protect themselves by quickly occupying neutral areas that the Perfectlanders hoped to have on their side. Then be aghast at the Loathesomites' large army, and insist upon its withdrawal to a point where the New Weapon might regain its full power as a threat. Meanwhile, call for a world plan to control the New Weapon, and do so in terms that would give you permanent control of even all *peaceable* applications of the instrument. And to round matters out, put the Loathesomites in the position of rejecting a treaty which your own

Senate would probably reject anyhow (for whatever its advantages to Perfectland, they would not be enough to satisfy the appetites of extremest nationalism).

Increase appropriations for long-range war against the Loathesomites. Make all possible attempts to line up allies. Then watch the budget of the Loathesomites, to see what they do next. If they set aside large amounts for defense, start a clamor that Perfectland must allocate still more money, effort, and materials for military purposes. Demand "guns instead of butter." (Or, in the Perfectland variant of Geopolitia's slogan: Universal Military Training and removal of the tax on oleomargarine.) If there is evidence that a large percentage of the Loathesomite budget is going for consumption goods rather than for war production, do not treat this as evidence of a peaceful intention. Rather, interpret it as evidence that the Loathesomite populace is dissatisfied, hence must be placated with a certain amount of peace goods. And gloat that only Perfectland is now in a position to overwhelm the world with armament production.

Or imagine this state of affairs: Imagine that Perfectland would build up areas abroad from which an attack upon the Loathesomites could be conveniently launched. But imagine that the inhabitants of these other areas don't relish the idea of being the battlefields for Perfectland campaigns. Imagine, further, that the officials of Perfectland encounter all sorts of contradictions in their attempts to build up such strong spots. In strengthening one of them, for instance, you raise fears among the inhabitants of another. Or you discover that they are all of them more like liabilities than assets; you discover that, in case of war, instead of having them to defend you, you'd have to weaken yourself in efforts to defend them. Puzzle over these problems for months. And then blandly offer all your quandaries as evidence that you have no warlike intentions. "How could we be thinking of war," you explain, "when there are so many problems in all these countries you accuse us of wanting as allies?" (Interpreting vexatious contradictions among the *means* as a sign that the *end* was not intended. As were one to say: "Obviously I don't try to do it, for I begin to find it can't be done.")

If Perfectland makes deals to arm countries thousands of miles from home, exult at its contributions to the cause of peace. But when the Loathesomites propose a treaty of friendship with a neighboring nation, so as to lessen possibilities of Perfectland attack through that territory, point with revulsion at this new evidence of Loathesomite expansion, aggression, and chicanery. Announce in advance that the terms of the treaty will be harsh. If, when the treaty is published, they turn out to be mild, you can first point to the mildness as evidence that Loathesomite power is weakening. Explain that, with the aid of Perfectland oratory, the neighbor of the Loathesomites was able to strike a hard bargain. Then, a few days later, when the incident is over, begin referring to the treaty in accordance with your original prophecies, as though it had all the harshness and aggressiveness you originally said it would have.

There was a time when Perfectland and the Loathesomites were allies against a common enemy? And during that time, Perfectland shipped large military supplies to the Loathesomites? Then, later, when Perfectland and the Loathesomites are at odds, and the rulers of Perfectland are calling for vastly increased armament, let them cite as evidence of Perfectland's good intentions towards the Loathesomites, the shipments made under the previous conditions. (You can leave unmentioned the fact that, though vast areas of the Loathesomites territories were laid waste during that war, while Perfectland's productive plant was mightily increased, the officials of Perfectland are still trying to collect on those shipments.)

In order to threaten the Loathesomites in areas ten thousand miles from home, demand fantastic increases in the military budget. Then explain to the people that a foreign power is to blame.

Call for billions to uphold unpopular regimes that, without your constant intervention and support, would quickly fall of their own weight. Blame this on the Loathesomites. Try to impose your form of government upon portions of the globe where conditions make it a total misfit, and blame your troubles there on the Loathesomites. (It would be like putting a Florida hotel in the Arctic, and blaming the Loathesomites when you ran into financial problems. Obviously, such resources are possible only to the device of Say Anything.)

If the Perfectland policy happens to coincide with the Loathesomite policy on some one particular issue, play down the agreement. If the Perfectland policy then shifts so that the two nations are again at odds, begin forthwith airing complaints of Loathesomite uncooperativeness. If the Perfectland policy then shifts back again, so that it again coincides with Loathesomite policy, warn that the Loathesomites are trying to "drive a wedge" between Perfectland and the Imperial Totter, a nation closely allied with Perfectland, but at the moment at odds with Perfecto officials.

To get massive military appropriations through the legislature, work up a war crisis. Talk excitedly of the impending Loathesomite threats. Prophesy that the Loathesomites are about to strike. After you get the appropriations, and there is no need to keep up such intense pother, you simply discover that the enemy is subsiding. You had prophesied that the Loathesomites were all poised to march upon territory you considered in your sphere of influence? And they didn't? Congratulate yourself that they were deterred by your strong attitude. If, next, it is found that something went wrong, so that fresh agitation is needed to get the appropriations, then discover all over again that the Loathesomites are ready to march. Even give the exact date, if you want. On "reliable authority." It doesn't matter. If, in response to your agitation against them, the Loathesomites show signs of taking precautions to protect themselves against attack, clamor that your point is proved: interpret the resistance provoked by your policy of threat as evidence that the policy was justified. If, on the other hand, they seek to end an idiotic armament race, then you should gloatingly broadcast the news as evidence that they are weak and frightened. In this way, even the most rudimentary sign of reasonableness, as an appeal for armament reduction, can be transformed into an inducement to still further armament, on the grounds that the policy is paying off. Further, given the animus, you will find no difficulty in gaining credence for both these views at once: that they want peace because their economy can't stand large military expenditures—and that they are preparing for further military adventures abroad.

Call for a fleet of warplanes that would take two years to build. And as a person in the know, explain to your audience that the Loathesomites won't be ready to fight for two years. If it turned out that three years were required to build the Perfectland fleet, then you could discover that the Loathesomites would not be ready to fight for three years. In fact, the Loathesomites won't be ready to fight until you are ready to fight them. Make this pattern so obvious, talk so much about Perfectland's comparative weakness at the moment, that nearly everybody must ask himself, "Well, since the war is inevitable, why don't the Loathesomites start it now, when they have the advantage?" And then have profound thinkers come forward with fears that the Loathesomites are reaching the same conclusion for themselves, and are in danger of striking at any moment. And when the Loathesomites, who do not need a war scare to keep their factories in full operation, still do not strike, then *gloat—gloat*—put forth all sorts of inside information about the internal weaknesses of their regime. For remember always: If they show signs of peacefulness, it is because they are too weak to fight; or if they show signs of resistance, it is because they are trying to conceal their weakness by bluster. But when you want big appropriations for your war industries, it is because the Loathesomites are so strong. In fact, the Loathesomites are anything and everything that you need them to be, for this one day's particular exhortation. And the animus thus built up can be relied upon to be its own protection, producing the atmosphere of the con game whereby the people are themselves eager to overlook the flimsiness of the propaganda, and are led to believe that their "spokesmen" really are speaking for them.

If the rulers of the Loathesomites express a willingness to negotiate with Perfectland in behalf of better international relations, and the hopes of people throughout the world are raised, at seeing light in the dungeon of malice, bide your time—and then, after a few weeks, recall the incident as an occasion when there had been general "uneasiness" and "suspicion" that a "big rapprochement" between Perfectland and the Loathesomites might develop. Glide easily over the worldwide distress when Perfectland officialdom had resented the "peace offensive." And "speak for" the people as though they had felt exactly the opposite of what they had felt, until they themselves accept the version of their "spokesmen."

If a given measure "for peace" is being pushed under militaristic auspices, to those citizens who distrust attempts to get peace by trafficking in ill will explain that the given measure is without bellicose implications. And to those who love the bellicose, explain that the Loathesomites understand only the language of force, and that your policies are a wholesome brandishing of weapons.

All told, the important factor in Saying Anything is the attitude, the animus. Hence, often, the device is reducible to a mere matter of Tonality. Any one instance of Tonality would be reducible to analysis in accordance with Aristotelian topics. But such individual treatment would not often repay the effort. One needs something more like a theory of gases. Hence one must proceed rather in line with the Benthamite shortcut, noting merely the common interest that animates a whole batch of "censorial" shifts between "eulogistic" and "dyslogistic" terms. Why seek to decide what topic is being exploited in a given instance? Once the attitude is established, once the audience has, over a period of time, been brought to expect the ill will as its daily bread, all a speaker need do is use tonalities that confirm the animus. Indeed, when things have been set vigorously in motion, only the slightest push is needed to keep them swinging. It may then even happen that the more trivial the tonality, the better. A mere expression like "the Loathesomites are at it again" might do as the newscaster's tithing for the day, his modest contribution to the methodical maintenance of international malice, the systematic debauching of human relations. Or perhaps a very judicious question will serve the purpose: "But can we hope that the Loathesomites will not interfere by asking to be represented too?" Or the tiniest suggestion of a snort when the Loathesomites are mentioned.

In building up this hypothetical example, we do not mean to imply that the Loathesomites, throughout such a controversy, would be meekly turning the other cheek. Say Anything, Say Both, Get Them Going and Coming, Cut In from Another Angle—once an issue is being considered in primarily terms of international malice, one can expect to find variants of these devices used by both sides, devices which deceive audiences so readily because the audiences, being in the position of fellow-conspirators, are so eager to deceive themselves.

"We didn't do it." "Only they did it." "Or at least, they did it first." As Machiavelli points out, if a ruler really wants to break faith, he need never be at a loss for an excuse. They *did* do it first—but only because everybody did it first. Trace the matter back far enough, and you get to the Tower of Babel. That is, you come upon the *essence* of the conspiratorial situation, the *essence* of wrangling alliances, a *universal* "priority" that, in the story of the Tower, is expressed *mythically* as an event actually occurring at some particular time and place in the past. But take the myth for what it is, a way of using quasi-historical words to designate a universal motive in the War of Words, and you realize why the charge that "they did it first" is so appealing. "All men did it first," in the sense that all men are thus essentially tempted. And they can at once admit and deny the charge by transforming a "Universal Myth" into a polemic, historical myth. Here the essential "All" becomes divided into a "We" and a "They," with "Us" invited to cleanse ourselves by assigning the unwanted elements to "Them" (ambiguities of consubstantiality and alienation that make for ritual purging by use of enemy as scapegoat).

Behind all such nationalistic "conspiracy" there lies such "spiritualization" as animates the Vigilante pattern: gratifying of a desire for violence by the moralizing of violence, representing the victim of it as a "bad" man who had done violence, and was being repaid in kind. The lure of the pattern explains why degenerate Christians make such perfect hoodlums (as instruments of mob "justice" for use in reactionary politics).

But though the inducement to Say Anything is most thorough in a rhetoric vowed to the cause of international malice, it is present, to a less drastic degree, in all factional, conspiratorial situations where "spokesmen *for*" some antagonistic group are furtively speaking *to* the group, and where the members of the group are prodded to adopt some particular animus as a sign that they are members in good standing.

In earlier pages we have considered rules of thumb in Aristotle for deriving materials for argument by reversing the arguments of your opponent. But when conditions are ripe for Saying Anything, the speaker might just as well get his material by reversing his own arguments. That is, he need not try to decide whether to say one thing or the opposite; he can Say Both. For it is not the argument that counts, but the animus behind it; and mutually contradictory arguments may be better than consistent ones in such cases, since they cover more ground. In fact, they are little more than a use of contrasted images for amplifying a single idea. And though the device of Getting Them Going and Coming (so that the opponent is "damned if he does and damned if he doesn't") is sometimes more inventive than the blunt Say Both device, the two obviously merge.

An instance of the second is discussed in Arthur Krock's column (*NYT*, 3/19/47). It seems that Gael Sullivan, an executive director for the Democratic National Committee, had figured out an ingenious way of putting the Republicans "in a hole" by calling upon them to endorse the Truman administration's foreign policy. If the Republicans did so, they "would become the 'Me Too' party, despite their control of Congress." And if they didn't, "a new charge of 'isolationism' and non-cooperation on a vital foreign issue could be laid against them." Mr. Krock was very indignant at this inventiveness on the part of a "handsome, self-assured young man from Chicago" who was "anxious to make a record for alertness" by turning a grave issue of foreign policy "to partisan advantage." Look up the item as an instance of epideictic, if you want to see a bright young man spanked in public (a "former college lecturer" ... a "former divinity student" ... "but he has 'played politics' with a callous city and national machine for many years" ... in contrast with Senator Vandenberg's "dignified protest" ... "and Senator Tom Connally followed him"). So all told, the Democrats were not allowed to get the Republicans Going and Coming, which meant that they were got Going and Coming Instead, as became apparent later when Republican orators explained that the bipartisan foreign policy had been their suggestion. And lo! if you didn't want the policy, you shouldn't want Truman. And if you did want the policy, then you should want a Republican president who could work still more closely with a Republican Congress.

However, at this point there is a possibility of Cutting In from Another Angle. That is, we had been told that the two-party system is the glory of American democracy. The voters are not compelled merely to make a choice between one platform and nothing, but can choose between opposite platforms. How then, asked Henry Wallace, Cutting In from Another Angle, do Republican and Democrat voters have a choice, if both parties are, by their own profession, united on a single policy?

This was a good device in itself. But it was running counter to an attitude already thoroughly established, by radio and press. We might call it an attempt to substitute a poorly subsidized dyslogistic tonality for a highly subsidized eulogistic one. The device of Cutting In is most effective when it is exploiting and confirming an established animus than when it is merely repartee by a minority against whom the animus is already being directed. As an instance of how much more effective the device is when it confirms the animus, consider this usage, in a newspaper whose readers were strongly against government ownership of any enterprises except such public services as must operate at a loss: A federal agency having published figures of its large profits on two federally owned and operated pipelines, figures designed to answer charges that political government in business is always "inefficient," the newspaper editor, speaking in the spirit of his advertisers, commented: "When the government goes into business, it apparently isn't as critical of profits as when it goes over the books of private enterprise." For its audience, it scored.

Once a tonality has been established, a rival orator must take the audience's susceptibilities to it for granted. Even if he is going to attempt changing them, as with Antony's gradual change of the mob's attitude towards the murderers of Caesar, he must begin by seeming to accept them. Yet think of a situation where the orator had not merely one audience to persuade, but many. Imagine his having been quite successful in remolding his first audience, as Antony was, by cautiously, imperceptibly drawing them from one step to the next. Then imagine that, before he had a chance to plead with other audiences, an adverse press printed reports of his first speech. Can't you see the headlines, to be read by audiences whom Antony has not yet addressed, and who accordingly still looked upon Brutus and his fellow-conspirators as saviors of the nation?

DOWN WITH BRUTUS, SAYS STOOGE OF DEPOSED TYRANT
CALLS FOR VENGEANCE AGAINST PATRIOTS

In a rabble-rousing address before a group of idlers in the marketplace, Mark Antony, a former darling of the slain would-be emperor, implied that the Roman people should take steps against the national liberators. Bluntly, he incited the very "stones of Rome to rise and mutiny." And he made no secret of the fact that, according to his party which aims to organize a conspiracy against the government, the freeing of Rome from the danger of dictatorship was nothing less than "bloody treason." He also read portions of what purported to be the ex-ruler's will, as a further inducement to the people to forget their gratitude to the Colleagues whose courageous act was mainly responsible for inaugurating the New Era.

Where such resources are available, those who have control over the tonalities have the purely materialistic equivalent of overwhelming eloquence. And attempts to cut in are necessarily difficult, when counter to the prevailing distribution of "intelligence," since in the end the method involves the transforming of the tonalities in which some crucial policy is named.

An instructive instance of simple *volte-face,* in the unstable alliance between business and government that is typical of our culture, occurred in the spring of 1947. For some time, the press had been printing, on its financial pages, statements by representative business leaders warning that prices were too high, and that a "correction" was imminent. These items were apparently preparation for a demand that the Government permit businessmen to agree on price cuts (agreements that, under prevailing laws, would be open to legal prosecution as collusion). Ostensibly aimed at lowering prices deliberately, the campaign was also intended to permit arrangements that could keep prices from dropping still further of themselves. But after some weeks of such preparatory warnings (interspersed with regrets that present regulations prevented businessmen from acting in concert), the President saw in these Tonalities an opportunity to Cut In from Another Angle, saying in effect that, unless business brought prices down, labor would be justified in asking for higher wages. *Immediately* the situation was changed. Talk of necessary price adjustments was forgotten (though one editor admitted in passing that "there is an opportunity for voluntary improvements of specific price situations"). But the editorial indignation was directed against the "not too subtle aside to the labor union leaders." And figures were promptly produced to show that wages were already high enough, if not too high. And the gravely unsettling effect of such official pronouncements was editorially regretted. (Further, as per our previous remarks on the role of government in a business culture, we should note the chance here to Get Them Going and Coming. If government economists warn against a market slump, and the slump does occur, it can be attributed to loss of confidence due to the government economists' warnings. If, on the other hand, they had not given warning, and the slump occurred, they can be blamed for their silence, which encouraged a false confidence, and thereby betrayed the public trust.)

Another way of cutting in might be called "esthetic." Thus when a charge has become so thoroughly established that it is obvious to everybody, it can be dismissed as "old stuff." This is a particularly effective flank attack (when confirming animus) since it practically puts a sanction upon corruption of long duration. For in the last analysis, the rhetorician's problem is a *stylistic* one, since he is dealing in *words*. And one requirement of style is *freshness*. But what steadier drag on the freshness of an expression is there than the prolonged continuance of the situation which calls for such expression? Hence, in effect, if a bad condition has persisted long enough, unless the rhetorician who would complain against it is unusually inventive, the very existence of the bad condition acts as the sanction for it, when the apologist cuts in with the objection that the rhetorical complaint is as dreary as the situation itself? Thus with George Seldes' valiant little sheet, *In Fact,* the saliency of its attacks against journalistic transgressions being blunted by the perennial ubiquity of the transgressions. One earnestly wishes that the rhetoric could be forever fresh, whereas it must forever hammer at the same points. Think of a carpenter who was required to find a new way of striking each blow, and you'll know what unwieldy obligations you can impose upon the rhetorician in such cases by cutting in from the esthetic angle.

The devices that Aristotle discussed are formal, or qualitative. Even his notion of amplification is such, as compared with the modern ability to Say Anything, when the tonality is *quantitatively* amplified through the great bureaucracies (of government, of press and radio chains: the Rhetoric Trusts). Here no torrential eloquence of a Demosthenes is necessary. Each rhetorician deals in tiny droplets of persuasion, until in their mere number and persistence they overwhelm their audience *physically*. Persuasion thereby takes on a more sadistic cast, like the proverbial Chinese torture. It is designed not so much to *convince* a man as to *wear him down*. And finally, in his semi-comatose state, he dreams fitfully. And in his dream he thinks that the same advertised Spirit is everywhere, and that it is no less than God Himself, speaking now not in resonant, Biblical accents, but in the dingy yet ubiquitous tonalities of hack journalism. Let us call this style the New Hygiene, for its slogan should be: Use Once and Throw Away. (Persuasion in the hands of men who spend all their lives with words, and will bequeath mankind not one sentence worth remembering, except perhaps as Herostratus is remembered for having destroyed the temple.) And perhaps, along with such traditional terms as faith, knowledge, opinion, belief, and conjecture, we should add, for the New Quantitative Rhetoric, the term worn-down-ness, to name the state of mind in an audience after it has been systematically assailed by a raging torrent of petty trickles.

However, there is one great danger in our diagnostic stress upon the device of Say Anything, as major resource in the modern, *quantitative* rhetoric. Elsewhere we have warned against the kind of interpretation which Thurman Arnold gets, in his *Folklore of Capitalism,* by treating the journalistic statements of many men as though they were all made by a single speaker. There is good farce in such a method; but it can make rhetoric seem more irrational than it ever is. Much of the inconsistency in the attempt to foster international ill will derives from the fact that the given animus is established differently by different persons. Individually, their views may not have such fantastic disarray as when thrown into one heap. And even when thus lumped together, they share the rationality of the conspiracy common to them all. That is, they derive their rationality, not from their relation to one another, but from their relation to the spirit, or animus, animating the lot. And that is rational precisely because it is *designing,* imbued with human *purpose.* We might say, not that it is irrational, but that it is only too drastically rational, possessing rationality on too malignly reduced a scale.

THEORY OF THE DEVICES

I

"Do not argue with everyone, nor practice on the man in the street," Aristotle says in his *Topics:* "for there are people with whom any argument is bound to degenerate." If you are dealing with someone who is "ready to try all means in order to seem not to be beaten," he says, it's legitimate to use any means you can to bring about your conclusion. "But it is not good form."

He has been considering how to reason from generally accepted opinions (he calls this "dialectical" reasoning), and how one can avoid saying anything that will obstruct him in an argument. His eight books of ergotistic scruples remind us of the turns, point-work, arabesques, and attitudes of formal dancing. Here is a realm of principle. But at the close he realistically refers us to the everyday world in which no holds are barred.

Somewhere in between is the area of the public debate. And in a book "by an old lawyer," Daniel F. Miller, published anonymously in Des Moines, 1880, *Rhetoric, as an Art of Persuasion,* we are admonished against some, "with heads full of learned lumber," who try to uphold all points in an argument instead of concentrating on the major ones. The writer explains:

> Here an unscrupulous opponent, if astute in argument, will avoid the strong points . . . and seizing on the weak ones only, refute them in detail with apparent zeal and confidence, and claim the need of success on the pretense that all the terms of the proposition discussed constitute unity in idea, and must all stand, or all go down together, as when a link in a chain is broken, the chain must necessarily separate.

But what if you feel that you are being misrepresented, though your cause is just? Would you not then seek to outwit your opponent by whatever means you could, like publishers who occasionally attempt to sell a good book by advertising it as if it were trash? Even though you resorted to means that could only be justified, Jesuitically, in terms of an ideal end? (Whereat there is the invitation to let an ideal end serve as justification for ever viler and viler means, until one is in the region of sheer duplicity, as with the religious hypocrisy of Tartuffe.)

Thus, if a man who knows nothing of economics proclaims that "all our troubles are due to labor unions," you might try to show other controversial matters which the government has not been able to solve. Whereupon, he begins anew: "That's it. It's the fault of the administration." You next try to show that both major parties were behind the laws in question, and he answers: "Yes, we have too much government interference already." You try to show that there are concealed taxes levied by businessmen on their customers as well as taxes levied outright by government, and he answers: "Taxes are too high already." You ploddingly qualify, "No, what I mean . . .," but suddenly another bright idea strikes him, and he announces: "There should be a high tax on labor unions. That's what the trouble is. Why, do you know—" and he goes into a tirade on corrupt labor leaders.

The faster you go, the faster spins the wheel. You are trying to make a point, not to defeat an opponent in an argument. And since your point involves a meeting of several factors, each one of these factors obviously can be the springboard for a new controversy. Your attempt to state your case by following him from point to point would be like trying to plug up a sieve by hastily moving a single cork from one hole to another. What can you do? Obviously, your only hope is to Cut In from Another Angle. You can't hope for a cure, but you might find a first-aid remedy. So, throwing the whole argument aside, you say: "You want to blame it all on the workers. I don't agree with you, but you're a fair man, and I'll make a deal with you. If you blame the workers for interfering with production on the days they strike, will you agree to praise them just as loudly on all the days they work?"

Or a Gentile shopkeeper confides to you, with an air of ominous prophecy: "You may think times are bad now, but wait until you see how things are a year from now. By that time the business of the whole country will be ruined. The Jews are starting up everywhere." What are you to do, if you feel that you should do more than merely keep your mouth shut? It is certainly no place for you to deliver a talk on the history and causes and political dangers of anti-Semitism. You must look for an *opportunistic* reply. There is, say, the fact that you and the shopkeeper are both Gentiles. So you perhaps try to throw him by yielding in the direction of this "racial" rapport. So: you laugh; you're enjoying it. And you protest jovially: "Come now, Mr. Butterfield, you are being too modest. Surely we Gentiles can make just as successful merchants as the Jews. Why, you know, Gentiles can outdo Jews in anything, if they really set their minds to it. Some of the greatest criminals in Alcatraz are Gentiles."

At the time when Churchill made his speech at Fulton, Missouri, inaugurating the long series of bellicose gestures directed at Russia, many earnest people objected. But the objections were all head-on. And the argument we heard that had the necessary flank attack was this remark by a subway rider: "A man shouldn't come to another country to say such things. He should make his speeches where he pays his taxes." One would have to think a long time before one could by deliberate design exploit xenophobia in such a "liberal" way as here happened in all simplicity.

The method has its dangers, unquestionably. One might call it "*P. M.* liberalism," since that newspaper often aimed to fight for the principles of liberalism by the use of such mildly unprincipled devices. The remark of the subway rider was reported in *P. M.* And we similarly recall the occasion of a fire in which a certain sportswoman lost twenty-six horses, on the day when an issue of *Time* magazine appeared with her picture on the cover. "That '*Time*' Cover Jinx Strikes Again," the *P. M.* headline announced. And the story listed "the series of incidents—or coincidences—that have hit famed sports figures in the last 15 years after their pictures had graced the red-bordered cover of the Luce magazine." Was not this item even bringing in superstition on the side of liberal politics?

Under some circumstances, as in a book, or when allotted a certain length of time for an address, you can round out a statement. But when you are conversationally criticizing a statement as it looks in one configuration, by trying to show how it would look in a totally different configuration, and where you could do this adequately only by building up the alternative configuration patiently, step by step, and especially where there are no rules, so that the opponent can interrupt at any time, or in his role as an unfriendly audience can simply refuse to make the effort necessary to follow you, every step in your exposition can be another source of haggling. In such cases, since one aspect of a question can be adequately understood only by placement in a context of other factors, and since each of these other factors is itself a controversial matter to someone who has not yet seen the relationship among them, usually a catch-as-catch-can argument is the only kind feasible.

Such rejoinders are hard enough when you are merely trying to score against an opponent. But they are still more troublesome when you aim not to rout him, but rather to take him for at least a little way along with you. Hence the temptation is to choose between flattery and silence. Or to lose patience and aim simply at an answer that will score. Politicians often use "character assassination" as their catch-as-catch-can rejoinder, since they are trying simply to rout their opponent, not to convince him, and their political theories are so tenuous that the only way the audience could tell the two candidates apart would be if one had been caught in a scandal.

But we are not greatly concerned here with rhetoric as argument. Argument usually involves sustained attack; but the characteristic rhetoric of today is done in quick raids, as with Indian warfare, guerrilla tactics, commando operations. It is neither good argument nor bad argument; it is not argument at all. For argument it substitutes *identification* and *dramatization.* An advertisement is doubtless reducible to enthymeme, or even sometimes syllogism. A slogan, "Superior People Buy X," depicting the consumption of X in expensive surroundings, might conceivably be reduced to some such form as: Expensive surroundings indicate superiority; you want to be superior; this product is shown before your very eyes in expensive surroundings; "therefore" you should identify yourself with and by this product which is itself identified with superiority. But though one might thus analytically reduce the advertisement, it has no such form. It offers no argument at all. It merely *identifies* X by association. And instead of sustained attack, it repeats the same quick raid over and over. (Indeed, our remarks on Say Anything could almost as accurately have been called Say the Same Thing—for the method aims at the constant reinforcement of one attitude.)

The Devices we have been considering are primarily matters of *style*. And for that reason, they readily bring us to confront matters of *personality*. (As per the formula: "*Le style, c'est l'homme même*"?)

II

Each kind of personality would have its corresponding kind of rhetoric, that might at times obtain advantages for the artificer, but might be used by him even at a loss, if it "epideictically" represented him as self-portraiture. Thus, with a man who identified his neighbors, not by saying, "They live in the house on the hill," or "They bought the Murdock place," but "They are the people that pulled our car out of the snow last winter," or "They are the first ones who phoned to say that they approved of my plans," or "They did it for us without charge"—with him one might use different devices than of the woman who, when her chickens began over-running a neighbor's vegetable garden, and he told her he did not mind, since he was through with the garden for that year, nonetheless she kept chasing them home with sticks, murmuring, "I don't want to be beholden to nobody." The first would bind by receiving. The second apparently would not bind at all. However, in other respects she was more generous than she suspected, doing acts of helpfulness that were beyond payment, but always greedily and complainingly demanding mean sums in exchange, so that her beneficiaries thought her as heartless as the villain in a melodrama—and every kindness she did gave the impression that she was foreclosing some poor widow's mortgage.

Obviously, the inventions here are restricted by the nature of the inventor, and would represent that nature regardless of results. And a wholly different list would arise, in such shifts between persuasion for advantage and the motive of pure expression, with a person who, feeling inadequate, and putting much store by appearances, was always lurking in tiny ways to make people pay him tribute (as they often did, without even realizing it, since his tests were secret). Thus if he could ask on a postcard what would require a long letter in reply, and if he received the letter, he felt that he had made his step forward for that day. And in order to be seen in a better seat, he would do as much scheming as a revolutionary might need to overthrow a government.

Possibly the most honest form of flattery is in showing a man that you associate him with his trivial traits, taking as the sign of his particular person, some indifferent detail that can go with many other persons. This is flattery because, though you may consider the trait neutral, when it is thus singled out as his the possessor furtively feels it to be eulogistic. Or the sign selected makes his personality at once objectively universal and fetishistically concretized. The flattered one becomes like an official whom journalists have built up, in the public eye, by the caricature of some one feature (like Theodore Roosevelt's teeth). The tribute suggests that you have paid attention—but for this very reason it may be resented if the attention is felt to encroach upon one's privacy, hence to threaten one's freedom. (Should a person have himself found a good expression for some really distinctive or essential aspect of his character, and should you construct a nickname for him out of this expression, thus as it were letting him name himself, you would have moved into more exacting areas of human relationship. For each time you spoke the name, you would suggest matters of motivation.)

We are here again confronting a distinction which we encountered in the first section of our *Rhetoric,* when considering Machiavelli's *The Prince.* We find that the Devices point towards two areas of motivation: the attempt to gain advantage in situations, and the sheer expression of personality. Thus, a friend said: "They had been meeting every Wednesday. But when they invited me, I insisted that they change the time to Thursday. I didn't see why I should accept the date *they* picked." In the offing, there were thoughts of advantage, but they were so general, so categorical, might we not rather treat the device as self-portraiture than as scheming? Some people can be reconciled only by joining to run down another (the standard condition of national alliances). Or, for a variant: Josephine praising Joseph only to spite Josephus (as with a critic who is generous to dead authors that he may more effectively condemn the living). Such devices may be more situational than personal.

Or the devices can be transformed into developments. Thus, Cringe knocks and you let in Bluster (as soon as he makes himself at home, like the dog that gets fat on two meals). But there can be a different development here: By saying little, Q goldened himself in; then growing garrulous he silvered himself out again.

Blandness is possible precisely because of the shifting between the rhetoric of design and the rhetoric of personality. Of some men: You can't show them hospitality without making them think they are doing you a favor to accept it; if you would treat them as equals, they will treat you as an inferior. Hence, unless asking for punishment, you must use devices against them even while befriending them. And note how advantage-seeking and personalities cross in this incident of the flower show: There were the beautiful flowers of the community exhibit, arranged formally; to view them was to walk from song to song, each an ordered symbolism inviting you to order your attitudes with similar symmetry; also there were judges, who awarded ribbons of merit—and out of their decisions emerged feuds that even survived the death of the feudists.

Invective is on its face competitive. Yet one may insult less through malice than because one loves resonance and invective is resonant. A martyr to the word, violating a sound principle of rhetoric cited by Quintilian, he'd rather sacrifice a friend than a wisecrack. Or some, when in doubt, attack, if they are under the sign of Napoleon, quite as they might have asked questions if they were under the sign of Socrates (the end in both cases being the same: to learn the disposition of forces by a quest).

Underneath all rhetoric lies this primary law: Salivation at the sign of the scraped plate. But it is matched by a counter-law: Fed appetites grow picky—and there the way is opened to the Ladder of Yearnings, the hierarchic hungers. Hence, though it is a personal trait to be a prima donna, there is an element of the prima donna in everyone. (Each prima donna feels grievously outraged by things which other prima donnas, with their own ideas of outrage, would hardly notice.)

A rhetoric of sheer display, eloquence for its own sake, "pure persuasion," the sustained and methodic use of linguistic resources through delight in the medium as such (in brief, the epideictic motive) becomes interwoven with hierarchic motives inasmuch as the proofs of such mastery are blanket claims to preferment of some sort. But we should also be prepared to reverse such observations, noting that though competitive conditions may lead to a rhetoric of advantage-seeking, there may also arise a mere "score psychosis." We mean: Persons may seek to score against one another, not for any particular gains, but merely through satisfaction in expressing the competitive attitude itself. In this sense, the rhetoric of the "catfight" can become a kind of epideictic, an oratory quite as weak in "ulterior purpose" as the cult of verbal ingenuity in the era of the "Second Sophistic." The art of scoring would here be an exercise over and above the thought of one's cronies as potential rivals, though it would most often be expressed through the materials provided by the experience of such rivalry (the fear of others) and would be sharpened by misgivings about oneself (for insofar as one has felt disloyal motives and repressed them, one may fear lest others felt the same motives but with less goodwill).

The cult of scoring for its own sake often derives from a narrowing of interests whereby the pettiest rivalries have the intensity of world issues. (Roundabout, they probably do represent the very issues which they ignore.) Often they go with the folding-up of people in retirement, particularly when association produces a community of such persons, who can no longer think of themselves as potential "influences" in the world at large, and seek to become despots in some tiny group, or to win the favor of such despots. The same motive can figure in the wrangling of children whose small realm of intimates is practically the compass of reality (or consciousness). Thus, when a rivalry between brothers becomes a "creative" situation that determines the quality of all their experience, the cult of scoring soon gets to the point where each may be willing even to set himself back a lot if only he can at the same time set the other back somewhat.

A friend said: "One of the most intense quarrels I ever knew had for its occasion a bottle of ink. Behind it was this situation: Two men, recently married, had been close friends before their marriage. Each now had property in a new realm of affection alien to the other's. And since property needs protection, often they were silent or evasive where they would formerly have been frank. Also, there were problems of timing. All four would have had to be in a mood of reconciliation simultaneously, for the accumulations of resentment to be swept away completely, as is sometimes possible with two friends at happy moments. Again, they were naïve about their women, each of whom was trying to break, or at least to greatly modify, the friends' former intimacy, and to 'own' her husband with a thoroughness not possible so long as the earlier friendship prevailed. The women did want all four to be friends, but they wanted the friendship removed to a purely social basis. Add further that the two family budgets were partly pooled, partly separate—and you had the condition for a bitter flare-up over a ten cent bottle of ink, with the use of whatever invective was available at the moment, until the 'pure' stage was reached, the love of scoring for its own sake, a sheer linguistic exercise, an epideictic of bad human relations."

But perhaps we should make a further discrimination here. Perhaps we are here using "epideictic" much in the way that De Quincy (as we noted in the first section) uses "eloquence" (to name the love of the medium for its own sake). Epideictic, as an art of display, comes closest to the "pure" motive De Quincey had in mind (adumbrating the *fin de siècle* slogan of Art for Art's Sake). But though one can inveigh and glorify through sheer love of linguistic exuberance, there is also a wide range of ulterior purposes for such expression, as when praise of a man may lead us to choose his policies (the demonstrative here reinforcing the deliberative) or when it prods a jury to pronounce in his favor (a reinforcement of forensic).

All told, then, we find these important shifts of motivation natural to the Devices: Of those expressions designed for an ulterior motive, some are for definite advantage, some are for preferment in a general way (we might say, they look *towards* preferment), and some are for sheer love of the art (as with "scoring" for its own sake). This last kind, however, might often be explained as expressions of personality, closer to Symbolic (or its special case, Poetic) than to Rhetoric proper. For even when apparently designed for advantage, such forms may be so much a matter of self-expression that the artificer adheres to them even when they bring disadvantage. (He may himself think that he is scheming for preferment, while in actuality he is trying to defeat himself. Thus, a man might insult people to keep from being prosperous, since prosperity would not go with his character, as were he physically weak and unconsciously felt that physical weakness did not belong with a good salary.)

III

This brings us to the distinction between conscious and unconscious motives, which we already considered somewhat when commenting on *voluntaria caecitas mentis*. Here one gets from Poetic to Rhetoric by adding deliberate design to any spontaneous expression. Thus, even such spontaneous poetic devices as figures of speech fall traditionally under the heading of rhetoric, as soon as they are methodically taught. And the symbolism of compulsive erotic gestures is transformed into an Ovidian rhetoric of flirtation, when it becomes a deliberate interchange of signs, the language of sexual affinity thereby being purposely reduced to a natural communication somewhat like that of grasshoppers alternately twitching their legs as they slowly maneuver themselves into position for mating.

Or in political matters, a ruler tends to ignore pleas until they become demands. And then he may condemn the demands as provocative and excessive. You can give this natural development a Machiavellian touch, in accordance with the principle of rhetoric we have been discussing, by stating it thus: "When the people are suffering, and plead, ignore the plea until it becomes a demand, and then condemn it as a provocation."

Or consider the development with our early ancestors in North America. When they first arrived, piously giving thanks to God and to their Indian hosts who taught them the local lore that would enable them to survive the severities of winter, surely no single one of them said to any other: "So long as we are weak, let us be graciousness itself in our dealings with these gullible savages. At this vulnerable stage, let us be as fair dealing as they are. And later, when we are firmly entrenched, will be time enough for us to cheat and rob and debauch them." Rather, there was a simple, Edenic response to both situations. In their first frailty and dependence upon the natives, the early settlers were naturally meek and grateful. Such an attitude most perfectly fitted their situation. And naturally they did not become overbearing until, with the immunity their meekness got them, they were able to build up power.

True, the meekness had its rhetorical use. The same is true of all ethical attitudes which bid for the benefits of cooperation in ways that make for private advantage. And so long as the natives and settlers were differentiated as "classes," this "universal" ethical mode contained the usual temporal possibilities, which would not be revealed until conditions had increased the relative strength of the settlers. Under such circumstances, only the most sophisticated and exacting of religious scruples (as in the Desert Movement of the fourth century) could have kept the newcomers from gradually changing their role until those who were guests gratefully accepting charity had become invaders sternly demanding a settlement. But these settlers were here to amass property, not (as with the ascetic cenobites of the Desert Movement) to renounce it. So the Indians found that, though Cringe had knocked, they had let in Bluster.

The Machiavellian gesture could, of course, be given to this development simply by treating the spontaneity of the original meekness in terms of its reversed outcome. You would thus transform the simplicity of a poetic response (the Sermon on the Mount is the monument to the poetry of meekness) into the complicity, or even duplicity, of a rhetorical device (as were the development made fully purposive at the start: "Let us be meek first and arrogant later").

For some years Hitler, with the connivance of many who were later to be counted among his enemies, worked a plausible variant of this device. Each step he took towards expanding the Third Reich was, in itself, too small to start a war over. And as soon as he had taken it, his propagandists began assuring one another, for all the world to hear: "Now at last we have got all we need. Now we can settle down"—whereupon, after a few months, or even weeks, a sudden small advance was made in some other area, followed promptly by the self-congratulations: "Now we have *really* got all we need. Now we can *really* settle down."

You can imagine the incident idealized as a Clown routine. First Clown points to sky. Second Clown gazes trustingly upwards. First Clown kicks him in the shins. Second Clown is indignant, rolls up his sleeves to prepare for battle. But First Clown is all smiles, fawns on him, offers him a drink, treats him as an old pal. Second Clown in mollified. They embrace, and start walking off together, arm in arm, whereat First Clown kicks Second Clown in the buttocks, immediately afterwards becoming once more the soul of ingratiation. Repeat *ad lib.*—or as many times as Hitler was encouraged to do, until the one occasion when (and he was justified in feeling indignant) the British Tories decided to end that routine, without having first let him know of their intention.

Hegel being a philosopher of the Development, and Marx being a materialist revision of Hegel, this problem of consciousness plagues the Marxists. For the Marxist view of capitalism takes it for granted that the missionary prepares the way for the army. In accordance with their doctrines, Marxists in all sincerity propose a united front with progressive bourgeois factions under conditions when all parties to the deal could profit. At the same time, their doctrine foretells the eventual liquidation of the liberals. Hence, they lack the conveniences of simplicity here. It is as though, instead of grounding their meekness in the Bible (with it "just so happening" that they turned to less "visionary" a language when they could afford to), they had approached the Indians with a document proclaiming: "Peace! Peace! We are all brothers. Be kind to us, and we can all profit by the collaboration, until the day when we are in a position to assume control over you." Or rather, that is how it looks to the indignant liberal, as he watches his kind being collaborated off the map. To the Marxist the all-important difference would be this: The class of Indians was categorically excluded from the class of white men, but the liberal can join the party of the proletariat, when the Development has got to the proper stage. Thus, what looks Machiavellian from the liberal point of view, which equates the death of liberalism with death of the person, can be offered in good faith from the Marxist point of view, which sees the person transfigured by the Development.

Question for readers. Comment on this development: In the early stages of the Second World War, Churchill established the slogan for relations between Britain and the United States: Give us the tools and we'll finish the job. Later, when the materials began arriving, the exhortations could be modified accordingly. Spokesmen could observe that the enemies of the Nazis were fighting "our" war too. And the public abroad could be encouraged to ask, in effect: "What do they think we are, their mercenaries?" Perhaps politicians as shrewd as Churchill and Roosevelt foresaw the second stage, and considered the first stage merely as the necessary way into it? Was it the settlers' plain simplicity? Or was it shrewd simplicity?

Or recall the episode in *The Brothers Karamazoff*, where several characters play a morbid kind of game in which each confesses the worst thing he had ever done. We once witnessed a similar game, played by some morbid adolescents, in one of their early bouts with alcohol. After several confessions, the spirit of competition began to take over, so that the list of transgressions became progressively meaner. Then one poor wretch, telling of a somewhat dingy sexual offense, of a sudden became professionally exalted just as he was finishing his story. In accordance with the rhetorical principle here under consideration, adding an element of purpose, he concluded: "And what is more, gentlemen, if everything goes as planned, I hope to commit this same offense again next week."

The purposive development can also, of course, be made into a rhetoric of the gods. For if the giving of gifts is poetic simplicity, and if the retracting of them may also be the same (as a ring is returned when an engagement is broken), the gift can be made into a vast cosmic plot when (as per Aristotle, *Rhetoric,* II, xxiii, 20): "Another topic consists in maintaining that the cause of something which is or has been is something which would generally, or possibly might, be the cause of it; for example, if one were to make a present of something to another, in order to cause him pain by depriving him of it," whereupon he cites from an unknown author: "It is not from benevolence that the deity bestows great blessings upon many, but in order that they may suffer more striking calamities"—and whether or not it be the favorite device of the gods, it is certainly a basic one of good drama.

Recall, in Mark Twain's *Life on the Mississippi,* the story of the childless foreigner and the young unmarried couple:

> In a Western city lived a rich and childless old foreigner and his wife; and in their family was a comely young girl—sort of friend, sort of servant. The young clerk of whom I have been speaking—whose name was not George Johnson, but who shall be called George Johnson for the purposes of this narrative—got acquainted with this young girl, and they sinned; and the old foreigner found them out and rebuked them. Being ashamed, they lied, and said they were married; that they had been privately married. Then the old foreigner's hurt was healed, and he forgave and blessed them. After that, they were able to continue their sin without concealment. By and by the foreigner's wife died; and presently he followed after her. Friends of the fam-

ily assembled to mourn; and among the mourners sat the two young sinners. The will was opened and solemnly read. It bequeathed every penny of that old man's great wealth to *Mrs. George Johnson!*

There was no such person. The young sinners fled forth then and did a very foolish thing: married themselves before an obscure justice of the peace, and got him to antedate the thing. That did no sort of good. The distant relatives flocked in and exposed the fraudful date with extreme suddenness and surprising ease, and carried off the fortune, leaving the Johnsons very legitimately, and legally, and irrevocably chained together in honorable marriage, but with not so much as a penny to bless themselves withal.

Imagine now that the old man had suspected the truth, and that instead of bequeathing the money to "Mrs. George Johnson" in all simplicity, he had done so with the deliberate intention that things should turn out as they did. You would thereby have transformed his conduct into a rhetorical device, a variant of blandness, perhaps, if he hinted at the ironic possibility, but did not show his hand unmistakably.

Where a given situation beneficial to some persons causes injustice to others, those who benefit by the situation may want to maintain it though the injustice as such is an unwanted by-product which they would quickly abolish if it did not arise from the same conditions as produce the benefits. Rhetorically, you can get startling results here by transferring the purpose from the situation to the injustice. That is, instead of saying, "Let us keep this beneficial situation, hoping that somehow we can remedy its unwanted injustice," you could say, "Let them suffer injustice, that we may profit by it."

That is, if you would point to an injustice *dramatically,* if you would bring it to *consciousness,* the most effective way of doing so is by making it a matter of *conscience.* And this you do by picturing it as *willed* (in one of the several modes available here: humor, satire, or ironic and grotesque expressions that forgo either smiling or laughter). Symbolically, there are dangers in the method. The poet who enacts his scruples thus indirectly, by picturing "hero-villains" who outrage these scruples, may become the victim of his own inventions. Our point is simply that the *rhetorical* motive behind the imagining of villainies may be far from any mere "projection" or "sublimation" of a "suppressed desire" to commit these villainies.

There is, of course, the "Gidean temptation" (to turn "thou shalt not" into "what would happen if . . ."—a tendency grounded especially in the fact that there is no negative in imagery). But we are trying to indicate a purely rhetorical motive here, over and above psychoanalytic ones. We are suggesting that a Shakespeare, for instance, could imagine deviations not so much through "suppressed criminal desires" as through having a fertile feeling for the society's norms. Hence, his rich dramatic *consciousness* invited to expressions made salient by appeal to *conscience,* an appeal that would be got by depicting the unwanted as willed (the portraiture of villainy).

It is said, for instance, that lobster meat is less tender if the lobsters are plunged into boiling water than if the water is gradually brought to a boil. Hence a chef, *as chef,* should prepare his lobsters in a manner that is atrociously barbarous from the *humanitarian* point of view. And the "loving" art of an expert who caters to the human palate can here remain wholly gentle, in the category of the amenities, only insofar as the slow torture of the dying animal is not "sympathetically" imagined. Once it is allowed to invade the chef's consciousness fully, it would place demands upon his conscience, compelling him to make a choice between his conscientiousness as chef and his conscientiousness as humanitarian. And if, after fully confronting the issue, he continued to prepare his lobsters by the harsh method (as regards the lobster) that happened to make a product most gentle to the human appetite, he could do so only by becoming, to the degree of his awareness, a *sadistic* chef. His "sadism," in other words, could arise only insofar as he "identified himself" with his victim. Otherwise, he is no more sadistic than we all are if it happens to be true that the ground must wince painfully with every step we take.

The child, tearing apart the wings of the butterfly in all innocence, is in a state of simplicity prior to cruelty. When it is old enough to think of such an act as the cause of unnecessary suffering, it has gone from "innocence" to "virtue." For henceforth, it must either renounce its pleasure, or become an accomplice in a cruel design (abandoning simplicity for complicity). Cruelty, sadism, is sympathy expressed perversely. It is an immature form of the ironic purgation in tragedy and comedy, where the audience's relation to the scapegoat as *katharma* contains simultaneously elements of identification and alienation.

In "objective" writing, the dramatizing of consciousness in terms of conscience can be contrived noncommittally through a villain. In argumentative dialogue the same skirting of censorship can be got by attributing the suspect views to a speaker for whom the author assumes no responsibility. But in "subjective" writing (or in the essayistic monologue) the author is taken to speak for himself, hence assumes responsibility for all statements. In these cases, consciousness may be established ironically, through *the author's own* outraging of conscience, unless the reader is willing to make complex ironic allowance for the nature of the form.

Thus, in one such "subjective" work, the author who was also spokesman for the fiction wrote, of persons who suffer under "brutalizing" conditions of livelihood:

> Let them be bred as other than mankind, give thought to the monstrous preparing of their characters. . . . Teach them that alleviation is neither possible nor to be desired, instruct them in hoglike appetites, nurture their brutality as we encourage in others affection. Do them at least this minimum of justice. Study them that their denigration may be thorough. Guide them downwards.

Here, by changing an indicative ("They are subject to bad conditions that threaten to dehumanize them") into an imperative ("Let us make them as unhuman as their situation"), the statement presents itself to the reader's consciousness in a way that affronts his conscience. The result is near to grotesque irony. It is on the road to satire. An out-and-out satiric treatment would be got, for instance, by a mock treatise on education: *Plan for Improving the Conditions of Persons Employed in Brutalizing Jobs. Educational Project for Making Them as Brutal as Their Work,* by the author of *The New Symmetry.*

During the early years of the Franklin Roosevelt administration, when the Communists had organized a high percentage of our liberal authors in a Writers' League, and many were trying to abide by the "party line" (as indicated to them by orators who were not themselves any too well versed in Marxism), we recall the remarks of Harold Rosenberg, made in consolation to a poor devil who had unintentionally offended by a speech that got him soundly rebuked by the guardians of the Faith. This earnest fellow was disconsolate over his fall from orthodoxy (it turned out that two weeks later the line shifted, and lo! he was redeemed)—and to him the ingeniously demonic Rosenberg explained: "The good party orator is not the man who bluntly repeats the line. There's not enough excitement in that, except when it comes from the very top. The lesser man should do a subtler job. He should always be on the verge of being suspect. 'Now he's going too far to the right,' the audience should tell itself in horror—but just at the last moment he swings back. 'Now he's going too far to the left'—and again, just in time, he regains his balance."

Maybe yes, maybe no, so far as the needs of the party are concerned. But it was certainly a perfect recipe for the rhetorical motive of poetry, or rather for that aspect of it which we here call the dramatic, or personalized translating of consciousness into the terms of conscience. And it explains why a literatum wholly "correct" as judged by the norms of faction is likely to be poor, like a Hollywood flag-wave.

IV

There is one notable virtue in the rhetorical stress upon the purposive. Such concern with the ways in which men are moved by their interests makes human conduct seem much more rational than do attempts to treat ritualistic motives as primary. (Bentham's utilitarianism is an instance of the first sort; an instance of the second would be Thurman Arnold's *Folklore of Capitalism,* where he plays up inconsistencies by ascribing them to love of ritual, and plays down the consistency of ulterior purpose that often animates such confusions.) On the other hand, there is a risk in making things look *too* purposive. For though words like "design," "plan," "plot," "scheme" suggest an element of rational purpose, they also have connotations of conspiracy. When the purposive element is too greatly stressed, even sheer errors can seem like monstrosities of cunning. This is a paranoid risk that lies about the edges of many Leftist attitudes toward capitalism as the all-powerful "bad father."

Hence, though rhetoric saves us from too irrational a view of human utterance by disclosing much rationality of purpose, we have seen how the result may become a new tyranny. For men may find so much evidence of the designing that human relations look like a vast plot in which all interchange is but a kind of persecution. At this point, however, we can turn from Rhetoric to Poetic (or, more broadly, to Symbolic), noting how the Devices serve the ends of self-portraiture ("identity"), in being reflections of the personality. The reader will now agree with us, we hope, in wanting to make so much of Chapter XXV in *The Prince,* with its shift from scene-act to agent-act motivations. (Here, after having made many sorts of developments "Machiavellian" by the rhetorical stress upon purpose, the author notes that a given ruler will tend to use the devices best suited to his character, even at times when they are not best suited to forward his interests in the given situation.)

However, the same line of thought suggests the possibility that at times the shift from design to portraiture can itself be a disguise. That is, just as the nineteenth-century stress upon the esthetic was nominally anti-rhetorical, hence had to smuggle in the rhetorical motive, might not much chicanery develop under the guise of personality, and be concealed, even to the artificer, beneath the cult of pure personality? Thus, one's very character may become a kind of plot. And at the very least, there are the obvious cases where people are exhorted to cultivate a "pleasing personality" as a rhetorical device (or to use other personal resources of winsomeness, the most intellectually disastrous being perhaps women's over-reliance upon "femininity" as a means of cajolery). Here the line between the Rhetorical and the Symbolic falls away. Such is likewise the case when a Rhetorical pose is, in a deeper sense, genuine (as with Oscar Wilde, who insisted upon the genuineness of the *poseur,* doubtless in his awareness that with him literary perversity was a true counterpart of sexual perversion). Psychotic "malingering" likewise falls in this indeterminate area, as the person who feigns illness for purposes of evasion really and truly is the sort of person who feigns illness for purposes of evasion.

The Gidean "esthetic criminal" (who commits crime not for advantage but for love of the art, as self-portraiture) responds to a kind of epideictic motive insofar as a poetic love of plot here finds expression in a cult of the plotter, or a love of design in a cult of the designing. But such rhetorical "freedom" is quite the same as Symbolic "necessity," since the deliberate choice to "be oneself" under such conditions is likewise a compulsion. A Rhetoric of advantage enters, insofar as the artificer's gestures are claims to distinction, however uncomfortable and even sacrificial. For they can be insignia proclaiming proud enrollment in a very noble but sinister heraldic line, ancestral blood that nurtures the strong stock of bastardy. (Cf. Gide's tributes to the *fils naturel,* whom he admires, we might say, as a source of bright new private enterprise.)

Character itself can, in turn, be considered in two ways: (1) one's identity as an individual (who rounds out his nature by acts in keeping with it); (2) one's identity as member of a class, in a particular position or social status, etc. Often those who treat "ritual" motives as primary in human conduct have in mind some such relations between agent and act whereby the agent "expresses himself in his conduct" (or, we might say, adopts such actions as "imitate" his nature or are "analogous with" it). Because such principles of "propriety" are not "rational" (in the narrowly *rationalistic* sense of the term), some critics who propound the priority of ritual and myth would treat them as "irrational."

But in any case, as we have said, the view of acts as the portraiture of character can ease somewhat the temptation to interpret them purely as "intrigue." And this point, at which Rhetoric retreats into Symbolic, must be remembered when one is contemplating human motives in their entirety. However, the view of act as merely the expression of an agent's identity can also, in its way, become intolerable, in suggesting that a man can but forever and inexorably name his number. When too strenuously pursued by such a demon of identity (in brief, by oneself), one does well to take flight into the areas of the Rhetorical Scramble, with its concern for the objectively designing, in contrast with the endless and inevitable restatement of one's unique nature, like a Leibnizian monad whose encounters with its fellows are but an unfolding from within.

Reviewing this problem of the shift between Rhetorical and Symbolic motives, let us see how it might qualify our previous remarks on the ways of the great Rhetoric Trusts and the unfairness that marks their utterances. We are admonished that this unfairness should not be attributed wholly to rhetorical misrepresentation. That is, the typical statements of such organizations are not uttered merely as acts designed to misrepresent the nature of the scene. Rather, they should be classified as the *spontaneous* acts of agents which the scene itself has selected. However unjust these statements are, motivationally they may be nearer to simplicity than a purely rhetorical analysis of their misrepresentations would indicate. The scene, we might say, leads to the selection of persons who are "naturally" and by training unfair in the gauging of international situations. And these agents, acting spontaneously in accordance with their nature, use a rhetoric of duplicity in the mere process of being themselves, quite as one could hardly call a bird a liar when, with a dragging wing, it seeks to lure us from the vicinity of its nest.

In sum, the positions in a given bureaucratic order have a nature of their own; hence persons who uncritically adapt themselves to the genius of these positions can then "spontaneously" respond to the conditions of their office. They need but have such a modicum of deliberate mental blindness as could be called a loyal dislike of biting the hand that feeds them.

However, the thought that agents selected and trained by the scene can "spontaneously" act in accordance with their nature without rhetorical duplicity as a motive requires in turn a correction. We should not assume, for instance, that a certain scene selects agents who are "naturally" unfair, or even trains them to be so. It selects people who are unfair, *not categorically, but in the particular way demanded by the scene.* In many other notable respects they may be the soul of honest dealings.

Somewhere in his Ethics, Spinoza observes that, although our languages have a word to name our delight in an enemy's misfortune, they lack a word to name our delight in a friend's good fortune. Even so, the fact that malice is everywhere does not make it prevail over other ingredients of motivation. True, if Prone has ten, Preen may try to take five from him; but if Prone has nothing, Preen may give him five. And we admit that, if only out of personal weakness, we could not possibly contemplate the field of Rhetoric as extensively and intensively as we do here, if we had to conclude that men, even in the Scramble, were motivated solely by malice and the lie. We must be *benevolently* caustic, even hoping ironically to find the irenic beneath the irate. And to any reader who might want to view human motives as Shakespeare's Timon of Athens did after his embitterment, we should observe that the "perfection" of malice and the lie is always impaired by *some* measure of forbearance and truth, if only as a device for making the vicious motive more effective. Indeed, where a reader would insist upon the more sinister genesis, we could at least demand that he pay full attention to the very real ways in which such origins are continually being transcended, so that aspects of truth and tolerance emerge, quite as men can fight effective wars only through abiding by the principles of cooperation, or as gregarious animals might originally have been kept together by the greedy desire of each to snatch whatever the others might find, yet the whole species might in time come to have community ways, with a genuine group motive, such as we might call a "herd instinct" (the Ancients gave it the more dramatistic name of "Imitation").

V

At the very least, we might deduce ethical ideals from demands made upon mankind by the *medium of communication.* And we might thereby reduce the ethical to the rhetorical without thereby "debunking" the ethical. In fact, the ethical *is* rhetorically engendered insofar as one must be, to some extent, a participant in the moral ideas he would impose upon others. And such ideas are an imagery that goads him to make himself over in its image.

Even if we began with Thrasymachus' proposition, in *The Republic,* that men censure injustice "through fear of being its victims, and not because they would not be unjust themselves," we could still note that the *universalization* of their fear acts as an *ethical injunction to the self,* quite as with the Golden Rule of Christianity. For instance, let us imagine an ethics which is rhetorically engendered in the directest way. The propounder of the ethic, let us say, tried to decide how *other* people should act for *his* benefit. He would arrive at commandments like this: "*Thou* shalt not kill *me.*" But the statement, as so phrased, is unfinished. For it has not yet received its *maximum generalization.* It is not yet wholly in the spirit of a "god-term," such as it must be if it is to be most thoroughly an ethic (and naturally, if our moral legislator is working out rules for his own protection, he will want them to be as thorough-going as possible). The advance towards a god-term is like the advance from titles to an overall Title of Titles. And an injunction made universal in this spirit should run: "Any thou shalt not kill any me." As so universalized, it becomes equally an injunction to the self. So, even if you proposed a debunker's approach to ethics in accordance with a highly simplified rhetoric of personal advantage, this "minimum approach to the ethical" would involve you in a principle of universalization that imposed the same law upon you. (This is probably but a quick and easy way of arriving at Kant's "categorical imperative." By universalization, freedom to legislate becomes the imposing of law upon oneself.)

We might put it thus: We are "naturally" or "spontaneously" fulfilling the demands and possibilities of reason (or of language) when we seek *summarizing* terms, a title of titles—and this movement, where freedom and order coincide, has as its ethical counterpart the desire for the universalizing of principles. That is, reason moves in the direction of freedom, moves towards the gratification of an ultimate formal desire, when it moves towards maximum generality of rules (that is, justice). The mind is thus "essentially" free as long as it can permit itself to aim at such universalization. Hence, Socrates in *The Republic* is looking for a definition of justice that would prevail over such restricted concepts of class justice as his Sophist opponents were proclaiming—and in this search lay the *rationality* of his quest. (We thus find rationality, language, universalization, justice, fulfillment, and freedom all interwoven with the desire for a summarizing title of titles, a *summa* which in theological terms was called "God.")

But if any situation requires that this direction be deliberately frustrated by inward checks placed upon one's thought, to that extent one is essentially frustrate, victimized by an *intrinsic* enslavement. Often modern liberal psychologists have concealed the true nature of frustration from us by treating of desires in too materialistic a sense. If Joseph works for John, yet cannot somehow contrive to complete the symmetry by sharing John's wife (the principle might be formulated as a proverb thus: "Chop John's wood, sweat in John's bed"), then the modern psychologist would tell us that Joseph suffers from a frustrated desire. By such a view, whatever you may want, and not get, is a frustration. And if you are frustrated intensely enough, you show signs of a "neurosis."

The psychologist of frustration in this sense may go a step further. He may note that the neurosis comes not from the mere frustrations, when they are felt to be imposed from without, but rather from their counterpart within, when the frustrated individual imposes thou-shalt-not's upon himself, suppressing and warping his desires until he is unsettled by a confusion of contrary impulses. This internal self-imposing of external restrictions obviously makes for a deeper kind of frustration than comes from the mere physical denials themselves. And such frustrating may be particularly discomforting in a society trained to value acquisition much more highly than patience (trained, that is, to seek for *methods* of acquisition, without a corresponding search for *methods* of patience).

But we are here asking whether there may not be a still profounder kind of frustration, due not to the denial of *things,* but to the denial of rational desire itself, a denial expressed in the deliberate refusal to aim at universalization ("justice"). In upholding a doctrine of racial supremacy, for instance, and in striving *conscientiously* to establish one's belief in this doctrine with all thoroughness, until its spirit had infused all one's thinking, would not one be imposing upon himself the most radical frustration of all, a frustration that denies the free turning of reason towards the rationality of universal principles?

We thought of this when reading an article, "Preface to Decision," by Donald Davidson, in the *Sewanee Review* (Summer 1945). We shall not attempt here to restate the author's arguments in favor of racial discrimination. We need note only that his avowed purpose is to find new answers to the "sociologists" who have discredited the doctrine of "white supremacy." Primarily the author bases his doctrine on the appeal to Custom. Custom is morality, in the South racial inequality is customary, hence moral persons, either white or Negro, should reaffirm the propriety of racial inequality.

"Custom," we might object, is no homogeneous thing. The monetary economy is also part of the South's customs—and insofar as it changes the nature of the South's economic structure, it is producing changes in custom. Further, where there are conflicts among customs, we might ask for a rationale of Law that will not merely uphold Custom (an impossibility, since some customs are breaking down others) but will seek to modify Custom in the direction of greater justice, or freedom.

However, it is not our purpose here to refute Mr. Davidson's article. We have given his thesis so sparsely that an answer on that level would be unfair. Our point, rather, is this: We were impressed by the fact that Mr. Davidson's article is obviously the work of a very sensitive, conscientious, and honest writer. It has sincerity and even depth. It is genuinely reactionary, whereas much said on the other side is superficial and false (censure of racial discrimination by people whose way of life is wholly out of line with their doctrines).

First, we should note how the article translates a view of racial essence into temporal terms by stressing the different historical derivations of Negroes and whites (in accordance with his proposition that the sociologists don't give proper attention "to history as a causal force"). And as magic often locates the concentration of the individual's personal essence in his proper name, so Mr. Davidson remarks of the sociologists' position:

> It is odd that a prime fact, like a name, should get left out. The original name of the Negro John Smith's slave ancestor may have been, in African, something like "Crocodile-killer" or "Spear-maker," a valiant and honorable name, but it was utterly lost when he was kidnapped into slavery or was sold to a slave-dealer by his own tribal chief.

Meditating upon this loss, Mr. Davidson observes: "It is a tragic business that the Negro John Smith cannot enjoy contemplating his own name in quite the same way the white man does, since there is hiatus or lurking humiliation where there ought to be a history." And in contrast with this "vital loss," the white John Smith "can think back for many centuries without discomfort, or often with pride, if he cares to." For "his history is with him wherever he goes."

> He does not have to bother to remember it consciously all the time, since it permeates the customs and institutions that the John Smiths and their ilk established and still maintain. But he will remember it instantly, from head to toe, if the Negro John Smith walks into the white waiting room and in any way seems to challenge the separate arrangements. At such a moment the historical element becomes the most powerful element in the whole environment of the two men, indeed in their very being. And white John Smith recalls that his grandfather before him, and his father and he afterwards, never at any time agreed to accept the Negro John Smith as a member of white society, save under such limitations as are symbolized by the separate waiting rooms and other more intricate but carefully ordered customs.

And as we have noted, in earlier pages of the *Rhetoric,* how the relation between social classes may be restated in sexual terms, we may note that the two lines of generation (the Negro and the white) are here mentioned with reference to "separate arrangements" of the waiting rooms (an association having ideas of privacy and pudency in the offing, enlisted covertly in the writer's cause, as a poetic, or novelistic reinforcement of his thesis).

Thus, we are not being ironical when we say that there is a certain kind of profoundness, and literary tact, in Mr. Davidson's suasion. But the thoroughness of his article, in thus adding roundabout suggestions of essence to his purely doctrinal opposing of southern Custom and sociologists' Law, brings a further reward. Towards the end, the author falls to admonishing the "liberals." He warns that, if they are influenced by the sociologists' view of "white supremacy," rather than by some such restatement as his, they will violate "the principle upon which the South has always insisted, implicitly or directly: that the Negro problem is a separate and special problem, to be dealt with upon separate and special basis, and that it throws all problems and all questions into confusion when its special nature is concealed or ignored." Is there not, he asks, a leadership "which would represent, not pressure groups, but majority opinion in the South as a whole?" And he continues:

> If there is no such Southern leadership, then we shall continue to drift, as we have been drifting, and shall confront the clever drives of the reformer with nothing but our old inertia. If we do thus drift, then a heavy responsibility falls upon those Southern "liberals" who are now so pertly and obviously active. They had better cultivate a healthy respect for that inertia, which, though it stands in regrettable contrast to the brilliant activity of the past, is nevertheless formidable, and may turn out to be inarticulateness rather than lack of concern.

Here was the point at which, of a sudden, we saw a further possibility, to which we have previously referred. For we felt that these remarks on "inertia" could be taken as a gloss on the author's own treatment of Custom as a non-rational category. And if this were so, we thought, the Agrarians' cult of irony might be examined as the literary counterpart of the "inertia" as so defined. There are many kinds of irony. There is a metaphysical irony, at contemplating the mystery of an existence that forever extends beyond the reach of operationalist terms. There is the irony of metaphor, which simultaneously says that A is and is not B. There is the irony of dialectic, and of the dramatic peripety. All such ironies as these need no cult of unreason to explain them; in fact, we can arrive at them by the most reasonable of methods. But there can also be the irony based on partial acquiescence to injustice. And this aspect of irony would not merely recognize the necessary limits of discursive reason; it would make a positive cult of the irrational.

Here, we thought, would arise a *radical* frustration, as contrasted with the frustrations studied by liberal psychology. It would intrinsically reflect enslavement, since it would deny itself the right to contemplate favorably the completion of the universalizing process. Universal irony, rooted in the Paradox of Substance, would here become confused with a hierarchic irony based on the idea of different classes or races as different in substance. Where racial inequality already prevailed, such irony would require a doctrine of "inertia" to complete it in the realm of political relations, since it would neither surrender present privileges nor intensify them. (That is, it would not grant equality to the descendants of manumitted slaves; but on the other hand, it would not want the formal return to slavery.) It would thus arrest conditions midway between contrary motivations. And insofar as the maintaining of such conditions maintains the given set of inequalities, the irony would be the insignia of privilege, a way of stylistically laying claim to class prerogatives, or of stylistically identifying oneself with them. In brief, it would be rhetorical, and an aspect of logomachy.

However, we do not intend to suggest that such irony (Empson would probably treat it as a variant of "pastoral") is confined to the cultural situation of the South. It happens to be especially noticeable there, because the customs, laws, and doctrines of racial segregation are so sharply defined. And it thereby reveals a condition intrinsic to all social hierarchies (which call for irony since they aim to "universalize" a principle of *inequality*). Indeed, we might even go a step further and note that the experiencing of an irony strongly tinged with the properties of class can lead to the fuller appreciation of irony in general. But behind the dialectics and dramatics of universal irony, there may be lurking the rhetoric of hierarchic irony—and we may be put on the track of the rhetorical temptation when we find overmuch zeal for the "irrational" as a social motive (the "irrational," that is, not as a recognized evil, but as the source of social and poetic good).

All told, the elements involved in the cult of irrationality as social good would seem to be these: (1) rational desire for order; (2) this desire is "rationally" gratified insofar as people can fit themselves advantageously into an order, preferably the prevailing order; (3) but the order necessarily involves a hierarchy, which has developed through a combination of personal merit, accident, and cultural continuity (the last being the customs that maintain a given set of institutions, with their necessary divergencies of role); (4) hence, a cult of "tradition"; (5) but this cult implies a sanction of injustice, insofar as the tradition perpetuates inequality of role ("property"); (6) hence, the cult of tradition frustrates the rational principle of universalization; (7) hence, irony and/or cult of irrationality as cultural counterpart of the hierarchic sanction. (Here sometimes arises the stress upon "ritual" as a primary motive of cultural expression. Also, cults of tradition, mysticism, and "inertia" as the "irrational" source of social benefit. In new hierarchies, the ironies and irrationalities may be concealed by antithesis, as their adherents see them mainly in contrast with the class structure of the old order.)

The thought may incidentally contribute somewhat to the problem of psychological "patterns." When is one conditioned to *particulars* (as when one is induced to love or hate some one person)—and when is a general attitude or "pattern" established (as when the loss of confidence in some one person is "transferred," becoming generally a loss of confidence)? One hears of "negativism" in children, for instance; but a negative attitude towards one thing must imply a positive attitude towards its contrary (at least in the sense that the child who disobeys at home might even be an obedient toady to the leader of his gang). Irony is a general attitude; a cult of irony would be a "pattern"; yet insofar as it was of class origin, there could be discriminations within it, depending upon its social implications. That is, there would be not just irony, but at least two kinds, a primary and a secondary. One would be a "universal" and non-rhetorical, including all men within it, but furtively partisan in the sense that it ironically acquiesced in the prevailing inequities. The other would be explicitly partisan, a doctrine of irony that was trained polemically against the expression of the enemy, denying the enemy categorically the perception of irony, rather than noting that the enemy's irony merely takes a *different form.*

VI

Though it is probably true that a form as complex as drama could arise only in a social texture made strongly hierarchic by the division of labor, we should recall that, within drama itself, there is a purely technical kind of irony, not reducible to terms of social inequality but inherent in the principles of drama as a literary gender. Let us, for instance, offer a hypothetical example of dramatic irony. We use a crass burlesque, since the nature of an audience's irony is thereby made most obvious:

The play opens. Prima: "Secunda, I received a beautiful letter from dear Stercus. So spontaneous a declaration of love. So obviously sincere. I will marry him immediately, and entrust him with control of all my money. Secunda, you are good, kind and true. Evangeline is coming to visit us soon. I know you will love each other. I hope she will model herself after you." End of first scene. Second scene; Secunda to Stercus: "She wept over the letter. And she never suspected that I had a hand in it. Within a week, we should be able to vanish with everything. Then we'll be free, Stercus, my dirty darling. But we must work fast. She talks of having someone come to visit her—and that may complicate things." Third scene; Stercus to Evangeline: "I know I am moody, and sullen, and poetic. I know you cannot understand my silences and strange absences. That's because you don't know what it's like when someone so unused to women as I am falls in love with someone so rare as you. A mysterious friend may help me to go away and never come back. I need you. If, some night, I phone you suddenly that I am ready to leave, would you leave with me?" Fourth scene; Evangeline to her nurse: "I want dear Stercus to meet Prima and Secunda. But he is so shy, I'm planning a surprise. I have arranged for a meeting without telling him. And I'm sure he'll be pleased, once he knows them." Fifth scene; First Detective to Second Detective: "We're on the track of Lefty Stercus, alias Don Juan de Alcatraz. He seems to be working with the same moll, but there are two other women involved. One's rich; the pair is probably set to trim her. And there's a younger one, who just left a convent. Let's go."

Here are the conditions for dramatic irony, as the audience sees acts which the persons involved interpret one way, but which it can interpret another, while knowing that its interpretation is correct. The gauging of the situation is at the same time preparation for a development. The irony may involve hierarchic factors, but it is at the same time preparation for a development. In the modern mystery story, where the audience cannot know until the end who committed the offense and for what reasons, this partial uncertainty about the relation of the characters to one another does not allow for so full and spontaneous a use of purely dramatic irony, though some character within the play may be ironic in attitude, or a *spirit* of irony may *brood* over the history as a whole. The greater stress upon knowledge (in modern scientism) may lead ironically towards a greater stress upon ignorance (rather than "pride") as the source of irony. Insofar as the audience is kept guessing who committed the offense, its knowledge of the situation is actually inferior to that of the villain, who knows of his villainy, but does not tell. Much of the attempt at "smartness" in the modern mystery thriller may be an attempt to compensate, by stylistic prodding, for the kind of formal intensity that is natural to classical irony in its fullest form. (One may note its hierarchic implications too, a counterpart to the hierarchic motive involved in the classical fear of "pride." For as fear of pride could reinforce a social status quo, so a scientist cult of smartness could go well with the ideals of people "on the make," actually or in their dreams of self-justification.)

If irony, got by the audience's superior knowledge of the characters' relationships, is intrinsic to the medium of classic drama, this very situation makes the drama a kind of beneficent con game wherein the playwright implicates the audience as an accomplice in his story. Similarly, the form can readily dissociate the two elements of blandness: simplicity can be assigned to the *dramatis persona,* when this very depicting of a simple character is a scheming on the author's part (who may, for instance, portray a Christlike refusal to strike, purely that the audience clamor all the more for vengeance).

Thus, in *Antony and Cleopatra,* when Enobarbus has deserted, leaving behind "his chests and treasure," Antony does not grow wrathful, but instead blames himself for having provoked such conduct:

> Go, Eros, send his treasure after him; do it;
> Detain no jot, I charge thee. Write to him—
> I will subscribe—gentle adieus and greetings;
> Say that I wish he never find more cause
> To change a master. O! my fortunes have
> Corrupted honest men. Dispatch. Enobarbus!

And as we soon learn, this kindness leads to Enobarbus' death. In the next scene, after he has been notified that his treasure has been delivered, Enobarbus laments:

> I am alone the villain of the earth,
> And feel I am so most. O Antony!
> Thou mine of bounty, how wouldst thou have paid
> My better service, when my turpitude
> Thou dost so crown with gold! This blows my heart:
> If swift thought break it not, a swifter mean
> Shall outstrike thought; but thought will do't, I feel
> I fight against thee! No: I will go seek
> Some ditch, wherein to die; the foul'st best fits
> My latter part of life.

Here the playwright is doing much the thing we are expected to admire Antony for not doing. He is arranging for Antony to make Enobarbus miserable (a petty, vindictive act to which the playwright stoops by making his hero too noble even to think of it).

Similarly, in *Measure for Measure,* the audience's privileged view of dramatic irony is transformed into the dissociation of simplicity and complicity when Shakespeare has the nunlike Isabella innocently speak to Angelo of his "potency." This expression by *Isabella* introduces the theme of *Angelo's* Puritan lechery, until he finds in her speech "such sense that my sense breeds with it." She was the first to Say the Word, uttering in simplicity what Angelo, the audience, and the "fantastic" Lucio (who is coaching her in persuasiveness) variously interpret in terms of complicity.

Imagine a situation in which Preen, thinking that Prone was about to murder him, shot Prone in self-defense. And as Prone lay dying, he let Preen know that in reality he had been bringing Preen a gift. If he did this as a rebuke to Preen, he would be wreaking Christian vengeance. Wretchedly, in his last few moments, he would be using the only competitive resource still left him. And so he would die a Great Rhetorician's death. The subtlety of the appeal in Caesar's dying words to Brutus resides in the fact that, within the play, as words spoken by one real man to another, they are *not* thus rhetorical. They are not said in rebuke; they are the simple utterance of sorrow. But as a device for affecting the audience, these same simple words of Caesar's *are* rhetorical. They have a competitive function. Shakespeare was being bland in thus, in the subtlest sense imaginable, saying the opposite, by making a cry, in itself uttered without rebuke, serve as the most dramatically poignant of rebukes.

Shakespeare does the same in surrounding Desdemona with Iago's ruttish imagery. For he thereby makes the audience, in its privileged ironic position, much more like *accomplices* of the villain than they suspect. Indeed Iago's vile imagery, Othello's noble jealousy, and Desdemona's virtue are all essential parts of a single idea, the idea of what we might call sexual property.

Iago's very duplicity thus becomes, in a sense, a kind of simplicity. For in greatly reducing the circumference of the terms in which Othello is persuaded to consider Desdemona, he induces Othello to drop many ingredients from the total recipe of motives (though without inducing the audience to do the same; for given their privileged position, Iago's simplification but prods the audience to greater complexity of awareness).

In real life, however, such a reduction of circumference, uncorrected by a privileged ironic position on the part of the audience, serves rhetorically to affect the audience quite as Iago's reduction affected Othello. This aspect of interpretation lends itself well to the paranoia of political faction, since everything seems to be taken care of, but in terms with too narrow a scope. And if a man makes a statement which by implication discredits the position of a certain faction, champions of the affronted faction may present it to their side as having no purpose but this one implied result.

VII

What are we after here? We have not been trying to approach the Devices pragmatically, as a rhetorical manual for instructing students in their use. Rather we aim at an ethical approach to them, a method of meditation or contemplation that should be part of a "way of life." Insofar as all men are in the Scramble, they will at times seek to outwit others, or will suffer from outwittings, or may want to expose devices intended for outwitting.

But though rhetoric itself is so often words for use in combat, ultimately *A Rhetoric of Motives* as we conceive it should be useful only in the sense that an attitude towards life might be called useful: useful not as a device for throwing an enemy, but for purposes of solace and placement, and for the cultivation of mental states that make one less likely to be hurt by enemies.

You go to see an old friend, whom you have known since childhood. You have fallen on evil days, but he is Prosperity Itself, as you feel oppressively, in walking past the Army of Officialdom between the switchboard and his office. He greets you with comfortable affability, swinging competently in his big swivel chair. You talk for a few moments. On some touchy matter you disagree with him. You say so—and to your astonishment (maybe even your eyes bulged with astonishment?) he rises. With Quiet Dignity, he has indicated that The Interview is Over. You leave. As you get to the street, it is raining hard. You stand in the entranceway of the building until, collar turned up and shoulders hunched, at a partial lull in the storm you dash for the subway.

Now, what are you going to do with that? Are you merely going to feel more forlorn than ever? Or are you going to poison your very marrow with promises that some day you will get even? Or are you going to kick a dog? Or drop into a dismal church and pray? Or walk furiously? Or lie all night wide-eyed? Or get drunk?

You may do a bit of all these things, and many more. But out of the confusion you might eventually come to a contemplative act: You might look upon the incident as a collector of curios valuing some new find. You make a place for it. You classify it. You ask how many other ways there are of Rising in Quiet Dignity to Indicate that the Interview is Over. You try to remember what the accompanying gestures were (the "imagery"). You wonder whether, in thus rising, your old friend was but handing down to you what had, by a superior in the office that very day, been handed down to him (the hierarchic motive, plus kicking a dog).

You haven't lied to yourself. You haven't turned the other cheek. You haven't tried to persuade yourself that you love the stinker all the more. You haven't made up fantasies of some great table-turning day in the future, when *you* can rise as a sign for *him* that the interview is over. You have not resolved merely to forget the incident. And you have by no means taken away all the pain.

But you have *moved in the direction of order*. You have moved towards the satisfaction of *placement*. An incident that might otherwise have been sheer desolation has been transformed into a minor acquisition. In a non-competitive way, you have increased your empire. Indeed, you need not even be embarrassed the next time you meet that same friend. For though there will henceforth be a further distance between you, you have found a new interest in him that somewhat compensates for the loss of earlier intimacy. You are now "collecting" him. You watch to see by exactly what other traits of character that unforgettable act of his was rounded out. Further, in all fairness, you watch to see what traits are directly the opposite of it. In time you discover how you had even held the weather against him that day, treating as part of his act your standing in the entrance looking at the downpour.

Surely you have been realistic enough. You have not been cynical. Even in time you may be just. And you have moved Stoically in the direction of order, solace, placement. Such is what we have in mind as the ultimate purpose for *A Rhetoric of Motives*.

Or if Q is returning from a visit, what kind of rhetorically inspirited report can be expected? Will it be malicious, to signify his solidarity with the home folks? Or sparse, to keep his listeners begging? Or enthusiastic, as an implied criticism of local shortcomings, like Tacitus praising the Germans to strike at the Romans? It becomes a professional delight to set up the problems, infer the answer on the basis of what you already know about Q's character, and then check against the actuality. Further, Q's report may not quite fit any of the categories you have listed for it. It may seem more motivated by desire for self-protection than by the tactics of appeal, if that is the sort Q is, or if certain images and gestures suggest that he is concealing important aspects of the incident. Or though you correctly anticipated his act in general, he gives it particular developments that you had not foreseen.

In sum, you recognize the prevalence of the Scramble, while striving to surmount agitation by connoisseurship. And above all, you watch for the goadings for the hierarchic principle, so near to the ironic roots of human relations.

Thus, each hunting season, we speculate: For every rabbit killed because somebody is hungry for rabbit, a thousand must die, to patch up the bold huntsmen's ailing egos, suffering from the severities of ambition. Similarly, a friend said: "Once, on a dull day in the fall, the low-hanging clouds made it easy to hear the gunshots in all the near valleys. I stood on the edge of the woods, watching two ducks that had been shot at, and were fleeing to another pond. I could tell when they arrived, since a battery of gunfire went up. Then I saw them again, with their necks straining, as they hurried into another valley, where again a valiant host met them with furious onslaught. Sometimes I could not see them; but I could tell by the sounds what pond they had flown to next. And I figured that there must have been no less than a battalion of warriors after those two bewildered ducks, which could have flown themselves weary, and no matter where they alighted on that first day of hunting season would have been met by gunfire. Then, I thought of some sensitive lady novelist, writing out of the memories of her childhood: describing the departure for the hunt, the sound of the guns over the hills, the servants, and the family relations, and finally the return of the father and the brothers with the limp-hanging game—the whole thing mixed with the pensive mystery of centuries and of the heroine's aching void (plus perhaps nostalgic suggestions of the glorious days of slavery). And I thought, that's how one might 'hierarchize' the forlorn flight of those two nameless, homeless ducks, dying that transcendence-hungry egos might live." How little of the hunt is stomach-goaded; how much is the crucifying of furry and feathery Christs sacrificed for the principle of human hierarchy.

But though we make much of the Scramble as a motive of rhetoric (scratch an anything and you will find a rhetorician), one would be wrong to think that discord gives rise only to discord. If you have observed human relations in any institution, such as an office or school, you soon note how the very *multiplication of conflicts* helps make matters run more smoothly, by calling forth tolerance and patience. Indeed, we might even state as a principle of bureaucracy that only by a great multiplication of conflicts cancelling out one another can the continuity of an institution be maintained. As new issues arise, people come to discover that their opponents of last week's issue are with them on this week's, while their allies of this week may be their enemies next. So they learn to go easy on one another, expecting alliances to be always somewhat on the bias. Thereby the institution manages to jog along, where a clear sustained alignment of forces would have split it as a pick splits ice. And the thought suggests at least this much in favor of empires: That to succeed, they must be liberal. For concord from discord is the counterpart of the *divide et impera* principle. . . . What we have here said, perhaps too lightheartedly, a Spanish proverb says grimly: "Trust your friends as though tomorrow they would be enemies, and bitter ones." Or this paragraph might be read as a materialistic gloss on the Angelic Doctor's remarks (*Summa;* Secunda Secundae; Q. XXIX, A. I: *Utrum Pax sit idem quod Concordia*) where it is written: "*Concordia importat unionem appetituum diversorum appetentium.*" Note also how a Romanian proverb, "Kiss the hand you cannot bite," at once exposes and confirms the hierarchic motive ("order"). And conversely, we could say in behalf of some "warmongers," much show of international ill will can arise purely through a disinclination to fight (as many Roosevelt supporters denounced him at all times but elections).

We could well claim Mark Twain as a source for a rhetoric of personal devices. His concern with ruses, stratagems, with the lore of gamblers, swindlers, and the like, is not so much moralistic as *appreciative*. His businessmen are not merely salesmen, they are orators, spellbinders, preferably given to selling poor stuff grandiloquently (partly perhaps because prices were not yet standardized, so that selling was largely of a conspiratorial nature, particularly among salesmen on the move; and partly because the business motive had not yet triumphed over the traditional theological and aristocratic resistances to it, so that financial scheming was viewed somewhat in the Balzacian perspective, and in keeping with the tone set by those engaged in the vast private plundering of the public domain). Typically, he quotes this example of spiritualization from "a now forgotten book" describing a "big operator":

> He appears to have been a most dexterous as well as consummate villain. When he traveled, his usual disguise was that of an itinerant preacher; and it is said that his discourses were very "soul-moving"—interesting the hearers so much that they forgot to look after their horses, which were carried away by his confederates while he was preaching.

Yet, though such out-and-out rogues as the King and the Duke in *Huckleberry Finn* were forever verbalizing for ulterior purposes, there is a purely epideictic motive in their oratory too. In a sense, they were as much lovers of the art as Tom Sawyer (when, supposedly aiding Jim to escape, he was actually introducing all sorts of unnecessary interferences, in accordance with his notions of esthetic propriety). Their duplicity was not just for gain, but was rather a kind of simplicity, an honest and spontaneous expression of their nature, as genuine as the motive of perennially repeated being Gertrude Stein was looking for.

In *The Making of Americans* Gertrude Stein came close to a systematic study of rhetorical devices in personal relations. Towards the end, for instance, when discussing how sensitiveness turns into suspicion, making a "simple thing" look like a "complicated thing," she writes:

> These then I am now describing who are completely for themselves suspicious ones, who have it in them to have emotion in them become suspicious before it is a real emotion of anything for anything about anything in them, these have it completely to be certain that every one is doing feeling seeing the thing that one is feeling doing seeing believing when such a one is not agreeing with them, when such a one is feeling thinking believing doing anything that such a one is doing that thing, for a mean or wicked or jealous or stupid or obstinate or cursed or religious reason, it is not a real feeling believing seeing realizing, that this one having suspicion in him is certain.

She then gives us the paradigm of an anecdote:

> One of such a kind of one once liked very well some one and then that one forgot to give this one five cents that this one had paid for that one and then this one hated that one, had no trust in that one for this one was certain that that one knowing that this one was too sensitive to be asking did not think it necessary to pay that one, he never could believe that any one forgot such a thing. This is an extreme thing of a way of feeling that is common to all of these of them.

You will note that, while using what look like the most concrete of words, she is here making a very abstract statement. (Few words are on a higher level of generalization than "this one" and "that one.") The five cents, also, we may assume to be an idealization. Surely the sorry affair involved at least five dollars. But five cents better gets the spirit of the thing. You will also note that her style permits her to make a virtue of necessity. For whereas you must ordinarily look for subterfuges that vary the wearisome of "this one" vs. "that one," or that try to make the various agents as distinct as possible while still stressing their purely functional significance, her style transforms those very liabilities into assets.

Primarily, however, her concern is not Rhetorical, but what we could call Symbolic. For at the point where the purposes of Rhetoric transform simplicity into complicity and duplicity, at the point where simplicity becomes complicated by ulterior motives, she is looking rather for the ways in which "this one's" or "that one's" doing is a simple expression of his identity. "Every one has their own being in them"—and the agent's acts are various ways of repeating his simple essence, or nature. (An estheticized version of the Leibnizian monadology? And with the possibility that the "making of Americans" might be universal, insofar as all human natures share a like essence?)

We have previously mentioned on several occasions our reasons for believing that Empson's notions on "pastoral" come under the heading of Rhetorical Devices (though, like Stein, with a strong tendency to lose the specifically Rhetorical motive in the Poetic or Symbolic).

Our own concern with such matters was first embodied throughout an early, rhetorically oriented novel, *Towards a Better Life*. In several chapters of that book, we attempted to adapt the style of the "case history" for purely literary purposes. That is, we had liked the results got by condensing human development into a few sentences—and to this end, we set up an aphorizing protagonist who, in quasi-essayistic style, here and there gave digests of differently motivated lives. Sometimes these were got by "idealizing" actual incidents or situations, with details omitted, changed, or added to suit the case. Sometimes the observations and reminiscences were wholly fictitious. But the method had a "whom the shoe fits" quality about it, as we found on one occasion after the book was published. At one point, without conscious memory of any actual incident at least, the protagonist wrote of a fictitious character: "If his companions were walking on the right side of the street and he suggested that they walk on the left, and if they crossed to the left because they did not care which side of the street they walked on, he took their acquiescence as a concession to his authority." After the book's publication, a charming friend, one of the last men we would suspect of such motives, took us aside and said, "That time we were walking on Sixth Avenue, and I suggested that we cross the street, I wasn't trying to be important. It was just that the sun was too hot where we were."

Since we there placed much reliance upon the ironic device we have described as a bringing to consciousness by an outraging of conscience, our emergent concern with the rhetoric of personal relations is given a sinister cast, for purposes of the fiction, not necessary to the study of devices as such. Conventions proper to the form invited us there to treat all rhetorically motivated acts as either conspiratorial or compulsive (conspiratorial when they were considered as strategies for handling situations, and compulsive when considered as the necessary and inevitable expression of the agent's nature).

Later, we began taking notes on a much more particularized kind of device: the manipulations of financial and legalistic symbolism by which the dominions of the great modern industrial dynasts were built up. But when, in the course of our research, we came upon the report of the so-called Pujo Investigation undertaken by Congress, we saw that only minor and marginal additions to the subject were still to be added. So we moved on, as we began speculating about the motivational realm behind the realm of business enterprise, the general motives of communication that shape human ambition, development, self-justification, and the like (*Permanence and Change,* which we originally thought of calling "Treatise on Communication"). In our next work, *Attitudes Toward History,* we attempted to treat literary genders (tragedy, comedy, satire, etc.) as symbolic devices for handling situations in life. The theory of "strategies" and "situations" was further generalized in *The Philosophy of Literary Form,* while we began plans for a book *On Human Relations,* a codifying of purely personal devices, and intended as the rounding-out of our concerns in *Permanence and Change* (a general theory of men's relation to the medium of communication) and *Attitudes Toward History* (on the "comedy" of human association). But, as we have elsewhere noted, we found that this intended third volume became a trilogy of its own (all based on a methodical concern with the "paradox of substance," which much modern thought was avoiding on the assumption that "substance" had been effectively outlawed from the best vocabularies).

In our earliest book of criticism, *Counter-Statement,* notably the section entitled "Lexicon Rhetoricae," our analysis of literary form in terms of the reader-writer relationship had treated of rhetorical tactics mainly at the point where they overlap upon poetic (the "scheming" being that of the benign sort that figures when the writer lays traps for his reader, and in the course of doing so, matures his statement beyond the confines of the emotional bias that goaded him to expression).

There is perhaps a "paranoid" motive in any such study of devices. But insofar as association with any group less inclusive than all mankind likewise has dissociative, or segregational, aspects, and certainly insofar as our modern world is burning with the zeal of restricted communities (the most intense being, of course, the nationalistic), there are plenty of realistic grounds for the contemplation of rhetorical devices in human relations (and for a concern with methods that will fill out the attitude).

Above all, we believe, although the devices can be considered pretty much in isolation of one another, one should watch for the ways in which the artificer is goaded by the motives of hierarchy. For as we have said, the desire for "order" is *rational,* but a given order is a "ladder," and the maintaining of a ladder of fixed discriminations involves "injustice," which is *irrational.*

In keeping with this situation, many of the devices used by the great Rhetoric Trusts exploit the fact that the antagonists are not on an equal footing. Thus, obviously, the power to Say Anything is greatly weakened in situations where an opponent can reply. (Many champions of national boastfulness seem to leave this consideration out of account, when they insist that our propaganda abroad be as rawly self-congratulatory as it is at home, and when they would commend the United States as a rightist paradise to a world in drastic need of political and economic reform.) The power of the Rhetoric Trusts, to build up either favorable or unfavorable animus towards a foreign power, depends mainly on their physical dominion over the communicative medium itself, as with press and radio chains, either private or governmental.

We can enjoy the rhetoric of private combat, on the other hand, because often the fight is between contestants who are relatively free in that they have equal opportunities. Particularly we admire a device when the victim of it sees it happening before his very eyes, sees his own position being methodically misrepresented, and though technically able to reply, is silenced purely by the dramatic skill of the device itself.

Thus, a friend said: "Once I went to a quite pretentious party on an evening when I was almost fantastically sleepy. After a few drinks, plus the smoke and heavy air, plus a brilliant conversationalist who told long anecdotes while I tried to keep him from wavering and appearing double, I was almost in a trance. I decided to get near an open window, in hopes that fresh air might revive me. So I began making my way slowly toward it. Just as I neared a doorway into an adjoining room, the hostess appeared, trailing an imposing train, its length in about the same proportion to her body as the tail of a comet is to the head. I stepped back to let her pass—but at that same moment a bright young fellow, snappy, brand new, came briskly by, and stepped squarely on the long ceremonial item. The next instant, the train was lying on the floor, and the queenly lady was transformed into a very angry hen with its tail feathers plucked. It seems that the insignia of her dignity had been merely clamped on, so no great harm was done. But as I looked at the suddenly denuded rear, as disillusioning as a stage set seen from behind, in my startled sleepiness I was about as horrified as though the lady's nude *cul* itself had suddenly popped forth. I was, I am sure, the very picture of horror—whereat, quick as a flash, the bright and briskly stepping one turned to me and said, reassuringly, 'That's all right, old man.' And I saw by the hate and scorn in the great lady's eyes, as they swept over me, that she thought I had stepped on the train. I moved away, speechless and befuddled." Here was free and equal combat. Our hero had been outwitted by an adversary who had no special privileges as regards access to the medium of communication itself. Here was a model of fair and open fighting. It is what we admire in the social "catfight," at its best. A similar condition marks the rhetoric of Demosthenes and Cicero. For though it can be outrageous in its stating of an issue, the opponent has exactly the same opportunities, before the same audience. But with rhetoric under the domination of the Rhetoric Trusts, there is a fantastic inequality of the opportunities permitted the rival factions. To combat a popular prejudice is handicap enough. To do so while granted but a fraction of the same technical facilities is to swim against Niagara Falls.

We take the War of Words to be inevitable. Indeed, a project that looks "towards the purification of war" should hope for not less of such battles, but many many more. It is only that grim disease of cooperation, nationalistic "total war," that must be outmoded, unless the human race itself is to become outmoded. War, in the sense of conflict and competition, is synonymous with vitality. But the more of it there is in civilized forms, the less need of it there may be in those burlesques of primitive substance-thinking we find in modern nationalism.

So much for the Theory of the Devices. Let us end piously, on an image. We propose to think of wrens, interrupting their song to scold; then in the very midst of scolding, they break into a new cascade of song. Would that all tempests could be tempests in a teapot. Would that all wars could be the turmoil of wrens. We would turn from the brontosaurian tramplings of the great Rhetoric Trusts, to a Cult of Wrens. We would think of the wrens, returning in the springtime:

> The wrens are back.
> Their liquid song, pouring across the lawn –
> (Or, if the sunlight pours, the wren's song glitters)
> Up from the porch, into the bedroom where
> It is the play of light across a pond,
> Sounding as small waves look: new copper coins

Between the seer and the sun. Therewith
Is made the contract between the brightly waked
Sleeper and his wren, neither the wren's
Nor his, but differently owned by both.
Behind the giving-forth, wren-history;
Man-history behind the taking-in.
(Define the city as a place where no
Wrens sing, as though April were seas of sand,
With spring not the burial of lilac,
The funeral of rebirth, the floral wreaths
For pollen, but heat quaking above stone.)
After magnetic storms that made all men
Uneasy, but those the most who feared the loss
Of salary or love –
The wrens are back.

Would that the Theory of the Devices could be thus under the Sign of the Wren. But unfortunately, the Rhetoric Trusts are everywhere about us. So we turn now to the suasive ways of the New Brontosaurs: press, radio, and bureau.

CHAPTER 2

Scientific Rhetoric

I. "FACTS" ARE *INTERPRETATIONS*

From the Aristotelian point of view, "scientific rhetoric" would be a contradiction in terms. For in Aristotle's usage, a statement becomes scientific in proportion as it departs from the rhetorical. We would call news "scientific" in the sense that it deals with information, or knowledge, and at its best this information is accurate. But news is "rhetorical" insofar as it forms attitudes or induces to action. As Augustine says in *De Doctrina Christiana,* information may be so persuasive that no further eloquence is needed for moving an audience ("*et fortasse rebus ipsis cognitis ita mouebuntur, ut eos non opus sit maioribus eloquentiae uiribus iam moueri*"). And we might similarly apply Aquinas (*Summa,* first part, Q.LXXX, A. II): "The appetible does not move the appetite except as it is apprehended" ("*appetibile non movet appetitum, nisi inquantum est apprehensum*").

If you say, "Attack him," the rhetorical factor is obvious. You are exhorting, persuading, calling to action. But if you say, "He is the enemy," the assertion is not in itself an exhortation. For the sake of the argument, let us say that you are stating the truth: The man *is* the enemy. Then, if you are speaking to a listener whose assumption is, "The enemy should be annihilated," your "scientific" statement of a "fact" is implicitly rhetorical, since it implies the injunction, "Annihilate him." Thus a "scientific" statement can become rhetorical, or the indicative can contain imperatives (as Freud notes how, in dreams, indicatives can be disguised optatives).

Too often we assume that we can get an adequate extra-philosophic report of "reality" by confining ourselves simply to "the facts." These "facts" are thought to exist wholly outside the realm of interpretation. Maybe they do. If you say that something will go up, and it goes down, the facts have spoken. But we must not assume that this kind of refutation, an ideal answer to all error, applies to any very large area of "the facts." For not only are many facts *interpretations* of the reporter; they are *selections* among his interpretations.

Indeed, one could not interpret without selecting, quite as one could not select without criteria of selection—whereat we are back in the realm of philosophy again, nor could we escape that realm merely by being haphazard or superficial in our selectivity. We do not avoid a philosophy merely by having a crude one. "The same facts" are reported differently in Moscow and Washington not because the reporters are crooks, but because they have different philosophies, theories of motives, interpretations. You can tremble at the thought, if you will: but when a man, hanging to his strap in the subway, reads a yellow journal, he is *meditating*. He is contemplating the motives of human action. He is pondering "representative" things. He is absorbing a philosophy, as written by reporters who probably despise philosophy, and take their trade to be the very opposite of it.

In sum, "the facts" gain added rhetorical power from the belief that, if "the facts" are but honestly given, they "speak for themselves." People do not usually realize that such positivistic and behavioristic tests of meaning apply only when the situation itself has been appropriately set for the test. In the laboratory we can set up controlled conditions which allow us to judge of behavior on a purely behavioristic basis. But when discussing events in the world at large, we must ourselves implicitly or explicitly supply the interpretive framework in terms of which the given action or event is to be judged. (We discussed this matter in the *Grammar*, particularly the pages on "Scope and Reduction.") A major resource of scientific rhetoric, encouraged by the views of a naively empiricist and positivistic science itself, resides in the focusing of attention upon the "fact" to be judged rather than upon the critical framework in which it is judged.

As a result, since the "fact" is believed to be "speaking for itself," people fail to note that there *is* no "fact" before them; there is nothing but a *report* of the "fact." That is, a newspaper is thought to be a body of *facts,* in the sense of something the opposite of mere words (as a thing is a fact in contrast with the word for the thing). But a newspaper is a body of *words.* Its statements are not merely the *grounds* of an interpretation; they are themselves interpretations. Hence, a falsely persuasive effect of news can result through deflecting the attention from the real center of the problem, which is always a *philosophic* one. And while we are invited to keep our attention upon the "facts" before us, we fail correspondingly to watch the point at which the magician is really performing his trick, as he implicitly builds up the frame of reference which should itself be in question. That is, since the report must be given through the medium of *terms,* it automatically fixes the terms by which the reported event is to be defined. And by repeatedly featuring stories in terms having a common bias, the "scientific" organ (that is, the medium for purveying information) is indirectly contributing to the enforcement of the particular terminology which perpetuates this bias.

A news story can thus be read as a *proof* whereas it should be read as a *to-be-proved.* To be proved, not in the sense that the reporter may be lying (we are assuming his goodwill), but in the sense that the very terminology of motives he uses implies a system of interpretation (that is, a "philosophy"), but avoids the many doubts and admonitions that go with a formal theory of interpretation.

A more critically admonitory word for "facts" that would still leave them with a certain priority would be "primary interpretations"—and the arrangement of such "facts" in a meaningful order might then be called "secondary interpretations." "Facts" suggests too much the idea that they presented themselves, and even wrote themselves. Yet words about "facts" (literally, *things done*) cannot themselves be facts, but can only be interpretations of those facts. (They can, of course, be facts for linguistic analysis. In a poem, the words are *acts,* hence "facts" of that poem. But this is not the order of facts the reporter has in mind, as when one semanticist advised his readers to consult *not words but facts,* and thereupon quoted, as an example of *facts,* the *words* of a not very reputable news weekly.)

Bernard M. Baruch, as reported in the *New York Times* (10/3/46): "I refuse to deal in emotional or political activities; as you know, I deal in facts." Mark Twain, *Life on the Mississippi:* "And mind you, emotions are among the toughest things in the world to manufacture out of whole cloth; it is easier to manufacture seven facts than one emotion." However, the more closely words are to be taken to be identical with facts, the better able are the words to *move* us. And though many people are skeptical of the press in the superficial sense (in suspecting that news is slanted in accordance with editorial policy), few are skeptical in the radical, or methodic sense that we are here considering: The newspaper, being not a set of "facts" (which are things and situations), but a set of interpretations (*reports* of things and situations), is *not antithetical to philosophy*, but is itself the *uncritical and unsystematic*, or *implicit*, philosophy. And confronting a news agency, we might ask ourselves: "How well can a business firm philosophize?"

The most drastically rudimentary problem in information as rhetoric: The "global" situation being what it is (the fate of the individual who would tend his own garden being willy-nilly involved in human relations universally, and most notably in the international dislocations due to the expansion of trade), much of what passes for "reality" necessarily reaches us solely through the medium of the news. Hence, except for a small circle of acquaintances whom we know intimately, "reality" must be for us largely what the great news-spreading agencies say it is. And since by this version of reality we are moved to action, if we believe any error, intentional or unintentional, in the representing of reality, we are, to that extent, prodded towards attitudes or actions correspondingly erroneous. For we act on the basis of reality as we know it. And where our understanding of reality is inadequate, our actions could be accurate only in cases of rare good luck. Also, of course, our errors often fail to do damage because we are comparatively powerless to act upon them (and the recognition of our powerlessness often leads us to abandon the whole matter).

If you corner a mild man, putting him into an extreme situation where he is threatened with dishonor, torture, or death, his response will be correspondingly extreme. Similarly, if the signs he sees clearly indicate that such an extreme situation threatens, insofar as his imagination is equal to this situation his responses again will be extreme. Contrarily, if the situation is not so at all, but if a constant bombardment of misinformation convinces him that it is so, again an extremity of response is likely. And though *in effect* his actions would be those of a maniac (since he would be acting in ways wholly unsuited to the realities of the actual situation) within the limited conditions of the information on which he is acting, he would be wholly *normal*. It is important to remember this, in trying to understand the ferocities of people falsely indoctrinated. They are not "fiends" intrinsically; they are acting much as people everywhere, on the average, would act, if what they believed to be the truth were actually the truth, and what they feared really should be feared. It is thus with ordinary people who, though not by nature much interested in politics, joined sinister political movements.

In sum: The rhetorical ingredient in "the news" resides primarily in the fact that, as regards vast areas of human relations about which we must adopt attitudes, or agree on policies, reality is little more than the news. And the "intelligence" upon which we must inevitably rely is not our own intelligence, but the purely mediatory "intelligence" of news-gathering and news-distributing agencies. Even under the best conditions, it would be a great struggle for men to see beyond the limitations of the medium.

About the "facts," of course, there can be endless dispute. At a time when the majority of the press was acting to discredit federal price control, for instance, one New York City newspaper published the photographs of several women who had purportedly been interviewed on the subject, and had declared themselves against price control. One of the women phoned the office of a rival newspaper, complaining that she had been misrepresented. And on further investigation, according to this rival paper, it was found that all the women had been similarly misrepresented. Obviously, it is not our purpose here to examine journalism of that sort, where the criticism would require a minute pitting of "fact" against "fact," in a task that even George Seldes could not stomach. We shall here be concerned only with the rhetoric of "honest" tendentiousness in the news. And even when we are using actual cases, to avoid haggling over "facts" we shall treat them as hypothetical. We shall, in brief, examine the rhetorical resources "natural" to the newspaper as a medium. We shall consider the main invitations or temptations to manipulation for persuasive purposes. And the reader can decide for himself to what extent he thinks newspapers deny themselves these opportunities.

Any "fact" reported about some person, organization, situation, nation, etc., could be analyzed along the lines of Aristotle's "places," as a device for favorably or unfavorably shaping the readers' attitudes. And the study of news as a kind of "oratory" should be grounded in such concern with ideas, images, and "opinions," as they are applied to either the "build-up" or the "smear." But besides such traditional resources of rhetoric, there are means of persuasion particularly characteristic of journalism as a medium. And we shall mainly consider these.

Here is another thing about "facts": If Mr. Q is a liar, and he lies, and the newspaper reports his lie accurately, this report is "factual." Many a newsman, skilled in sizing up conditions, yet required to forward official handouts that he knows to be corrupt, will put the false words in quotation marks, which escape the notice, or the proper evaluation, of the reader. (That is, the quotation marks around the official utterance may mean, for the reporter, "I assume no responsibility for this." To the reader they may mean, "This has official sanction.")

"It is a fact" that so-and-so said such-and-such about conditions. (Maybe he is lying, or wrong, but "it is a fact" that he said so.) "It is a fact" that so-and-so said such-and-such about the future. (Though newspapers are supposedly designed to tell you *what happened,* you'll be surprised if you ever stop to ask yourself just how much of the "news" is about *things that may or may not happen, or positively will not happen.*) "It is a fact" that "certain persons who did not want their identity disclosed" said such-and-such. (And that could be true, even if nobody but the reporter himself had said it.)

II. HEADLINE-THINKING

In considering the resources intrinsic to the newspaper as a medium, we should mention first a purely *quantitative* rhetoric, in the sheer volume and placement of news: featuring, a size of headlines, even type and color of headlines. A rumor boldly dominating the front page today has what the old scholastics might have called "more being" than its authoritative but inconspicuous denial will have the next day. And since there can be a true report of a false rumor, the *tenor* of the rumor, rather than its dubiousness, can be played up—while the later correction can be made without corresponding appeal to the imagination.

The resources of quantitative rhetoric are so obvious, one can hardly bring oneself to mention them. Yet every day our gauging of "reality" is formed and deformed by this sheerly mechanical device. Here is "truth" in terms of a pageantry that, if it's on the stands at three o'clock, must make way for a new version of the world at five. Here is supposedly the very "essence" of experience, depicted in accordance with the Genius of the Headlines.

The Genius of the Headlines. Had there been headlines in Biblical times, news of the Sermon on the Mount might have been featured, thus:

Revivalist Addresses Hill Throng

Promises Seekers Success

Or for Paul:

"Better Marry Than Burn"

Asserts Noted Apostle

We can think of them, in Monday's reports of sermons. Or a modern one:

"Love is All"

Says Visiting Bishop

We can only guess to what extent our very meditations upon human existence itself have become but a reflex of headline-thinking. For even poets and novelists, when they attempt to be "universal" (or should we say "global"?) in their expression, seem often to be writing "cultural trends" that they have contemplated, not at first hand, but through the medium of the news, as assembled by a business firm.

Did not Archibald MacLeish, in his verse play, *Panic,* unconsciously pay the greatest tribute of all to the newspaper? In his introduction he says: "The rhythms of contemporary American speech . . . are nervous, not muscular; excited, not deliberate; vivid, not proud. . . . The voices of men talking intently to each other in the offices of the mills or on the streets of this country *descend from* stressed syllables; they do not *rise toward* stressed syllables as do the voices of men speaking in Shakespeare's plays." Maybe yes, maybe no. Phrases like "Get going," "shut up," "what do you mean," "he never got to first base," "you're telling me," "he's on the spot," when they don't rise, seem to be spondaic rather than descending.

But omission of the definite and indefinite article from headlines, plus the preference for short words, will often throw the accent to the first syllable, giving an effect that could be perfectly described as "nervous," "excited," "vivid," rather than "muscular," "deliberate," "proud." Thus, looking on one front page, chosen at random, we find these typical beginnings: "Broad Nationalization Plank" . . . "Truman to Deliver" . . . "Tito, Defiant, Says" . . . "Marshall to Resist" . . . "West Willing to Discuss" . . . "No Draft Likely Before" . . . "8 Communist Chiefs" . . . "3D Ave. Plea" . . . "Czechoslovak Army Demoralized" (a tabloid would probably reduce it to something like "Czech Forces Split"). And now, turning to the MacLeish play, we find lines like these, where "A Woman" is speaking:

Men die: houses
Fall among kitchen flowers.
Families scatter. Children
Wander the roads building of
Broken boxes shelter.

People do not speak like that. But headlines do, and the poet has transformed the quality of the headline into a ritual, a style (aptly sin-

gling out the headline *conventions*, the only aspect of news-writing that
lends itself to ritual). And this stylized speech is obviously of the same
texture as the following lines which one character reads from a news
ticker:

> Atlanta . . . Seaman's National . . . branch closed.
>
> Indianapolis . . . People's and Guaranty . . . closes.
>
> Frankfort . . . Farm Mortgage . . . forced closing ——

Or as the words of these "Men's Voices," reading:

> Bankers summoned to conference.
>
> Mister McGafferty summons . . .
>
> Government calls on McGafferty.

The poet pays a still further tribute to the medium. For while the play
pictures the entire collapse of a society's economic institutions, through
all disarray the organs of "intelligence" remain in perfect operation,
acting like a Greek messenger to bring in reports, from the outside
world, on the inexorable unfolding of Fate. Does he not here spontaneously identify the journalist medium even with the ultimates of human
reason and universal destiny?

But we do agree that the poet caught the very essence of news, considered as a style. For that essence is in the genius of the headline, the
distinctive feature of news, considered as rhetoric. This in turn involves
three major resources: selectivity, reduction (or "gist"), and tonality.
All three are parts of a single rhetorical complex. Insofar as is possible,
we shall try to consider them separately. But at the same time we shall
note their interwovenness.

III. SELECTIVITY

Approaching the matter of selectivity roundabout, a former friend said:

> When I was a student, and striving for a knowledge of literature, I looked
> above all else for those packed moments when something was expressed with
> exceptional rightness. Gradually I collected a set of such expressions (Matthew
> Arnold might have called them "touchstones"), and would try to decide what
> elements in them made them good. Later I began to think of life not only in the
> "universal" way that goes with poetry and philosophy, but also with regard to
> the particulars of history, "current events." Here entered the newspaper.
>   Naturally, I tried to approach journalism with the same 'appreciative'
> attitude I had taken towards good literature. And why not? For didn't the

headlines constantly call attention to notable pronouncements on the state of the world by prominent public figures?

These headlines troubled me—and it was years before I clearly discovered why. Day after day some platitude, uttered by one pompous ass after another (or, as I learned later, his ghost), would be clamorously greeted by the press as though some new step in human understanding had been taken. Puzzled, but sure that my elders must be discerning profundities which escaped me, I examined the remarks for traces of resonance, imagery, or epigrammatic sharpness, and could find nothing.

Each day there would be a vast stir over some putty-like pronouncement or other that didn't seem much different from the things I had been reading for the last several months, or even years. And their dullness was made even more apparent by their being in headlines.

Obviously, I was discovering the difference between poetic and journalistic tests of the outstanding, between two tests of the "representative." I was being forced to learn that the pronouncements were being quoted precisely because they had no saliency, that the very dullness of the statements was what made editors want to feature them with such untiring avidity. I was to learn that their value was their standardized *selectivity,* their use for keeping the mind in a certain frame, for purposes of policy.

A news item reporting a bad situation in some quarter which it is the editorial policy of the paper to denigrate may be quite literally true; indeed, a whole series of such articles may be quite literally true; yet the articles could be falsely tendentious in the sense that they do not give a *properly rounded picture* of the situation reported, but are "truths" selected for a particular polemic purpose. Hence, although they could be placed in the category of science or knowledge, since they are "true information," the partiality of their truth makes them rhetorically persuasive in the worst sense. News, when given point in headlines, can be as restricted in its emphasis as a short story or lyric designed to make a single mood prevail throughout the entire universe of discourse.

Hence, there is a certain blandness behind journalists' insistence upon full freedom to gather information in areas which, for political reasons, are to be presented in an unfavorable light. In effect, they are but demanding a better opportunity to work adversely upon the imaginations of their readers. For if they have few stories on which to base the attitudes which they would inculcate, they confront a technical embarrassment. They must ground the desired attitude in an ever-changing procession of specific details (all different in their particularities, though similarly directed or weighted). And if reporters cannot range freely in the area to be thus adversely reported, the editors lack sufficient daily embodiment for their policies, and must rely too greatly upon overt editorializing, with too great abstractness in the appeal through commonplaces. News-wise, a situation remains "news" insofar as one day there can be a story about Mr. Q in this situation, the next day about Mr. X, etc.

From the standpoint of an ulterior motive, the ever-changing details of each day's news (when treated to perpetuate a fixed attitude on the part of the readers) are but the varied reindividuations of a single underlying form, concretions (in terms of particulars, or "images") that bring the abstract "principle" or "idea" into the realm of *feeling*.

Since the newspaper is supposed to be representative of the day's events, and must select representative cases, all such choices, besides resting on philosophical assumptions, invite readers to accept the same underlying assumptions. Here again we encounter the rhetorical ingredient in so-called "informative" matter, since selected "facts" that pass as "reconnaissance," or "preparation for action," are really *inducement to action*.

Closely allied to selectivity is the rhetoric of timing. There being much disrelatedness in a newspaper, as one jumps from item to item, out of this very disrelatedness a rhetoric of juxtaposition can arise. Thus, at a time when an exchange of letters between the President and the Pope was published, one newspaper also printed a photograph: "The Emperor of Japan Bows His Head" . . . "Emperor Hirohito in the chapel of a Catholic church at Akita during a recent inspection tour of the northern part of the country." It was a minimal bow, just enough to pass the test with the caption-writer's assistance. But being publicized on that day, it helped enlist the gods of old Japan on the side of the One God, an important alignment politically as well since it went along with a drive to make our citizens think favorably of plans to restore the power of the Japanese cartels. At the same time, a prominent radio commentator began publicly debating with himself whether the Emperor was near conversion to Christianity, the newsman's quandaries thus helping identify the ex-divinity with the Prince of Peace, the Roman Pontiff, and the rebuilding of the Japanese war potential.

There is also the timing of a news release to coincide with organizational designs. On the whole, that topic belongs more properly under the Rhetoric of Bureaucracy; but we might now consider this instance of honest selectivity: There are said to be somewhere between 6,000 and 8,000 laws filed at each session of Congress. Somewhat less than 2,000 of these are passed. Obviously, there would here be possibilities for "creative news about the future" (news that would be a disguised form of "deliberative oratory" insofar as it was designed to bring about the kind of future best suited to the editorial policies). For reports can be sent from Washington, singling out certain of the bills that were filed for consideration. Wholly "true" stories about them can be featured. A series of wholly "true" interviews with their sponsors and other sympathetic public figures can be printed. There can be auxiliary stories about the situation which the proposed laws are meant to control—and these stories need not, in themselves, be any the less "true" than stories of an opposite tendency, which would likewise have their kind of truth to commend them. All such focusing of attention upon a topic could be expected to have an "educative" effect upon the public (for remember that the newspaper is our primary medium of "adult education"). And it could be "educative" not simply in the sense of a rounded and well-balanced representation, but in the sense of indoctrination.

Here is a normal instance of selectivity: An anti-Nazi Protestant minister is brought to the United States, for possible use against the Left in Germany. He is built up for his role as a hero of the resistance to Hitler within Germany, at a time when Nazism had prevailed most strongly. Returning to his country, he joins with Socialists to combat the *political* influence of the Vatican. Whereupon a new version of his year under Hitler promptly comes into being. It is discovered that he had avowed "his sympathy with Nazi aims," that he never vigorously opposed Nazi ideology, that his only opposition to the Nazis had been his struggles to save some autonomy for his own church, that during his sojourn in a concentration camp he had been in what was called "honorable confinement," with many comforts and conveniences, that he had denied the principle of German national guilt, that he had been anti-Semitic and had minimized the extent of anti-Semitism in Germany. Of a sudden, these became "the" facts about him, in the very press that would not have found a single one worth considering had his policies remained in good favor. This is the usual "now it can be told" kind of selectivity, dictated by changes of policy. . . . The thought is no startling disclosure, but must be restated here, for systematic purposes, when we are considering how the press could give you exclusively bless-facts or damn-facts about the same subject, *and be "honest" in either case,* though goading you to one or the other of two completely opposite policies. (For we are not talking about falsified news. We are talking about only the most reputable press, which yet somehow deals in so pliable a kind of "truth" that it can without lying invite you to say either yes or no, as the editor prefers. And that is the quality of "reality" got through news as a source of "adult education.")

If the press of your nation would foster ill will towards another nation, it may give its readers the impression, say, that the scientists of that other nation are inferior. (This is a good "place" to utilize in our society, owing to the prestige of technology.) Then let a leading scientist in that other nation come into conflict with the authorities. And lo! of a sudden the press of your nation will be vibrant with accounts of this scientist's high repute among his colleagues throughout the world.

When the effects of selectivity have made themselves felt, there can be added rhetorical increment. For though a reader knows that tendentious news must to some extent be discounted, such knowledge can be in turn counteracted by the motives of the "con game," previously discussed. That is, after the reader's attitudes have been formed by the selectivity of the news he read, he may himself conspire with the editor in demanding that he be cheated by the continuation of such selectivity. And he might even stop buying his favorite paper if it tried to give him a truly rounded version of reality.

Here are instances where the selectivity threatens to pass beyond truth, yet technically is within bounds: The Maritime Commission wanted one government to return 96 ships which it had been operating under lend-lease agreements signed during the war. Since there was much effort at the time to promote popular ill will towards that government, we heard this story on three different broadcasts, as an item of general news interest. The next day, from a page of specialized shipping news, we learned that the same Commission called for the return of three times as many vessels, operated by another nation, "in 'direct competition' with the American merchant marine, at rates more favorable to foreign operators." But policy did not favor the building of public ill will against the nation operating the much larger number of our ships. Hence, the three broadcasts could "honestly" mention only the item that contributed to ill will against the government operating the smaller number.

Again: On one broadcast, it was reported that a United Nations commission in Greece, there largely at the instigation of our government, "was fired on by guerrillas." Just a few minutes before, we had heard, on another station, that the members of the commission had been caught in a crossfire between guerrillas and nationalist troops. Note that, even if the report of the crossfire were true, the report of the commission's being fired on by one side would be *selectively* true.

Photographs are obviously tendentious in the sense that they can "tell the truth" about either hovels or palaces. But there are even moments in a single act which, if taken by themselves, abstracted from their proper sequence, become rhetorically weighted. Thus, a speaker addressing a large audience must, like an opera singer, fall into oral postures which look quite grotesque if permanently held in a snapshot. There are firm moments too—and the editor can "honestly" select one or the other. In 1944, a news weekly published side by side two campaign photographs of F. D. Roosevelt, both "true" but one "dyslogistic." The rhetorical resources of "honest" selectivity could never be more obvious. One was all brightness, alertness, competence, smile—the humane leader. The other was droop, gasp, evade—and above all, such exhaustion as could not possibly cope with the responsibilities of another presidential term. Neither was doctored. Both truly represented moments in the life of the same man (or of any man, for that matter). So much for them, as "science." As rhetoric, they "proved opposites."

Where the story is told by a photograph, the caption can do the work of the headline. If you would observe an extreme case of "creative" work in this field, look up the story on "Life in Bulgaria," as depicted in *Life* magazine for May 12, 1947. One photograph is of an old man, with two children, a quite human theme, a genre picture, "universal" in its touching juxtaposition of youth and age. Caption: "Only the Old and Very Young Escape Red Training." Another: A picture of powerful-chested men singing vigorously, in chorus. As much sheer songfulness as a mere photograph could possibly convey. One can imagine a political censor's great delight in having his country represented by such evidence of vigor and fervor. Caption: "Cultural Escape. Bulgars' Frustrated Talents are Poured Into All the Arts." (The reasoning would seem to imply that a *feeble* love of art would be evidence of a *good* culture.) Again: Picture of three old men, humorous old codgers, of a sort that could pose as cracker-barrel philosophers in a genre painting of New England life. They look friendly, and comfortable. Caption: "Three Old Men Dream of Vanished Hopes Under Emblems of Bulgaria's New Order." Finally: Photograph of students and girl teacher on athletic field. She is teaching them how to kick what looks like a soccer ball. The snapshot shows her leg outstretched, at the moment when her foot is in contact with the ball. Caption explains: "Their Russian Trained Leader Teaches Them a Kick That Resembles the Famed Goose Step." You need not know "the facts" about Bulgaria to judge those pictures. You need merely compare the pictures with their captions.

Paradoxically, one especially persuasive aspect of selectivity in headline-thinking is the *quietus*, a rhetorical device that is by the nature of the case imperceptible, but can have a tremendous effect upon the citizens' understanding of reality. Where reality is perceived through the press (as in much political information), the mere slighting of an emergent political trend can be a more effective "refutation" than whole pages of invective. And if the political trend does gain popular prestige despite such slighting, a subtler, more Machiavellian variant of the quietus would be available. There can be a flurry of publicity, during which the news of the new trend is given fair coverage. Then, after a few days, the subject can be dropped again. Rhetorically, such a change says in effect: "When the movement was a matter of public interest, we gave it ample consideration. But we no longer give it space because it is no longer of public interest." This device can be pointed up by comments in editorials, and by columnists and correspondents, that refer in passing to the rapid subsidence of the movement. Rhetorically, the most effective use of headlines-in-reverse would be the absolute quietus. Next in effectiveness would be this "irruptive quietus," the lapse into silence after publicity. And if this in turn fails, there remains the standard resource of selectivity, the featuring of stories that represent the opposing philosophy, or terminology of motives, which the given newspaper favors.

IV. REDUCTION ("GIST")

If a political candidate delivered an address lasting two hours, and if nearly every sentence of that address was sound and appealing, but there was one erring paragraph, the headline writer for a newspaper backing a rival candidate could "honestly" report, as the very essence of the address, that one erring paragraph. Thus John L. Lewis once nonplussed a Senate Committee before which he was testifying by posing as the champion of free enterprise, at a time when bodies like the National Association of Manufacturers were backing this slogan. But at one point, when asked how to stop country-wide strikes, he expressed himself a bit unguardedly: "Until we change our form of government, we can't do anything about it. If you want a totalitarian form of government you can do all those things." Whereupon, the headlines: "Lewis Sees U.S. Powerless / To Prevent Coal Strikes / Unless It Goes Totalitarian." Obviously, Lewis thought there could be many ways of preventing coal strikes without totalitarianism. For instance, some strikes might be prevented by government pressure on the operators. But as John Dewey once said, you can't say everything at once. And a partial statement could be seized upon, for polemic reporting, as the very essence of Lewis's testimony.

A Methodist bishop delivers an address warning that, unless we modify our ways of dealing with Russia, we are headed for war. Thanks to the rhetorical resources of gist, this address can be "honestly" head-lined: "Oxnam Holds War / With Russia Sure."

The requirement that the "gist" be put into the headlines practically demands such treatment of Papal pronouncements as we considered under Spiritualization (as combined with the Spokesman device). For instance, we have heard many charges that relief supplies from America were being distributed in war-devastated countries on the basis of polit-ical allegiance. There have been charges and counter-charges, as Left, Right, and Moderate governments have all been accused of such prac-tices. Many conservative papers in the United States, for instance, printed stories from correspondents in China, showing how the Nation-alists interfered even with the shipment of medical supplies to the popu-lation in Communist-dominated areas. Accordingly, the Pontiff could justly complain that relief was "in some countries tagged with a price, the price of adherence to a political party." But as reduced by a gist-loving reporter, this universal position could be factionalized thus: "Pope in New Plea for Fight on Reds. Pius Says Communist Tyranny Replaces Nazis. Sees U.S. Aid Used Politically." (Needless to remind you, though the reporter found the Pope's words "marked by bluntness and vigor," there was no mention of either Communists or Nazis in his address.) And lest the reader think of Nationalist China, the helpful reporter explained: "Vatican circles said his words could be applied to all Communist-dominated countries. They saw a particular reference to Yugoslavia, Albania and other countries where they said the Commu-nist party had been using UNRRA supplies as a political weapon to win over peoples or to coerce them into supporting the party's policy."

If a sweeping program is announced by a political party, along with a criticism of those in the party who might not be wholly behind it, the headline can, with "scientific" factuality, play up the incidental criticism as hinting at possible dissent within the party. Thereby the program itself would be presented in the light of a weakness, whereas actually it may have inaugurated a new era of strength. Thus, the story of sweeping reforms could be honestly reduced to such headlines as these: "Rift in X-ist Ranks Indicated."

Gist can readily take the diplomacy out of diplomacy, when that's what the writer wants it to do. Thus, the Iranian minister was quoted in a brief dispatch as saying: "As I have always considered it the utmost necessity for Iran to gain the friendship and good relation of our great neighbor, Russia, I expect them not to darken the hearts of their friends in Iran by untrue statements." The headline for this item was: "Moscow Lies, Ghavam Says."

At a time when Sweden signed a bilateral trade pact with Soviet Russia, and the United States protested in diplomatic language, both Sweden and Russia answered in diplomatic language. But one newspaper gave the gist of Sweden's answer, thus: "Sweden to Stand on Soviet Accord. Reply Voices Surprise at U.S. Protest and Insists Trade Policies Are Liberal." But it gave the gist of Russia's thus: "Soviet Rebukes U.S. on Trade Pact Note. Says, in Effect, That Russia's Negotiations With Sweden Are None of Our Business." The nearest we come to this expression in the actual statement is an assertion that Sweden and Soviet Russia "stand in no need to make point of consultation with the United States on the favorableness or unfavorableness of a trade agreement."

One news item, presented in a way designed to create animus against strikers, used the running head, "Defiance of U.S. Hinted." (Defiance itself, of course, is capable of two quite distinct tones. Not many months previously, a business official had been depicted in the press as a hero for defying federal regulations. But the tone now identified defiance with Red Ruin.) The actual report, however, was a quite honest statement of the case. In keeping with the recognized democratic practice of citing representative persons, the reporter had quoted *one* striker ("who declined to be named") as saying: "If the government issues an order to seize the telephone industry . . . it should remember that a piece of paper will not operate the nation's telephone system." But in accordance with the ethics of "gist," this remark could be reduced in headlines to ominous talk of defiance against our country. (The business official, of course, had defied the *administration*, whereas the anonymous worker had defied the whole nation.) Such reduction amounts to *amplification*.

In reducing a story to its gist, one can choose between explanatory motives and sheer behavioral description. For instance, one nation demands large reparations of another. Behaviorally treated, this might not look so good. Hence, the sheer behavioral "fact" could be given, if the purpose was to give the reader a bad impression. But if the headline writer would give a good impression, he can reduce the story motivationally, thus:

Britain Asks $11,520,000,000

in Reparations from Italy

To Offset Russia's Claims

Bargaining Move

(We shall return to this point when discussing tonality.)

On other occasions the headline can reinforce the *apparent* motives of a statement. Thus, at a time when the United States was trying to forestall strong United Nations action against Franco Spain by proposing a *weak* measure which it wanted to make look sufficiently strong to be acceptable as a substitute for a truly strong measure, the gist of the U. S. resolution was in one paper presented thus: "U. S. Calls on Franco to Quit. Or for Spain to Depose Him." The reduction here was made in accordance with the *apparent* purpose of the measure, the information itself thus being set in a frame that reinforced the deflective rhetoric.

When a debater begins, he says, "I am going to prove . . .," etc. In his peroration, he says, "I have proved . . .," etc. From the standpoint of rhetoric, a headline is exordium and peroration rolled into one, without being formally recognized as either. It is the *thesis of an argument* masked as the "gist" of some "facts." Often it can do its rhetorical work most effectively if the reader does not read beyond the headline, or if he reads only the few opening sentences that seem most to confirm it. (See the sixth paragraph in this section for an illustration.)

The principle of reduction has been well illustrated by comic excess in a series of *New Yorker* cartoons varying the theme of mental undressing. For instance, a married couple passing a flashily dressed woman. Above the wife is a thought balloon, indicating that she sees only the other woman's clothes. The man's balloon indicates that he is in thought stripping her naked. Another variant: Mohammedan in hotel lobby, reducing all the women to a hypothetical state of nakedness. Another: Man passing draped manikin in shop window; in his mind's eye he sees the manikin undraped, with exposed metal rods for joints at knees and elbows. A number of the *Harvard Lampoon,* burlesquing this series, showed a hot blond highstepping before a funeral parlor. The undertaker is leaning in the doorway; his thought balloon shows her lying with pointed breasts, nude, on a mortuary slab. It is good to recall these overly zealous reductions of a subject matter to its "essence" when one is considering (a) the selectivity of news items in general, and (b) the selectivity-stop-selectivity in the headlines of such items.

V. TITHING BY TONALITY

The greatest embarrassment that besets the analyst of news rhetoric is a procedure we have called "tithing." "Tithing" is our word for the journalistic building of animus by countless strokes of style, each so trivial that you can hardly bring yourself to point out its tiny inclination. As you see the infinitesimal but endlessly repeated reinforcement of an attitude, by different particulars, through months and years, you collect a body of testimony each item of which is as microscopic as bacteria, yet so powerful in the mass as to threaten the very foundations of human society, particularly in an age which has so many new means of destruction as ours, goading us in our unimaginative moments to try using the new weapons as a cure for economic ills inborn to our society.

If a foreign nation's ambassador to our shores so much as shows his ignorance of baseball, and it is editorial policy to keep alive a feeling of ill will towards that nation, then the ambassador's failure to appear at a certain game is a matter for headlines, a news item rushed by wire throughout the country, and picked up by all editors who would so "tithe." Or, the editor may keep alive a series of petty annoyances, tiny stories selected for their almost imperceptible nuisance value, in conveying the general impression that there is something unwholesome about the quarters which these foreigners inhabit. There is a large amount of such items, which the student of journalistic "tithing" begins to encounter in even the best newspapers, once he is vowed to watch the styles of the press as carefully as he might scrutinize the inventions of good literature. Perhaps no other medium of expression in all history could adhere to so mean a kind of persecution without producing a universal nausea that neither readers nor writers could endure. Yet in the journalistic medium, it can often be the norm, almost our cultural bread—and majestic forests are destroyed daily, to keep it vigorous.

In "tithing" we encounter the most characteristic aspect of the quantitative rhetoric natural to the newspaper as a form. The power resides not in the brilliance of the message, but in the efficiency of the technology by which an idea can be institutionally amplified until it is equivalent, in its suasiveness, to an evangelical doctrine like Christianity, vibrant with intellect and poetry. This is the rhetoric of small profit made stupendous by big turnover. Here is the rule, not of great, demonic malice but of petty malice, a threat created by the mild peccadillos of a man who would borrow four books when intending to return three, or insists upon paying but is too slow in reaching for the check, or routs out a friend at midnight to hear an abject confession, and at the crucial moment in his unburdening, lies. Here is the superficial kind of vice that overestimates the size of its cronies' parade and underestimates the adversaries'. Here is the art of the negligible, made monstrous.

"Tithing," then, is the establishing of an attitude by trivial effects that become important in the aggregate. The very triviality of the device adds to its effectiveness, if there is a constant opportunity to repeat it, in varying details. It is difficult to cite examples, because they are in their very essence made not for close attention but for inattention. As soon as one singles them out, one realizes that they are the exact opposite of Matthew Arnold's "touchstones." But we must list a few (dwelling upon the negligible):

A radio newscaster reports a political party's attempt to "overthrow" a government. The word is technically accurate, as applied to parliamentary regimes in Europe where such administrative upsets are a normal aspect of the democratic process. But it has different connotations for the uninformed in the United States, to whom it is synonymous with revolution. And the announcer, if he would gain maximum disapproval for the party's act, can leave this distinction unexplained.

A Congressman traveling in Britain is reported to have found evidence that the Russians had spread distrust of U.S. capitalism among the public. (Ignoring the long tradition of *Fabian* criticism indigenous to England, the report makes the fruits of that movement look like a mere reflex of Russian influence as though Shaw had learned his socialism from Stalin.)

A bomb is tossed into the headquarters of a Leftist organization. The incident is reported on the radio as "an indication of the ill feeling between the Left and the Right." By this tiny stylistic turn, the victims become as guilty as the perpetrators.

In one news story, where some United States soldiers were arrested for crossing the boundaries of a nation towards which our press wanted to promote an attitude of ill will, the report even contrived to make it look bad that the soldiers had been handled "with kid gloves" during their detention. The favorable treatment suggested a kind of fawning, unwholesome attitude on the part of the jailers.

When the United States was backing a dictatorial regime in Turkey, a news story described the country as "poised halfway between the Oriental despotism of her Ottoman past and a republican democracy of the future." The idea of a reformed Turkish government at some hypothetical date in the future is thus used as "news" of Turkey now. Yet democracy would be possible *only* if the Turks could get rid of such regimes as our government was subsidizing there. The talk of a coming change thus serves as an argument for the very subsidy that would prevent or delay the change.

Such tithing involves "tonality" in the sense that it implies a tone of voice. But whereas tonality is implied in headlines, it can be explicitly present in the "intelligence" communicated by radio. Thus we heard two programs in succession, on free time granted by a radio network, the first stating the position of the Congress of Industrial Organizations, the second that of the National Association of Manufacturers. The announcer, of course, disclaimed the broadcasting company's responsibility for the views expressed on either program. But he mentioned the name of the National Association of Manufacturers in a natural and pleasant tone of voice, whereas he had previously pronounced the syllables "C. I. O" in accents that were solemn, even ominous.

The point might seem trivial; any single instance of "tithing," when considered in isolation, usually is trivial. But on the subject of tonalities, and their importance, remember this: Recall the occasion when Mae West appeared on the same program with Charlie McCarthy. Recall the scandal that broke after this program and that has, we believe, kept Mae West off the air ever since. For listeners throughout the nation had resented what they considered the lewd suggestiveness of her lines. Yet experts in such matters had scanned the script in advance of the broadcast, and had found nothing to censor. For they had read the lines without imagining the tonalities which Mae West would impart to them.

Hence, we take it seriously when we hear newscasters who pronounce the names of foreign diplomats outlandishly, if they represent countries against which they would promote ill will. Or in programs designed to "dramatize" the news, advocates of disfavored policies may be represented as speaking in foreign, crude, or bellicose accents, or in whatever other tonalities may, in the given situation, contribute a "dyslogistic" effect. We heard an announcer on a major network first so "muscovite" a Russian official's name that it sounded like a series of snorts and growls, and then proceed to "quote" him, thus: "a r-r-rude inter-r-fer-r-rence oon Hoongahrian eentayrnel affairss wheech ees nut payrmeesseeble."

A U.S. Senator dramatically announced that he had received a "reliable, authentic report" from Russia disclosing what the headlines called a "Giant Hunt for Minerals." This information was presented in ominous tonalities, suggesting that certain sinister activities had fortunately been uncovered in time by the sources of underground information to which the Senator had access. The story detailed the plans with alarming factuality, an enterprise of "more than 800 expeditions incorporating a host of some 60,000 scientists, engineers, technicians and workers. . . . " And so on. And the Senator was said to be turning over this intelligence to a Senate Committee, that our industrialists might be properly warned. Where "facts" failed, the absence of facts could serve to reinforce the same sinister tonalities, as the dispatch exposing the vast network of expeditions added: "But whether it is concerned with uranium or other fissionable materials was not specified." Later it was learned that the "startling disclosures" had been got by the simple expedient of changing the tonalities in a U.S.S.R. Information Bulletin. The document had been openly and proudly distributed by the Russian Embassy, to acquaint the world with what it considers the virtues of its economy. Everything that had been reported there in a tone of self-congratulation was reproduced in the news story almost word for word, but in a tone of profound shock. Everything that had been said openly was presented as though uncovered by stealth.

However, the shift of tonalities in this incident is not yet finished. For we get this story from Arthur Krock's column (*NYT,* 5/27/47), except that we ourselves modify the tonalities of Mr. Krock, who himself tells of it in the tonalities of grievance. For, Mr. Krock explains, Moscow propagandists would doubtless find "sinister reasons" behind the fact that a two-week-old Bulletin publicly issued by the Soviet Embassy should suddenly be flaunted before the nation as the exposing of a secret. Furthermore, he explains,

> It will perhaps be useless to point out that "Monday morning journalism," a weakness in the American press system, is partly responsible for the incident. Yet that—and not a concerted intention to mislead, exaggerate or pass off used goods as fresh—is at least half the explanation.

(Incidentally, as regards this instance of tonal translation, we will concede: So long as nationalistic aims are overstressed, any nation's efforts at self-improvement are liable to be construed somewhere as conspiracy.)

At a time when the airplane industry was in great need of orders, and there were promises that a "crisis psychology" would get it back into financially profitable production, a headline in a religious newspaper tithed thus: "America Looks to the Sky."

We read one news story reporting the statements of a speaker who had adversely criticized both the United States and another nation, towards which the press would foster ill will. Only criticism of the other nation was featured in the headlines. Criticism of the United States was relegated to the end of the article, under a subhead which, if read only in connection with the headline, seemed like a further adverse reference to the other nation, since the headlines gave no indication that the United States was mentioned at all. Doubtless this was an accident—but it was of such a sort that, if the reader but ran his eye over the page, as he does with so many headlines, the arrangement would make its peculiar contribution to "tithing."

During the Italian elections in April 1948, when the Vatican so boldly intervened in political affairs, we thought what an easy opportunity our press could have had, if it had wanted to report the campaign in tonalities appropriate to our traditional stress upon separation of Church and State. But of course, our press had reasons for exploiting other tonalities, since De Gasperi was as much their candidate as the Vatican's.

We felt similarly about a Budapest dispatch noting that Esperanto was being revived with government support in the Danube Valley. The story, using mild antithesis, contrasted the "Southeastern European Esperantists" with "their former colleagues in western countries," who still believe that the language should remain "politically neutral." Since this story was published at a time when the press was on the lookout for "rifts behind the iron curtain," we felt that an opportunity had been missed to link the story with that timely topic. The last paragraph of the dispatch reads:

> Some of the Hungarian government leaders favor Russian over Esperanto as a second language, Mr. Kokeny said. However, Esperantists here got another boost last week, because Hungary's new President, Arpad Szakasits, is keen on Esperanto.

If we exploited this last paragraph for tithing, the item could have been "tonalized" thus:

Hungarians Hope to Offset
Influence of Russian

Officials Back Esperanto
as Second Language for
Danube Valley

Tonality being a kind of implied identification, when the resources of tonality are threatened, outright identification may be needed to recover its effectiveness. Thus, recall the time when, along with praise of the two-party system, the press had established good tonalities for references to "the bipartisan foreign policy of the Administration," and

Henry Wallace, cutting in from another angle, had sought to reverse the tonalities, on the ground that the bipartisan policy gave the people no alternative. One reporter writing from Washington pointed out that this same expression, "bipartisan foreign policy by the Administration," had been used the week before by another witness at a Congressional hearing. And at that time "The committee had spent nearly half an hour vainly trying to get a categorical reply . . . to the charge that he had belonged to the Young Communist League." Obviously, by this device, the tonality which Wallace had threatened is protected by identifying his tonality with another word which the press had already strongly endowed with dyslogistic tonalities. (We are not suggesting that there is anything particularly reprehensible in such rhetoric. We are merely pointing out that it *is* rhetoric. There is deception here only insofar as a reader might think he is reading "facts" *as distinct from* rhetorical manipulation.)

In "tithing," even the absence of news is news, and even the failure to establish an accusation is an accusation. Thus, a "spy scare" or a "witch hunt" engineered by some Congressional committee could serve its purposes even though no single charge could be legally proved. For if one person after another is publicly questioned on suspicion of being secretly a member of Faction X, though each of them indignantly denies the charge, you have material for a succession of headlines that keep the name of Faction X vibrant with dyslogistic tonalities. Hence, where the Department of Justice or the Federal Bureau of Investigation might advise against an inquiry, on the grounds that the evidence is insufficient to convict, and that some manifestly innocent persons would be victimized, a Congressional committee might hold it nonetheless, purely for its use in the headlines. And the journalistic flurry could serve the Congressional investigators thus: If they can intensify the dyslogistic tonalities of Faction X, then they can discredit an emergent Faction Y (which is still tonally unsettled) by flatly identifying it with Faction X. This is perhaps but a roundabout way of approaching the standard use of amplification in political oratory whereby reform is endowed with the tonalities of revolution. Since there are reformist elements in revolution, revolutionaries may temporarily ally themselves with a reformist party as the one least distant from their own aims—whereupon reformists and revolutionaries having united on the *reformist* aims they share, a sufficiently strong reactivating of the public's resistance to revolutionaries may serve to identify the reformist party with the tonalities of its *revolutionary* wing.

Once things get to swinging, even the sheer denial of a rumor can reinforce its value. Thus, if the military wanted Congress to vote a large war budget in peacetime, and wanted to frighten the public so that they would not protest such expenditures, their spokesman in the administration might announce before a Congressional committee that unidentified submarines were reported to have been seen near our coast. Later, after the story had been featured in the press as the originators had intended it to be, the spokesman could blandly call upon the public not to be alarmed (thereby offering material for further alarming headlines). He could explain that an effort would be made to verify whether the submarines were those of a foreign power, since they might turn out to be our own. And "in all fairness" he could point out that it is quite legitimate for foreign submarines to sail the high seas anywhere they choose (thereby using even a "reassurance" as a further incentive to believe in the sinister possibilities of the rumor). The official could also disclaim any idea as to what nation these hypothetical submarines might belong, while the free press could contribute its part by indicating that the ominous elusive shapes (now in headlines said to "prowl") belonged to one particular power against which the public was then being goaded. (As for the seeing of the shapes themselves, you might even with confidence expect them to be glimpsed by earnest souls in Middle Western ponds, as a match for other prodigies, seen flying in mysterious ways across the heavens and dutifully reported in the press, with great military experts grimly announcing that a thorough investigation was under way.)

Once an audience is thoroughly conditioned by tonalities, the correct reporting of an adversary's statement can be a further step in deception. The Nazi propagandists, for instance, frequently quoted the criticisms of their enemies. But the reader received these through an attitudinal fog that made it impossible to know them for what they were. Establish the attitude that a certain kind of criticism is sheer slander, and quotations from it can seem to corroborate you rather than refute you.

We should also consider a means whereby "behavioral" reporting can contribute to tonality. Thus, if Primus insulted Secundus yesterday, and Secundus strikes him today, then as regards merely today's "facts," the news is that Secundus struck Primus. If only today's blow were described, with no mention of yesterday's insult as its incitement, such a report would be what we mean by "behavioral" description as a rhetorical device. Sometimes "behavioral" reporting can "honestly" disregard motivational elements which, if included in the definition of the act, would critically alter its appearance. Thus, if an act was done under duress, but in itself looked "handsome," a sheerly behavioral account of it, however accurate, would have "good" implications not possible to a full motivational description (which would have to mention the duress). Hence, a behavioral style could be a convenient rhetoric of "honest" misrepresentation when a strong nation forces a certain policy upon a weak nation. The press of the strong nation could signalize the compliance in headlines that play up the decisiveness of the act itself and pass over the grudging motives for it.

Here is another instance of the way in which a behavioral reduction may give an impression quite different from the motivational account. Thus, a reporter tells of conditions in Breslau under Polish rule. He honestly describes what the first headlines call a "minor miracle" in reviving the ruined city. He honestly reports the nature of the fighting there during the war, as the Red Russians fought street by street against the Germans and a force of Russian deserters. But for any one who dares not read the story itself, the second headline, reduced to a purely behavioral account, gives a quite different idea by referring to present restorations "After Russian Troops Plundered City." Since the headline thus so strongly sets the tone, there is even the possibility that many who do read the article, with the usual inattention to which newspapers are geared, would remember the resonance of the headline rather than the "gist-less" muddle of the story in detail.

If you were reporting of a nation which recently suffered an unprovoked attack by a powerful enemy but which now had a government you would discredit, you might confine yourself to behavioral facts about conditions now. These would comprise the present hardships and the political order you would discredit. For behaviorally, the past suffering would be no act now. Hence, dismissing it, you could simply identify the present hardships with the prevailing political order. You need not say so. Your statement, formally, may amount only to this: "The hardships are such-and-such *and* the political order is such-and-such." But if your report is read by a reader for whom the tonalities have already been set against this political structure, your behavioral account both exploits and confirms these tonalities. It says, in effect: "The hardships are such-and-such *because* the political order is such-and-such." Maybe it is, maybe it isn't. Behaviorally, you can suggest such a conclusion without making any such literal statement at all.

At one stage of reconversion after the Second World War, a great many war factories having been closed as a result of official action, the discharged workers naturally began looking for work elsewhere. There was nothing else for them to do. Later, when it was decided that war production had been curtailed at a greater rate than revised plans called for, this situation was described as one in which too many workers had been "abandoning war work for peace-time occupations." After some of the war factories were reopened, it was announced that the workers were "gradually returning." In other words, the purely behavioral account of the workers' movements made it look as though their departure from war factories and their return had been motivated by choice, whereas they left the factories when there were no jobs and returned when there were. The purely behavioral statement thus helped reinforce the anti-labor "tithing" in which our press was then exceptionally active.

Similarly, at one stage in the quarrels between the Kuomintang and the Chinese Communists, an agreement was reached, but soon fresh disturbances arose when the Kuomintang began violating the agreement. However, the dispatches from China did not state the matter thus bluntly, in causal terms. Rather, we were told, the difficulties resulted from "Kuomintang efforts to obtain the approval of the Communists and other parties to some revisions in the previous agreements." Purely behavioral description here attains to blandness. Your enemy breaks his agreement with you, and promptly announces to the world that you are being stubborn and uncooperative in resisting attempts to arrive at a new agreement.

In the special session of this same Eightieth Congress, the Republicans wanted to avoid passing the sort of remedial legislation advocated in their recently adopted political platform. They also wanted to avoid the resentment of the public. So they began the session by introducing a measure that was sure to provoke a filibuster of Southern Democrats. Repeatedly, over the radio at that time, we heard news broadcasts announcing that the Republicans "could not break" the filibuster. Behaviorally, this statement was completely accurate. Motivationally, they "could not break" the filibuster because so many of their members did not want to.

We heard an ingenious variant of behavioral reporting over the radio on May Day, 1947. Since both Communist and non-Communist workers celebrate this day, and since the occasion is also marked by military parades in Moscow, a broadcaster could report that the demonstrations throughout the world were "timed to coincide with the display of military might in Moscow's Red Square." The military display in Moscow being timed to coincide with the workers' parades elsewhere, one could, by using "timed" in a purely behavioral sense, say that the parades were timed to coincide with the military display (somewhat as one could say that the army's pace was timed to keep step with a certain private).

Similarly, when, sometime after the nationalization of the coal mines in Britain, there was a disastrous snowstorm that interrupted transport and caused many hardships, including a fuel shortage, we heard one of the country's most respected commentators refer in a newsreel to "the coal crisis in Britain following the nationalization of the mines." Later, the speaker told of the snow, but without mentioning the mines. The two items were left disrelated, each with its own orbit of behavior.

The behavioral style could also at times be used by a newsman to "get across" a disclosure that would not be feasible if described motivation-ally. Thus, at a time when, according to President Truman's frankly rhe-torical blasts, Congressional investigations of "Communism in the United States government" were being used as a deflection, to keep the headlines filled with reports of Congressional activity at a time when nothing was being done by Congress to remedy the nation's growing economic plight, we heard one reporter explain that the investigating of Communism was taking the zeal out of plans for domestic improve-ments. This phrasing is but a "behavioral" translation of President Tru-man's polemical version. We have previously discussed the ways whereby one can transform an accident into a rhetorical device by treating the result as intentional. Here is the opposite resource: An intended result can be translated back from rhetorical analysis into "pure news" by presentation as a non-purposive event. Yet the rhetorical implications are there for one who would "read between the lines" by translating the behavioral style into the motivational.

The rhetorical choice between "behavioral" and "motivational" description could be treated as a variant of the shift between idealiza-tion and materialization, discussed in the previous chapter. But gener-ally the "censorious" nature of the mind-body pair is obvious, whereas the use of behavioral reporting for "honest misrepresentation" is hard to detect and harder still to prove.

We might recall here our earlier concern with Jeremy Bentham's *Table of the Springs of Action,* the locus classicus for the study of "censorious" terms that "have the force, but not the form, of an argument." Bentham's analysis of such "appellatives" is basic to the matter of "tonalities." In negotiations between nations, for instance, there are occasions when par-ties seek to mediate their differences; there are other times when they choose to be intransigent. Hence, by treating compromise in the tonalities that go with words like "compliance," "adaptability," "reasonableness," we can set it up as a fixed principle of good conduct. And we thereby automatically rule out tonalities that would place compromise in the same bin with "weakness," "cowardice," "vacillation," "defeat," and the like. Similarly, intransigence may be treated in the tonalities that go with firmness, steadfastness, uprightness, stern loyalty to principle; or it may be likened to stubbornness, pig-headedness, unimaginativeness, lack of sympathy.

"Tonalities" are not quite the same as Bentham's "censorious appellatives," however. Carrying out the Bentham principle, we should call "foolhardiness" in the enemy what we call "bravery" in an ally. Or we might refer to Communism simply as "totalitarianism," thereby identifying it with Fascism, while capitalism could be called "democracy" ("democracy" now being a word with good tone, though earlier in our history it was of dubious quality, "republic" and "democracy" confronting each other almost as antithetical modes of government).

That is, Bentham's principle concerns the possibility of a choice between words of opposite emotional weighting. We are concerned with a further aspect: the deliberate *imparting* of emotional weighting to a word by the use of tone. In practice, the two merge into each other, and reinforce each other. However, they can be differentiated. For where a tonality is not established, we can establish it by suggestion, in using it *as though it were* established.

For instance, we praise ourselves as a nation by talk of our high *idealism* in international policies that net some of our citizens large profits. But when Henry Wallace backed the project for sixty million jobs, his statement was discredited as the *idealism* of an irresponsible visionary, in contrast with the soundness and wholesomeness of realistic businessmen. This must have been rhetoric; for businessmen are not stupid, and within a few months there were more than sixty millions at work. However the important thing for our purposes is to note that the manipulation was contrived, not by shifting between "eulogistic" or "dyslogistic" terms, but by using the same term both eulogistically and dyslogistically. Here the choice would be between tonalities rather than between appellatives. (We are making a choice strictly between appellatives when we shift between idealistic and materialistic names for a given motivation. And we are strictly using tonalities when we use the same word in different emotional weightings, depending on whose ox is gored. But more broadly, identification by either of these methods could be called either "censorious appellatives" or "tonalities.")

Similarly, looking back at a time when efforts were being made to establish federal unemployment insurance, we recall how the press used "insecurity" as a good word, when praising the momentous role that insecurity played in stimulating capitalist production. Yet a few months later, after the insurance laws had been passed, the press began a new campaign, attempting to prevent further legislative reform. And how was this policy commended? By using "insecurity" as a term with *dyslogistic* tonalities. Business, we were told, was suffering from a sense of insecurity. The heads of enterprise could not plan because of uncertainty about the laws still to be enacted by Congress.

The nature of Rhetoric, as an art that "proves opposites," here comes to a head in the situation whereby any term can be found to contain two opposing sets of hidden modifiers. Thus, if debaters were given "Idealism" or "Insecurity" as topics, they could deliver opposing orations, detailing the virtues or the vices of their subject. And such possibilities of amplification are secretly concentrated in any topic. Thus, if an indoctrinated Nazi used the two sentences, "The Jew did it" and "The Aryan did it," the shift in tonality would not be confined to "Jew" and "Aryan." Secretly, the word "did" would be correspondingly modified. "Did" in the first sentence would have connotations of botching or scheming. In the second, it would have the connotations of Caesar Augustus' accomplishments, as one who came upon a city of brick and left it a city of marble. (After the Great Aryan, Berlin's marble was rubble.)

Without tonality, no tribal cohesion. Rhetoric as a pragmatic means of inducing collective action begins in tone. A newcomer "belongs" when he has mastered the tonal subtleties of his group, when he knows spontaneously what he is expected to mention in accents of approval, scorn, boredom, apprehension, amusement, and the like. While students are being taught a formal lore, they are scrupulously picking up some such informal lore (largely from other students whose prestige enables them to set the tone). Often you can find a teacher burlesqued in the tonalities of his students, as they, by sheer shading of the voice, let in or keep out authors, cultural movements, even whole civilizations. Thus, an academic friend said of an anti-philosophic colleague: "When one of his students remarks of another, 'He is majoring in philosophy,' there is such firm and quiet repugnance in the words, no dignitary ever spoke with more authoritative disparagement of a menial."

True, though the setting of tone is of major importance in controlling responses, and the headline is particularly effective in setting the tone, there are definite limits beyond which the manipulator of tonal suggestion cannot go, especially since headlines do not permit the gradual modification of tone exemplified in Antony's speech before the mob after the death of Caesar. However, such transitions are possible, through headlines over a period of time. For instance, the late Heywood Broun, at a time when he was head of the journalists' Guild, called attention to an arrangement whereby an editor could lead his readers into a policy by first having it expressed by one of his columnists. And only after the policy had been built up gradually in such "independent" columns would the paper itself assume responsibility for it. If, when it was first being recommended in the column, it was enough of a change to evoke letters of protest (Broun pointed out), the editor could disclaim responsibility, citing the columnist's deviation from editorial policy as proof that the press was free.

As regards the effects of journalistic tithing by tonality, the critic should bear one important consideration in mind. News being addressed to an inattentive audience (diametrically opposite to the attention given by experts to poetry or critical prose), newspapers have become so perfectly adapted to inattention, they doubtless demand it. Hence, probably a fantastic amount of "tithing" is probably necessary to make something really sink in. Accordingly, if one reads such a medium with the close attention that he would pay to dignified texts, one may get a false impression of the rhetoric. Surely much of the excess in journalism (as in the systematic fomenting of international ill will) should be greatly discounted, when one is judging of its effects upon readers. Readers resist strongly, not in deliberate protest, but by their state of great distraction.

The rhetorical element in the news increases in direct proportion to its democratization. Thus, the organized purveying of news begins in confidential information to "insiders." It develops as an extension of the diplomatic pouch, spreading beyond "political government," to extend ever widening areas of "business government." And as its range of readers increases, its motive changes. Where the information is confidential, its function is sufficiently served if the report is accurate and relevant. The purchaser, concerned with questions of advantage, wants the news unadorned. He wants to hear of all important developments, both favorable and unfavorable, if only they bear upon his chances of profit and loss. He need not read such reports for their "human interest," their "dramatic value." His involvement in his own practical designs, with their promises and risks, can supply this motive for him (and any further need for dramatic exercise he can get from sports, art, sex, etc.). So far as news is concerned, he needs ask only to know exactly what is going on. And he is willing to pay a relatively high price for such information, a price far above the mechanical cost of gathering and distributing the information.

Eventually, however, a different element enters. News becomes democratized. His underlings read the same daily paper as he does. And men of his sort pay large subsidies that enable the paper to be sold to the general public at a much lower price than its actual cost of production.

At this stage, he does not want the news merely to be accurate. He wants it to take into account the susceptibilities of the public at large. Whereas a statement made "confidentially" need only be accurate and relevant, he will feel differently about it if it is designed to be "over-heard" by people of many sorts, with interests other than his. When so many are listening, as he himself wants them to be, considerations of tact enter. News ceases to be a mere preparation for action (as with reconnaissance informing him about the actual disposition of forces). It becomes inducement to action (thus requiring stylizations that may serve his special interests better by being addressed in part to the general public rather than to him alone, and by aiming to affect the attitude of this public as well as telling him how things stand).

To an extent, he may thus become a victim of his own demands. He may come to believe the rhetorically tinctured version of reality which he thinks best for others. We should not assign a Machiavellian over-simplification to his role. He probably thinks at least partially in terms of the treatment he would prefer for those who are "overhearing." But at the same time, you will usually find him subscribing to a *different kind of news service,* closer to the sort that prevailed before the news was democratized. We refer to the reports issued by private news agencies, "news letters" that, as measured by the sheer quantity of news purchasable for a given sum, are thousands of times more expensive. And whereas he may himself want the daily press to play up and play down possibilities selectively for the purpose of affecting the general public's attitudes, he wants the confidential news service to state exactly how things stand. We should add this reservation, however: Often the King's ambassadors told him not just what was, but what he wanted to hear—and we can expect "confidential" advice in news services to show a like trend.

VI. NEWS AS DRAMA

A former friend said: "I spent one summer writing in the country, where the newspaper arrived in the mails about one o'clock, after I had been working on my book for about four hours. What a fantastic situation.

Imagine it for yourself. You have been writing steadily. Your work has fallen into a sustained pace. You have set up a kind of inner rhythm. The postman arrives, bringing the newspaper. You open it, glance over the headlines. Of a sudden a mob has smashed down your door and swarms into the room, pushing, shouting, trampling riotously. Everything is rage, roar, yap. Yap, howl, shriek, screech, heckle, heckle, heckle. On the mail at one, the news has arrived. Today's reality is here."

The problem of "reality," when headlines transform rhetorically designed statements into "news" (that is, reports about "truth"), was illustrated quite well in an article by Hanson W. Baldwin (*NYT,* 7/17/47), where he was decrying the emphasis on the "weakness" of United States military strength. He said that statements by various officials and military men, stressing the elements of weakness in our war machine, "of course, have been intended for domestic consumption as part of a drive to secure the passage of universal military training and to impress Congress with the need for more funds for the armed services." But "unfortunately" these statements "are transmitted abroad and, because of the official source of these statements, they are bound to make" an "international impression" that can only be "inimical to the best interests of the United States." Presumably we needed two "realities" for that Thursday, July 17th—one for our domestic purposes (saying, in effect, "truly, we are weak") and another for our international purposes (saying, "line up with us, for we are mighty").

Richard L. Strout, writing in the *Christian Science Monitor* (3/26/48), made a remark much to our purposes: "The separation of executive and legislature in the American governmental system often results in the use of 'shock' or 'scare' tactics to get quick congressional results in emergencies." The point incidentally indicates how readily the discussion of news as rhetoric leads into the rhetoric of bureaucracy. And, furthermore, it indicates why Situational matters wholly beyond the verbal must often be considered when the rhetoric of the press is being studied. Intrinsically, the use of "shock" or "scare" tactics makes for the "newsworthy" since it is "dramatic" (news as sheer story, told without "ulterior purpose"). Extrinsically, as rhetorical design, such stories may be treated in a way that adjusts them to certain bureaucratic purposes (in accordance with our remarks on "tithing" by "tonalities").

The remark by Mr. Strout was in connection with a Navy Secretary's story of mysterious submarines seen off the Pacific Coast. The next day, the *Monitor* printed an editorial containing some highly commendable comment on that same device:

The sport of sighting sea serpents will now take a back seat. If less than twenty "enemy submarines" are sighted in the next month we shall lose faith in the American imagination. But fortunately serious folk will have second thoughts about the submarine story. They will note that "off our shores" actually was nowhere nearer than 200 miles and in one case nearer Russia than the American mainland. They will wonder about how you identify a periscope "seen at night." They will surmise that American submarines are also cruising far from home.

Walter Lippman, criticizing the Truman administration's use of what has been called "crisis psychology," put the matter thus: "The trouble with using excitement as a device to pass necessary measures is that it aggravates the crisis which the measures are designed to deal with." He also was referring with distaste to this submarine episode, which he also linked with the way of launching the administration's policies in Turkey and Greece.

About this same time, a dispatch from Moscow in the *Christian Science Monitor* (4/7/48) reported:

> The war talk and alarmism in other countries, where full and untrammeled reports are available about what is going on, finds little parallel just now in the Moscow press. . . .
>
> One gains the impression that perhaps nowhere else in the world is there as little popular awareness of the current "war of nerves" widely attributed to Soviet moves, as there is among the people of Moscow.

Take it as you will, certainly on those days "world reality" was greatly different as seen through a Moscow newspaper and as seen through ours. And according to such testimony as we have just quoted, the "reality" in ours was greatly heightened by headlines which a free press constructed out of the Truman administration's rhetoric, as shaped by the bureaucratic necessity, in our governmental system, of having to work up a false "crisis" to *force* through Congress the desired appropriations.

During the negotiations between Russia and the Western powers in the attempt to ease the "Berlin crisis" (summer of 1948), Herbert L. Matthews sent a dispatch from London (*NYT,* 8/2/48) saying of arrangements for rapid, secret negotiations: "This mechanism is important because all three Governments [that is, U.S., Great Britain, and France] and especially Washington believe that war or peace may well depend on the diplomatic skill employed by the Western Allies freed of the pressure of public opinion." This statement followed a long period of turbulent polemics during which the "free" press had participated vociferously at every step in every international conference. We were then told repeat-edly by editors that the best results could be got by thus having every step in the delicate diplomatic maneuvers immediately broadcast as in the blow-by-blow description of a prizefight.

Presumably, at that time, many influential diplomats of the Western nations wanted such interference in the treaty negotiations. For as we noted before, a supposedly "rebellious" press, using tonalities that treat compromise as "betrayal of sacred principles," can greatly strengthen the hand of envoys determined to get an agreement on their terms or none. And when worsening conditions later made it imperative that treaties be signed, the press *was* excluded from the negotiations with the diplomatic "leaking" of news reduced to a minimum.

There is one notable difference between step-by-step reports of treaty negotiations and a blow-by-blow account of a prizefight. Though both kinds of news are "dramatic," depicting the moves of antagonists in a conflict, the description of the sporting event is in itself as "neutral" as the narrator can humanly be in such situations, however inflamed the audience's passions; but the reports of the international deliberations were dramatized by the most aggressive use of "tithing" and "tonality." Hence, the reference to "the pressure of public opinion" in the London dispatch quoted above might more accurately be read as "public response to the rhetoric of the news," particularly since the tithing involved zealous use of what we have called the Say Anything device.

This is not merely a matter of what one wag, burlesquing the Wilso-nian slogan for the rejection of secret diplomacy, called "open conflicts openly arrived at." The public was not present at the conference by proxy as they can be present by proxy at a prizefight. Of course, even in accounts of sporting events, the audience can get a deceptive impression. We recall one prizefight, for instance, which the spectators considered a poor one, but which the radio men, possibly responding in part to the excitement of the narrative job itself, made highly "dramatic." Here was a paradoxical kind of swindling, whereby absent listeners were cheated into enjoying a good "drama" at second hand while the spectators actu-ally present were being bored. And there was much complaining after-wards, particularly by newspaper writers who were in competition with the ringside radio reporters. But at least the false dramatizing of the news in such cases is not got by a rhetorical goading to partisanship through tithing. (If the sports contest were reported in the political style, one fighter's blows would be treated as threats and provocations, while the other's were mentioned in the tonalities proper to long-suffering and

calm retaliation regrettably made necessary by the outlandish aggressiveness of his opponent.) Yet though we would despise such a method
of reporting a mere entertainment, we take it as the norm for news of the
political "reality" we receive through the press. Here, if we read with the
attitude set by the headlines, we receive not the material for a decision,
but a decision implicit in the stylized treatment of the material.

The essence of journalistic dramatization is revealed in this foible:
That first estimates of damage and death in reports of a catastrophe are
usually much higher than the final accounting (which, of course, rates
smaller headlines). Usually, catastrophe is minimized only when there
are political reasons for weakening the purely dramatic value of the
event, as in reports of losses suffered by the journal's own side in battle.
(Even here, the usual exaggeration can be expected, if there are factional reasons for playing up the disaster as a basis for criticizing persons in authority.) Ordinarily, conflict is more newsworthy than agreement (except when an agreement strengthens a party in a conflict). And
even newspapers themselves sometimes warn us against the ill-propor-
tioned view of reality we can get from the ways in which certain news is
featured. Thus recently a syndicated article signed by Charles A. Lind-
bergh stated that airplanes seem more dangerous than other forms of
transport because air accidents rate bigger headlines (and doubtless
they would have told us this even though the air companies were not big
advertisers). And an article by Clifton Daniel, "Secret Diplomacy
Revives in Europe" (NYT, 8/30/48), noting that information about the
negotiations of diplomats "has been withheld from the public as a matter of deliberate policy by the four major powers," contains such
remarks as these: Some English newspapers, far from complaining,
"have taken the trouble to express their approval" ... "The Daily
Express recently wrote that 'rightful secrecy' was surrounding the Moscow talks" ... The Economist said that decision to keep the discussions
on the Italian colonies secret was taken "very sensibly" ... The Daily
Graphic noted that "secret diplomacy is an improvement on public
bickering" ... it is hoped that negotiations have a better chance of success if the negotiators "are not obliged to play to the press gallery every
day, thereby ruffling each other's tempers" ... "Britons look askance at
the boisterous American practice of trying every case in the newspapers" ... since commentators in the Western press don't know what is
going on, "There have been no charges of perfidy against the Soviet
negotiators" ... and finally, "The nerves of the newspaper readers and
radio listeners in all countries also have been spared, and, they no doubt

are grateful for this tiny respite from the chip-on-the-shoulder journalism and propaganda." However, when the misleading effect of the newspaper's dramatic overstress upon conflict and calamity is mentioned, the statement is usually made in "neutral" terms, not "censoriously," somewhat as though one were referring to a natural condition (the dramatic overstress being in response to a demand of "human nature" generally). Journalists will accuse bodies like the House Un-American Activities Committee of seeking, not justice, but headlines, without thereby concluding that newspapers are a party to the injustice.

On this matter of "human nature" (considerations that make news impinge upon Poetic, or more generally, Symbolic), R. L. Duffus, in a review of a privately financed report, *A Free and Responsible Press* (*NYT* Book Review, 3/30/47), writes: "A newspaper devoted largely to undramatized 'significant' news would not last long. This is human nature—not journalistic nature." But let's stop to consider how the motives of journalistic dramatization operate.

First, there is the principle of reduction. A Congressman, let us say, begins with some measure which he backs in comparative isolation. There is a special interest motivating some powerful group of his own constituents, and he would back a Congressional measure favorable to this group. However, in Washington, despite himself, he finds that he must confront a more inclusive range of considerations. He must somehow reconcile his measure with measures by other Congressmen representing interests more or less at odds with his. Hence, "horse-trading," the normal political compromises which his political enemies will excoriate with slogans like, "You scratch my back and I'll scratch yours," while themselves necessarily engaged in the same practices.

But the making of a deal is not enough. His representing of a local interest calls for a wider justification, since he is part of a body presumably legislating for the best interests of the nation as a whole. So he will, if possible, commend his measure in terms of wider scope, reducing it to some slogan involving the general welfare.

As a politician, he is a "time-server." He is concerned with day-to-day struggles for advantage. Accordingly, what would be more natural than for him to recommend his measure in terms of whatever feasible controversy is at the moment uppermost in the headlines? There may be many "universal" topics in terms of which he might propose his measure. But the strongest one would be a timely topic then being featured by the press. If he could identify his measure with this topic, either genuinely or spuriously, he might hope for the maximum of persuasion.

Next year the particular topic might be a dead one, but now it was very much alive. And whatever measures he proposed next year, he could seek to identify with the topic then most timely.

Suppose, however, that the topic uppermost at the time concerns bad relations with a foreign country. The Congressman will then seek to give his measure the appearance of maximum relevancy and urgency by recommending it in terms of this foreign controversy, whether it has any direct bearing upon the controversy or not. If he can manage to do this, his measure will have "dramatic" interest; hence his handouts to the press may get published, under challenging headlines, whereas the same measure would have been ignored, or given poor publicity, if it were merely "undramatized 'significant' news."

Thus, as a result, even measures to do with purely domestic policies will be "dramatized" by translation into terms of the current international controversy, insofar as the politician-rhetorician can find the necessary verbal contrivances. Hence, from another angle, there is a further batch of material that serves the ends of "tithing," and adds to international ill will, since a mean-tempered utterance, full of fire and challenge, would be more "dramatic" than an even-tempered one that did not exploit nationalist antagonisms.

Thus, when public rage is being whipped up (when "get tough" methods of diplomacy have been decided on, and the people are goaded accordingly), the mere existence of such a timely topic makes for its amplification. Every lawmaker will strive mightily to find a venomous device whereby his measure will win in the scramble for citation in the press; hence he will try to dramatize it by finding some means whereby it can be identified with the fund of public resentment already accumulated. And in thus seeking to profit by such frenzy, his publicity will also help contribute to it. For as we have said, the establishment of a tonality may be considered as an underlying form which each day is individuated by translation into new subject matter. It can be kept alive only by this method, by constant slight variations on the theme. Hence, any measure "dramatically" recommended in terms of the given tonality will also by the same token add its mite to that day's reactivating of the tonality.

All told, it is true that the demand for drama is human. In the last analysis, it could be treated as a secularization of the motives for Christian worship, since drama requires conflict, and conflict demands a victim, and the victims featured in the dramatized news are mean day-to-day replicas of the suffering Christ. (We recall a talk by Joseph Campbell, in which he quoted a mystic formula, "Split the stick, and there is

Jesus." In this respect, the drama of the news in modern civilization is a splinter of Christianity. We heard one radio newscaster who, before pausing for a commercial, promised his listeners: "We'll give you another heart-breaking story in exactly sixty seconds." The other aspect of Christ, as the way to salvation, has its journalistic replica in the promissory function of the *advertisements,* themselves also an aspect of dramatized news.) Yet not human nature, but "journalistic nature," must be held responsible for the excesses of dramatization in the news. And in any case, let us note how a purely "esthetic" policy (cult of the dramatic *per se*) comes to serve the ends of international polemics in ways that serve special interests. News dramatized by identification with a timely topic conceals, behind the dramatization, the special interests favored by the exploiting of that particular timely topic.

On the radio, the sheerly technical desire to make news interesting can lead to the cultivating of international malice. For antithesis is a major device of rhetorical effectiveness. And since a newscaster will naturally seek to step up the intensity of his message as much as possible, there is always the invitation to exploit the most intense of all antitheses, those involving a strong prejudice of the audience. But whereas newspapers often take a frankly factional stand in domestic matters, and thereby aim their appeal at some portion of the public as regards political alignment, the radio usually aims at a broader appeal, transcending local choices. Hence, a commentator who would intensify his remarks by placing his listeners in dramatic opposition to some enemy doctrine will try as far as possible to use kinds of antithesis not likely to alienate any large section of the public. The perfect solution for this problem in dramatization is obviously the use of items that exploit animus against a foreign nation with which our nation is at odds. Further, the idea of a foreign enemy, built up as national scapegoat, provides a topic that uses antithesis to unite speaker and audience as joint participants in a common resentment (a good condition for effective communication). Thus, the invitation is so insistent, that it could take exceptional scruples to resist it, whereas there are other incentives for not resisting it, since it can so easily pass as high public spirit, even in the mind of the artificer, while it may also fit well with the motives of the bureaucratic order to which the rhetorician owes his employment.

There is nothing exceptional about the principle of ill will in the news. Consider Florida's delight in news of hard Northern winters, and particularly its headlines about bad weather in California. News that spreads international ill will can be but an extension of this same motive.

Yet there seems to be an assumption that rhetorically weighted reporting of domestic factions is the same in principle as tithing by tonality in the accounts of our dealings with foreign nations. But there is an important difference between parliamentary battles and the controversies of diplomacy. All the disputants in a parliamentary battle fall within the same judicature, and their conflicts are settled within the orbit of litigation. But diplomatic controversies concern matters that transcend the means of litigation. Though we do have a "World Court," and some faint rudiments of world federalism in the United Nations, in the last analysis there is no governmental structure larger than the governments of the large nations. Hence, the threat of force as the court of last resort lurks behind all disputes between great nations. And for this reason, we must not take it for granted that the parliamentary wrangle within a nation would be culturally the same as wrangling in international controversies. The second kind requires diplomacy (rather than the appeal to public indignation as a bargaining device) precisely because nations in dispute are armed, whereas litigants within a nation are unarmed.

Indeed, the incentive to the cultivation of intense ill will against a nation with which we are at odds is so great that a somewhat organizational aspect of rhetoric threatens to figure here too. The very habit of fairness, in an institution or individual, can set the conditions for an added persuasiveness in unfairness, as when a reliable poll of public opinion begins rigging its questions, or a formerly judicious commentator decides that henceforth he will slant his statements (partially lying on the grounds that the people cannot act properly if told the plain truth; for in their state of ignorance and distraction, a partial lie by oversimplification might bring them nearer to the true response than would a whole truth with all its complications). There is a Jesuitical propriety in such a decision; there is a measure of honesty and justice in it; but once the rhetorician has made such a choice, he must be exceptionally imaginative, intelligent, virtuous, or lucky, not to become demoralized and eventually deserve his enemies' charges against him. (Here again we come upon aspects of the Hierarchic Anguish, as the technician seeks to fit himself into an Order, which he loves for its regularity as well as its privileges, but whose privileges, unless accurately criticized, produce drastic irregularity.)

One can suspect that people are better off if they get their tragic catharsis from purely imaginary stories than when they depend upon "documentary" reports of real victims and real horrors (a kind of catharsis too much like that of the Roman circus, where the populace could not be satisfied with symbolic killings but demanded the slaughter of live human offerings). But a primary stress upon news purely for its "dramatic" value can at least give one a better chance to "see around the corner" of editorially slanted news than is the rule under totalitarian coordination.

A "liberal" newspaper item may represent both the reality of an event in itself and the various special interests affected by that event. There is here a muddle of reader preferences, editorial policies (in the purely technical sense), and response to authorities or pressure groups (including financial backers). And these various interests of representation do not always coincide with one another. Hence, particularly when a story first "breaks," it may be featured for its "dramatic" value alone, regardless of its tendentious implications, which may be inimical to other interests. And several days may elapse before editorial policy crystallizes.

For often, when a story first breaks, if it has news value it will be presented purely on its merits as news, regardless of ulterior purposes beyond sheer appeal. Thus, when the Russians gave out word that our diplomats had begun peace feelers, this announcement was promptly featured in our press, regardless of editorial policy. It was not until later that "tithing" and "tonalities" were resumed, as the press (having adopted Bernard Baruch's octogenarian term "cold war" for what once would have been called "polemic," or maybe even simply "rhetoric") now went a step further in the same direction by labeling the Soviet moves a "peace offensive." Thus, in the first announcements, the story was given purely for its news value, for its sales appeal as a "sensation," and only later was the public required to understand it in accordance with whatever line would fit the "bipartisan foreign policy."

But at a corresponding stage in wholly "coordinated" news publishing, the story would simply have been suppressed until the government authorities had definitively decided what attitude toward it they wanted their public to adopt. There would simply be no stage wherein the story would be released without reference to rhetorical design, purely as drama, the incentive being not to mold readers but simply to attract them as customers.

Under politically coordinated censorship, an unwieldy event would simply "not exist," so far as public consciousness was concerned, until the proper officials had decided how it was to be presented (not as "drama," but as political rhetoric). Hence, the public would have much less opportunity to glimpse the many-sidedness of the event than if it had been presented only in accordance with bureaucratic design.

You may even insist that this liberal leeway (allowing for a purely "dramatic" test of news over and above its serviceability for some special cause) is due to no higher motive than competition. If one paper doesn't exploit such news for all it is worth in terms of sheer "human interest," irrespective of rhetorical wrighting, its competitors will. But even if this be the primary motive, it is in itself a "non-political" one, appealing to a wider dramatic interest than political faction alone; and thus it enables us better to see around the corner of an ideology in its most efficient embodiment (as under centralized bureaucratic censorship). And apologists for our "free" press doubtless have some such considerations in mind when they insist that dramatic criteria transcend the pressure of special interests.

In sum: We must be careful in interpreting the monopolistic aspects of the news. True, much of "reality" reaches us over the wires of three great news-gathering bureaucracies which are no more deft in perception and communication than one could expect any business agency to be. And their version of reality is likely to reflect the special interests of the particular bureaucratic order served by the given personnel. But we must guard against a rhetorical tendency to point up criticism by likening the ways of such agencies to the coordination of the news under Fascism. Capitalism does have Fascist temptations; but it also has genuine liberal virtues.

Yet while recognizing the justice in these claims, we must not allow them to count for too much. Since dramatic value is tied, by the timely topic, to the exploiting of animus which the news agencies themselves have built up, it can be almost identical with the interests of owners and pressure groups. Hence, a long sequence of tithing by tonality, which at once exploits and confirms a popular prejudice in accordance with editorial preferences, can be justified purely as dramatic expediency, or can as properly be condemned as tendentious selectivity dictated by ulterior motives. And since apologists for our press and radio will always congratulate themselves on its freedom from the dictatorial control exercised by totalitarian regimes, one can find them speaking otherwise only when they fall to quarreling among themselves. Thus, an editor had asserted that the views of the radio newscaster are controlled, whereas the newspaper "is free to speak as it pleases." Whereat Elmer Davis, speaking with some indignation over station WJZ (7:15 P.M.—9/24/47), denied this allegation, pointing out that the newspaper "is free to speak as its *owner* pleases." A few weeks before, an editor of the *New York Times* had indignantly denied this same charge, when it was made by a spokesman for the Soviet press. We do not assume, however, that Mr. Davis was consciously allying himself with the Russian position. In such a battle, he would doubtless have been on the side of the local editor. And only because he was so resolutely facing in one direction did he accidentally expose himself to attack from another. However, we are not here required to take sides in the controversy. Our present purpose is to point out how a dyslogistic charge of "pressure" might be identical with a eulogistic praise in terms of "drama," so that two champions of news as *appeal to human interest in general* might with justice interpret each other's motives as *subjection to special interests*.

Furthermore, where a story is given purely for its dramatic value, and where the purely dramatic value would interfere with the tonalities maintained as rhetorical policy, the effect can be offset by printing alongside it another story which reaffirms the tonalities. Or the two can be brought together under one head, so that the purely dramatic story which would alter the tonalities can share them nonetheless. At one time, for instance, the Russians proposed that both the United States and Russia retire from Korea. Since the Russians alone were supposed to be the "imperialists" there, this proposal was embarrassing. Yet it merited prompt publication as sheer drama. One newspaper solved the problem neatly by putting two stories under one head, thus: "Soviet Asks Korea Occupation End / As Russian Spy Ring Is Reported."

There is a variant of "dramatic value" in news having cosmic connotations, as with the astrological marvels that Elizabethan playwrights used for giving regal dignity to their plots. Here universal design seems to intervene purposively in the human order, so that accidents become fate-laden. Thus, when Congress finally approved the European Recovery Program, some enterprising newsman is reported to have calculated that the number of hours spent by the Senate in debate, before passing the measure, corresponded to the number of the majority voting in its favor, while the extra number of minutes above the total number of hours corresponded to the votes of the dissenting minority. This marriage of ancient numerology and the modern stopwatch led to results evidently deemed so momentous that we heard the "facts" announced over three different news broadcasts. The stories of the "flying saucers" that were frequently reported in the news about this same time would be another instance of such tithing by cosmically tinged tonalities, as they vaguely combined the thought of meteorological prodigies with suggestions of possible new enemy weapons, ghoulish in nature, that might invade us from the skies, somewhat as mechanical Men from Mars. Such stories gain "dramatic value" when fears of some foreign menace have been aroused; hence, they especially rate journalistic attention at such times. And since nothing is more dramatic than the thought of destiny as a partner in human motives, though such stories may be chosen solely for their dramatic value, they provide an increment of their own, contributing to the very fear from which they borrow their effectiveness.

As featuring had its invincible rhetorical counterpart in the quietus, so there is a rhetorical equivalent to dramatization. This device we might call a deliberate *Failing to Realize* the position of an opponent. The report can be "factually" true, yet it is so designed that it does not make the matter live in the reader's imagination. No invective here: one can simply "damn by faint reporting."

Only professional literary critics are likely to detect how thoroughly this device of failing to realize can be used in "honest" reporting of inimical policies. You can lay it down as a law: Whenever a speaker is eloquent in a cause you do not favor, and you would report his speech "factually" without allowing him the persuasiveness of his eloquence, tell it in your own words, reduce it without quotation, or select for quotation sentences which, without their proper preparation in the address, are lame or even repugnant.

You can watch the process best, perhaps, in book reviewing, where the reviewer can "scientifically" kill a stylistically engendered effect by telling of it in his own words, without style, or can kill an effect that depends upon development by citing the conclusion without adequately explaining the development. For instance, the work under review may have been designed to make the reader at home in a certain set of terms, terms that become clear within the universe of discourse; and the writer may sum up his position by bringing several of such terms together in one sentence; whereupon a critic can conceal misrepresentation beneath the appearance of great "factuality" by singling out that summarizing sentence and citing it as a typical example of the author's expository style, without giving the reader the necessary preparatory knowledge supplied by its context. Or if a writer, in stating a position, at some point translates it into a specialized terminology, to indicate its relevance for specialists to whom such terminology is most "natural," hence most persuasive, the critic can quote only that exceptional passage as a typical instance. It is as though a French author had somewhere quoted Cicero in Latin, and a reviewer were to select that passage as representative of the writer's French.

Thus, a major way of being "factually" true while weighting the report to one side is by failing to "realize" both positions with equal thoroughness. Thus, when the question of aid to Franco Spain was being considered by the United Nations, Léon Jouhaux, secretary general of the French General Confederation of Trade Unions, made a strong plea for aid to the anti-Franco Spanish. According to a report in a leading New York paper, this address, which strongly attacked a United States resolution, "was acclaimed as perhaps the most eloquent made before any committee of the General Assembly." Yet *only one sentence* of it was quoted directly in the news story. Otherwise, we were granted about four inches of lame paraphrase by the reporter himself. The same news item, on the other hand, gave a long report of the statement by a Latin American pro-Franco orator, and all of a purely pedestrian speech by a U.S. Senator. In saying that the French speech was most eloquent, the reporter told his readers news unwelcome to the policy of his newspaper. In giving but a fragment of the speech, and that lamely, in his own words, the reporter could make sure this "fact" was not realized for his readers. (We most decidedly do not mean that the ruse was intentional. We don't know whether it was or not. We cite it simply as an illustration of a device that lends itself readily to reporting as a medium. The reader can decide for himself whether he thinks the opportunity is likely to be exploited.)

The piecemeal nature of news, coupled with dramatization and the exploiting of timely topics, adapts news rhetoric well to "crusading." However, the tonalities which the press itself has helped build up favor minor reforms (such as a flurry of agitation against some merely symptomatic "vice ring") that usually serve rhetorically as deflections of more thoroughgoing criticism. Or (as with a northern Republican newspaper's articles on mistreatment of Negroes in the South) "crusading" may be an electioneering device (more properly belonging under the Rhetoric of Bureaucracy). Except for the elements we center in the headline, the "places" used in arousing public spirit on such matters are not specific to news-writing as a medium, but could be analyzed in keeping with the traditional lists, as in Aristotle. For a superior recent "crusade" of this sort, see Bert Andrews' *Washington Witch Hunt*, built around stories in the *New York Herald-Tribune* exposing excesses committed by the House Committee on Un-American Activities. These articles were "tendentious" reporting in the most admirable sense, and well deserved the 1947 Pulitzer Prize for journalism. Particularly effective is the transcript excerpted word for word from the testimony wherein "Mr. Blank" is defending himself before his superiors against an unspecified charge. These pages have almost the weirdness of episodes in Kafka's fantasy of bureaucracy, *The Trial*. And later the author does well to note the irony, when the official who had invited the victim to talk thus blindly for the record ("for the purpose of permitting you to have a complete record" . . . "I am making that statement for the record" . . . "send anything over to him you want to incorporate in the record" . . . "you send it over and we'll slap it in the file," a dozen such in a few pages) was himself under fire, pleading for the very specification of charges he had refused to Mr. Blank.

Commercial advertisements might fall under the heading of dramatized news, with various graphic devices intensifying the role of headlines (might not typical advertisements be reducible to headlines and subheads?). The "promises" (the nature of the "goods" as a way of secular salvation) would be analyzable along Aristotelian lines (thus perhaps a concern always with the underlying Hierarchic motive that invites consumer acquiescence through the assumption that the financially "adjusted" are the morally "justified").

We should here mention also a special form of advertisement, a kind of open letter to the public (often so entitled), a statement that is admittedly special pleading by representatives of some faction. In early 1942, for instance, when maximum production of war goods was necessary and leaders of the automotive industry were said by their critics to be delaying the conversion of their plants until they could strike the most advantageous bargain with the government, the Congress of Industrial Organizations printed paid advertisements presenting their case. In such "news," the informative element is on its face rhetorical (frankly designed to persuade). Thus, ironically, overtly tendentious advertising of this sort puts the reader in a more judicious frame of mind than news proper, which pleads under the guise of sheer "factuality."

The quietus here is got simply by refusal to accept the advertisement. Thus, newspapers refuse to publish advertisements of George Seldes' *In Fact,* that checks on their delinquencies. (Among other things, that little weekly has kept its readers informed on the way in which the quietus has been applied to news items telling of medical experiments on the relation between cancer and tobacco. Though stories about the progress of medical knowledge are naturally newsworthy, since they so directly concern physical and mental well-being, the press here for once has shown great restraint in denying itself appeal to human interest through news items that might pain some of its biggest advertisers.)

In closing, as regards "human nature's demand" for drama: We should perhaps note one important distinction between journalistic and formal drama. The "documentary" element in dramatized news, despite

214 I The War of Words

its selectivity, is thought to be a literal representation of reality ("factuality" rather than *proportion* being the test of such "truth"). But formal drama, however it sways us, never deceives us into forgetting that it is a fiction. Formal drama thus provides a much richer dialectical exercise than comes of reading dramatized news. With news drama, we shuttle between credulity and incredulity. In formal drama, there is no such problem of "authority"; we believe only what we see, not what we are told, and the belief itself is qualified always by the absolute knowledge that what we are seeing is not *literally* true (though the documentary emphasis of modern naturalism often cuts away some of the complexity here). In news drama, illusion is enslavement. With the metaphorical nature of drama proper, illusion is freedom.

VII. POLLS, FORUMS, ACCOUNTANCY

Polls and forums should be considered here, because of their informative element. In forums, there is some opportunity for a kind of blandness, since those in charge of the arrangements can plan for one side to be more strongly defended. A discussion would to that extent be "rigged," and questions giving a speaker particularly effective opportunities could be "planted" in the audience. Or, in the case of a studio audience, it could be so "screened" that its selected expression of attitude had a persuasive effect upon the "secondary audience" listening on the radio. But such matters belong better under the Rhetoric of Bureaucracy where the factor of non-verbal maneuvering is uppermost. For our present purposes, the center of rhetorical weighting in polls and forums is to be sought in the nature of questions as such.

Let us begin with an example which, though absurd in itself, clearly reveals an important formal element. At a time when anti-Russian slogans were prevalent, we heard on the radio (we did not catch the source) news of some temperance organization which demanded that all candidates for office pledge themselves to abstain from alcohol. The question was framed thus: "Do you promise to refrain from all alcoholic liquors, particularly vodka?"

Note, for our present purposes, that the last two words of this question are assertive rather than interrogative. The rest of the sentence asks whether the candidate will refrain from drinking. But the last two words are more like a proposition; saying in effect: "One should be anti-Russian." Or: "We take it for granted that you, and all other of our citizens worth saving, are anti-Russian." By the reference to vodka, the cause of temperance is identified with something like the "bipartisan foreign policy of the Administration." The question is quite worth pondering from the formal point of view, since the appendage reveals the *assertive* nature implicit in questions.

Surely, no work is more comprehensively assertive than Saint Thomas Aquinas' *Summa Theologica,* systematically stating the most minute details of Catholic belief. Yet every proposition is first presented as a question, to which false answers are given, with a contrary view, before Aquinas rephrases his question as a "Conclusion," which he next explains, following his explanation by a refutation of the false answers. Indeed, each group of assertions is called a "Question." Spontaneously, by this method, a statement such as "Sacred doctrine is a science" would be introduced stylistically in this form: "Is sacred doctrine a science?"

In part the method is a reflex of pedagogy, where the assertions of a doctrine are impressed upon the memory and the success of their indoctrination is tested, by the quiz. But there are further considerations here in keeping with our previous consideration that the Latin, *quaero,* means not only to question, but to seek (quest). Thus, we noted, Anselm's formula, *fides quaerens intellectum,* might in itself be given two quite different translations. It might be taken to mean, "Faith questioning intellect" (that is, faith controlling intellect). Or it might be taken to mean, "Faith seeking intellect" (that is, faith looking for its translation into the vocabulary of logic—the sort of thinking that eventually developed into theories like Eduard von Hartmann's post-Hegelian, pre-Spenglerian *Philosophy of the Unconscious,* viewing life as a development from vague instinctual urges into a perfection and clarity of form that is at the same time a kind of dying).

Typically liberal pedagogy (doubtless influenced by the Cartesian principle of organized doubt) has developed the question as quest to a point where its assertive nature is submerged. That is, the question is not merely a stylized way of leading into the answer which was there before the question. It is, rather, a "heuristic" question, posed to the researcher or experimenter, who is then committed to go in search of the answer.

Where the question involves an operational answer, it can be as factually heuristic as it seems to be. That is, a physicist may ask, "What will happen under such-and-such conditions?" He may then set up the conditions, and find the answer. In form, as has often been noted, this process is a kind of dialectic. By arranging the conditions, the experimenter puts a question to nature in such a form that nature gives an intelligible answer.

The thought reveals the dialectical form likewise lurking beneath questions of a more purely doctrinal sort (questions that can't be answered by a physical experiment, but involve rather a reasoned accumulation of the relevant "facts," a mixture of research and logic). The dialectical element is somewhat concealed here by the form. The researcher thinks of himself as merely seeking the data that provide the answer to his question. But actually, both perception and evaluation of such "facts" involve the participation of criticism by "the enemy," and the attempt to so modify one's position that objections are forestalled. Hence, underlying such search, there is somewhat the form used by Aquinas in the *Summa*. The question is posed; antagonistic possibilities are considered; against them all a contrary authoritative view is posed; the conclusion is stated and "proved," and the statement is used to disprove the positions of real or hypothetical antagonists. (The processes may be intermingled, rather than thus presented in orderly analysis. The "authority" may be some "facts" assembled by other researchers, but taken on faith. The "refutation" may not be absolute, but may be done rather by modifying one's own assertion to admit antagonistic positions somewhat, a method also frequently used by Aquinas. But basically, it is "dialectical," and involves the maturing of a statement by subjecting the question to helpful doubts.)

The prestige of the physical sciences, with their stress upon quantification, can introduce a false positivism here. The biologist says what can be said about motives as considered in terms of biology; the economist says what can be said about motives as considered in terms proper to his specialty. Whereupon some inquirer may ask himself, "*To what extent* are humans moved by biological motives, and *to what extent* are they moved by economic ones?" The question is unanswerable, but it *looks* answerable. It might conceivably be answerable in some particular instance of motivation—but it would still not be answerable in general. (That is, not answerable in terms of a *quantity*.)

But these possibilities of shifts from one specialty to another indicate a very important "fact" about such questions. The more they have the appearance of being purely truth-seeking questions (rather than stylized ways of translating a statement of doctrine), the more thoroughly is there a level of sheer assertion lurking beneath them. If the question is posed in economic terms, it implicitly asserts a preference for consideration of motives in such terms. Similarly, a biological question is an implicit assertion for biology as a specialty. Such questions are "leading questions" in the sense that they select a terminology and there are kinds of answer implicit in the terminology (kinds that are further restricted insofar as the questioner prefers some one school within his specialty). In this sense, again, the vocabulary implicitly contains a channelizing of answers; and questions posed within such terms are but stylized restatements of the vocabulary's original genius.

Insofar as the various vocabularies become identified with particular social institutions, a concern with their kinds of questions may promise preferment for those apt at dealing in such questions. The questions thus become insignia, endowed with elements extrinsic to them as questions. Some of them, for instance, lead to academic opportunities which may give a good question-poser a berth for life, if he is apt at guiding new candidates through the maze of questions, until they too can qualify by inventing projects for still more questions. Since life can be transformed into an infinity of questions, the number of inquiries need be limited only by the number of grants and subsidies.

Or consider Chapter VI of Gulliver's voyage to Brobdingnag, which is based on the satiric use of questions as assertions. The King's inquiries about the methods of government in Gulliver's homeland are in themselves moral indictments. Thus, in discussing the creation of new lords, he wanted to know "Whether the humor of the prince, a sum of money to a court lady, or a prime minister, or a design of strengthening a party opposite to the public interest, ever happened to be motives in those advancements." And when discussing the large and sometimes ruinous sums spent by candidates for election to the House of Commons, "he desired to know whether such zealous gentlemen could have any views of refunding themselves for the charges and trouble they were at, by sacrificing the public good to the designs of a weak and vicious prince in conjunction with a corrupted ministry." Question, inquiry, curiosity are all but stylistic variants of the same satiric pointing, as when Swift writes:

> He was still at a loss how a kingdom could run out of its estate like a private person. He asked me, who were our creditors; and where we should find money to pay them. He wondered to hear me talk of such chargeable and extensive wars; that certainly we must be a quarrelsome people, or live among very bad neighbors, and that our generals must need be richer than our kings. He asked what business we had out of our own islands, unless upon the score of trade or treaty, or to defend the coasts with our fleet. Above all, he was amazed to hear me talk of a mercenary standing army in the midst of peace, and among a free people. He said, if we were governed by our own consent in the persons of our representatives, he could not imagine of whom we were afraid, or against whom we were to fight; and would hear my opinion, whether a private man's house might not better be defended by himself, his children, and family, than by half a dozen rascals picked up

at a venture in the streets, for small wages, who might get a hundred times more by cutting their throats.

Remove the clear satiric intent, which frankly puts the reader on his guard, use the same method "factually" by the selection of questions of either a "what is wrong with?" or "what are the main advantages of?" sort (depending upon one's preference for eulogistic or dyslogistic implications), and you have an opportunity for "honest" rhetorical bias in your poll.

The assertion implicit in questions is also revealed in the polite style whereby commands are phrased as questions. And the question form can temper the severity of a proposition, thus: The austere research organization plans to issue a pamphlet, "X Trades With the Enemy." But before copy is sent to the printer, a hasty office conference is called. Whereupon somebody suggests an alteration. The suggestion is adopted unanimously. And the pamphlet appears under the judicious title, "X Trades With the Enemy?"

For our present purposes it is enough to keep in mind the assertive genius implicit in questions. Here is the element out of which questions can function rhetorically as "leading questions," owing to the many almost unnoticeable ways in which they can imply an answer. At the very best, questions can be deflective, in that they propose to consider a problem in one set of terms, whereas some other set of terms may bring us closer to its roots. (Thus, when economic concerns are *reflected* in theological terms, the *selection* of questions purely internal to the theological terminology could *deflect* answers to the economic problem. Or questions of "self-criticism" posed *within* an orbit of terms may deflect criticism *from without* that orbit of terms.) We have previously cited, as an instance of how subtle the leading question can be, the keen analysis by Arthur Kornhauser, "Are Public Opinion Polls Fair to Organized Labor?" (in *The Public Opinion Quarterly,* Winter 1946–47).

There are notable respects in which accountancy should be considered an humble, but very persuasive kind of "scientific rhetoric." For the computing of a company's assets and earnings, though "factual," is not an inevitable matter. There are many perfectly honest and orthodox practices of accountancy whereby a version of reality expressed in financial terms can be "stylized," with a saving of vast sums that would otherwise have had to be paid as taxes, were a different style of accounting used. The mere fact that the cost of new equipment can quite legitimately be charged against a company's earnings for a few years, or spread proportionately over several years, is in itself evidence that the accountant's version of the taxable earnings for any given year can be made to vary considerably. If the costs of new equipment were bunched into war years, for instance, the books would show reduced earnings at a time when taxes on earnings were highest; and by the same token a statement of larger earnings could be issued in subsequent peace years when the tax rate was reduced. There are no "sharp practices" in such procedures. They mark the wholly honest use of the resources indigenous to the symbols of accountancy.

Similarly, in the period of high profits during and after the Second World War, a fiction of accountancy was utilized to cut the income tax of high-paid executives. By this device, part of the salary was withheld by the company as a deferred payment. In accordance with the laws and rulings then prevailing, the employee could not be taxed until he actually received the money. Hence, if only a portion of his salary were paid at the time, he could "persuade" the tax officials that he rated under a lower income bracket than his total income called for. And if he received the remainder, say, after retirement from active service, it too would be taxed at a lower rate. But, had payment not been partially postponed, the amounts due the government on his salary at the year when he earned it would have been much higher, owing to the graduated nature of the income tax. Such humble rhetoric has no Demosthenic resonance, but the difference it makes adds up to drachmas enough to have bought the whole peninsula of classic Greece.

Indeed, businessmen value the rhetoric of accountancy so highly that private finance is jealous to impose upon the government a much less florid style. Thus, many expenditures that a private corporation might list as "assets" would, in the style allowed to the government, have to be classed as "debts," so that we spontaneously think of loans to business in the positive sense of an upbuilding, whereas we think of corresponding loans to government as a mere mounting of the public debt. Indeed, the styles both legal and financial imposed upon our political government are so much more severe than those permitted our many business governments that political government began incorporating its agencies, to profit by the greater latitude of movement granted to commercial corporations.

Many of such devices are entertainingly considered in Thurman Arnold's work on *The Folklore of Capitalism* (an anthropological title for what might be more accurately called *Studies in the Rhetoric of Capitalism*).

On July 20, 1947, the *New York Times* announced a new report by the Department of Commerce, "a comprehensive and wholly revised study of the national economy of the United States since 1929." We need not attempt summarizing here the changes of method in computing the national income. Sufficient for our purposes is the writer's statement that "a rise in profits under the obsolete method of measuring them after taxes is transformed into a drop in profits when they are calculated before taxes with the new formula." Here, obviously, are two "realities," each of which could honestly serve a different rhetorical purpose. If a man makes a dollar, and is taxed twenty cents, he has netted only eighty cents. But if he makes ninety cents, and is taxed four cents, he nets eighty-six cents. Compute his profits by the first formula, and he makes less than if you computed it by the second, even though he actually gets more by the second dispensation. Hence, you could truthfully use whichever of these methods best suited your rhetorical designs. Thus, here too, with correct figures, you could meet Aristotle's definition of rhetoric as a medium that "proves opposites."

At one period in 1947 when our biggest businesses were showing embarrassingly large profits, newspaper writers began publicizing a bookkeeping device whereby the figures could be considerably lessened (without, of course, lessening the actual profits themselves). Charges against depreciation had been traditionally based on the original cost, plus the probable period of utilization. In brief, if you bought a machine for a hundred dollars, and you expected it to last five years, you might reasonably compute the depreciation at twenty dollars a year. Hence, whatever profits you made from the machine annually, you could deduct twenty dollars as the average yearly charge against depreciation of your machine. But the New Accountancy pointed out that, in a period of mounting costs, this machine at the end of five years would require a much more expensive one as replacement. Hence, businesses were advised to set aside larger sums for depreciation, based on the probable costs of the equipment which they would eventually need for replacement. By this arrangement, a percentage of the profits could appear in the company's financial statement under another name. We are not suggesting that there is anything wrong with the practice itself. Such "special reserves" for depreciation were not computed against earnings for the purpose of cutting income tax. They were taxed by the government accountants purely and simply as earnings. We would merely note how, rhetorically, they allowed for a rationalization whereby the extent of the profits could be minimized (in accordance with the publicized contention that wages rather than corporate profits were responsible for inflated prices). Thus, at a time when corporate profits were exceptionally high, the National Association of Manufacturers could lump wages and salaries on one side, as against *dividends* on the other. Here was a perfectly honest rhetorical accountancy whereby all profits set aside for future investment would escape computation as earnings, while all salaries paid to the large executives would be included with the wages paid to the factory workers.

About this same period, another innovation of accountancy came to the fore, obviously for its rhetorical value. Whereas orthodox economists compute profits on the basis of a company's "net worth" (its total outstanding stock, plus accumulated surplus), apologists eager to put the case for business in the best light began using another "yardstick." They began stressing the small profit made on each dollar of sales. By the second method of computation, at a time when meat packers were making very large profits (as computed on the basis of net worth), their accountant-rhetoricians could announce profits of only a fraction of a cent on each pound of meat. And C. I. O. accountant-rhetoricians, analyzing Armour's profits in 1946, showed that they amounted to 2.6 per cent, when computed on sales, whereas they were nearly 16 per cent when the traditional method of accountancy was used. On another occasion they showed how, even accepting the new rhetoric of computation, a rival rhetorician can produce quite different results with it. For instance, beginning with meat packers' advertisements proclaiming a profit of 1.8 cents on each dollar spent on meat, they show, as you add profits all along the line, the ultimate consumer pays more than 30 cents profit. Thus, without falsification of "the facts" themselves, by mere "goodwill" in one's manipulation of them, one can arrive at quite different views of "reality." Might we call such rhetorical choices, such range of mathematical stylization, "*enargeia* by statistics"?

Again, note that we are not here concerned with out-and-out misrepresentation. We are discussing not lies, but the tendentious selection of "hard facts." If the directors of one company, Corporation A, privately bought up the stock of Corporation B (bought it up, that is, not in their role as directors of Corporation A, but as private investors), and if they then, in their role as directors, bought the stock at much more than it was worth, Corporation A might then "honestly" show on its books a much higher valuation than the property itself was worth. And if it was a public utility, its accountants might ask the right to charge the public such a rate for services as provided a "reasonable return" on the *fictitious* valuation. Here, still, we should remain in the realm of "truth," so far as the figures of accountancy were concerned. And indeed, all over our nation there are public utilities which are permitted by public service commissions to charge on the basis of stock values thus "watered" in the past, by one device or another. However, when accountancy works so closely with organizational practices, perhaps we should consider it rather when discussing the Rhetoric of Bureaucracy.

The corresponding rhetoric of the quietus here would be the use of confusing or insufficient bookkeeping methods. Perhaps someday, unless the records are carefully obliterated by that time, some scholar will publish an analysis of the rhetorical unction in which the loans of the Reconstruction Finance Corporation seem to have been presented. Apparently the accountancy here favored a semi-quietus kind of lackadaisicality, an easygoing rhetorical style that covers the disposition of something like fifteen billion dollars on a more or less friendly basis.

CHAPTER 3

[Notes toward] The Rhetoric of Bureaucracy

This chapter is entitled "[Notes toward] The Rhetoric of Bureaucracy" to signal that it is based on incomplete, unrevised drafts and notes available in Burke's papers at Penn State.—Eds.

The officeholder, when at peace with his office, the underling content to have superiors because he in turn has underlings, the bureaucrat at home in the bureaucratic structure—there is nothing new about this situation, except perhaps its greater *percentage*. It makes for what Karl Jaspers has called *die Herrschaft des Apparats*. In *Die Geistige Situation der Zeit* (ringing many variations on a theme that would, from the standpoint of our pentad, fall under the head of Agency dyslogistically interpreted), he writes of the bureaucratic machine needed to manage the workers who serve the industrial machines; he considers the possibilities of careers built upon advancement within the bureaucracy and by means of the bureaucracy; he labels the cultural situation "*Geist als Mittel*" (spirit employed as a mere instrument of adjustment, rather than as a ground of motives in its own right); he talks of control by the unscrupulous, quick to size up a situation, and skilled at management because they have a good average approach to people. "State, community, factory, business—everything is done through bureaucracy. Everything typical of our times needs numbers, hence must be organized." And he stresses the premium that such cultural conditions place upon shrewdness, cleverness, and aggressiveness.

Yet it is also quite possible that many such men have put their lives together in accordance with rudimentary laws of piety whereby the abstract relations of office become infused with the spirit of familial motives formed in childhood. In the subtle ways of identification, they have probably "integrated" past and present by an idealistic merger of their early "pre-political" selves with their later natures as functions of the agencies by which they are employed. Their later life is thus made consubstantial even with their infancy. And the usual ambiguities of substance prevail here, their adult situation being at once of like substance with their childhood situation and distinct from it, so that they move in a kind of mild somnambulism, as the persons figuring in their lives now borrow magical properties from real or imagined likeness to persons figuring in their childhood. Their existence is a kind of lived poem, capable of interpretation on various levels, ranging from the purely utilitarian and rationalistic at one end to the intra-uterine at the other (as were they, in their office, drawing sustenance from a vast placenta in which they basked like beings gently sprayed with the benign nutrient rays of an invisible, internal sun).

Such, probably, is the Edenic source of motives in men at those moments when their jobs become for them womb, cradle, berth, parent, sun, fertilizing, rain, spirit, ground, king, instrument, and God, all in one—moments perhaps that exist not in time, but in essence, as the ultimate conclusion of their work, which is a striving towards complete integration and so prods them to find their situation emblematic of this unitary end.

Some such piety as this, we may assume, is the principle behind the Protestant view of secular work as itself monastic, a glimpse into the depths of motives too exacting for men to retain continuously, so that they become moved, or at least think they are moved, merely by the hope of individual gain that presents itself in terms of the day's contingencies, until a man's whole universe of vision, at least so far as his intensest efforts are concerned, may become narrowed to the problems involved in the struggle for freedom to buy cheap and sell dear.

But whatever it may be in its ultimate pious, poetic, Edenic motivation, as regards the rhetoric of the Scramble such a principle of ultimate integration allows for a kind of "corporate identity" whereby the individual derives his very substance from the temporal institution which he serves. And this condition gives rise to many possibilities disintegrative or falsely integrative.

First, note a kind of "corporate boasting," a vicarious sharing in the dignity (or supposed dignity) of the "substantial body" with which one feels oneself consubstantial. A slave must thus boast "corporately" of his vicarious share in the prominence of his master's family, feeling himself a spiritual participant in those holdings in which he is a part, not as owner, but as owned. Or we see a variant of such corporate boasting in the New England chauffeur who, telling of a party he attended, quietly gave assurance that it had included "only servants of the best families." It is the basis of appeal for the rhetoric of public relations counsels, hired to build up a sense of "company loyalty" by so channelizing men's pious "loyalty to the sources of their being" that they may be encouraged to take delight in the company's powers vicariously, being moved by the magic of obedience to superiors, and accepting *insignia* of reward rather in partial substitution for monetary returns. It is, of course, behind all group identifications, with party, nation, sect, race, region, etc.—and as such is the rhetoric behind the market for professional sports, whereby one may choose as one's own advocate a fighter with whom one will never have any personal contact whatsoever, or may be led, by the exploiting of "local spirit," to take as representative of the community a team composed of hired men not one of whom need be of local origin or locally engaged in any way other than by the ties of his acts as a professional athlete.

Hence the rhetorician may appeal to the resources of "corporate boasting," whereby the more modest and unassuming a man may be as an individual person, the more outrageously he may be attached compensatorily to some figure (institutional or personal, or a person treated as charismatic vessel of some institutional substance) qualified to act vicariously as his champion (a rhetorical situation which has unfortunate effects internationally, since a man individually humble may become overbearing in his role as "representative" of his nation's prowess, or, putting it the other way round, in his assumption that the national power represents him).

"Appreciation" allows for corporate boasting of a not very drastic sort, in that one can share vicariously in the worth of the work appreciated. The device is caricatured in the figure of the *nouveau riche* who, on the assumption that everything can be bought, finally sets out to buy himself "culture," and for this transaction hires art experts to do his appreciating for him, in collecting a batch of authenticated old masters at his expense. By such resources, the man who has never really read one book in all his life can become the owner of an excellent library. And the true admirer of some work may feel his own identity endangered if a critic belittles it, as with the struggling author who wrote letters to the editor each time the name of Shakespeare was mentioned slightingly, until one day, after making himself quite miserable, he decided that Shakespeare's reputation was quite able to take care of itself, and immediately afterwards realized that his excessive defensiveness on this count had been a roundabout way of promising himself that he too would produce great works.

The consubstantiality of corporate identity can serve as Edenic ground for all rhetorical devices assisting in the "socialization of losses," as with the fictions that identify nations with their nationals, whereby the financial, industrial, diplomatic, and military resources belonging to the people as a whole are expended to the special profit of capital invested abroad in ways unprofitable to the nation as a whole. A variant comes to light in the disputes between Britain and the United States on the one side and the Soviet Union on the other, concerning reparations payments from Italy. "We" proposed to forgo such payments entirely, asking that Russia do the same; but at the same time a great deal was being done by both Britain and the United States in behalf of their nationals. The Soviet Union could not make such a dissociation; its claims could only be made in behalf of the nation as a whole; but in our structure, there is the fortunate ambiguity (fortunate from the standpoint of our nationals) whereby nation and nationals are one when it comes to paying the bills (hence, the nation can pay a high percentage of the bills) whereas nation and nationals are distinct when it comes to pocketing the profits (indeed, our statesmen and politicians are expected to puzzle out ways of making these profits collectible, if only by devices whereby we as a nation advance loans which enable the foreign countries to pay our investors as individuals, in exchange for a small income tax paid grudgingly). You may take it as a principle underlying the rhetoric of nationalism that one way for private individuals to take money from the national treasury is to have the sums sent abroad as uncollectible loans advanced by us as a *nation,* but with clauses guaranteeing that a large portion of this money will be returned as payments to our *nationals,* as a newspaper put it, when discussing the problem of reparations after the First World War: "United States representatives have pointed out that after World War I the United States paid for Germany's essential imports while other countries collected the reparations" (*NYT,* 7/15/46). But from the standpoint of our present distinctions, this is not quite accurate enough; some secondary distinctions are necessary: We *as a nation* advanced sums to Germany; Germany *as a nation* handed over these sums as reparations payments to other *nations;* and these other nations paid a large percentage of these sums to *individual inves-*

tors in the United States. Thus, it was not merely a case of the United States being filched by taking over a lot of bad debts; it was a case of the United States taking over these debts until, with the help of the losses we incurred *as a nation,* our bankers were able to recoup on their own investments and make still more as discount when floating other loans.

The same corporate principle can also, as embodied in the doctrine of original sin, serve as unifying device (in branding all with the same mark, that is, in ascribing the same motive to all), and as a means of solace (in encouraging the transgressor to feel that, however black his transgressions, all other people are "in principle" transgressors too). "We are all plagiarists," said the plagiarist; "for the very structure of our language is stolen from the common treasury of our culture."

Purification by scapegoat similarly involves "corporate" identification, with the Jew playing a specially "favored" role as scapegoat in the Christian myth. Hence, in the degenerate vestiges of Christianity that characterize modern business enterprise, it seems a foregone conclusion that, after each speculative orgy, when the scandal breaks, some Jewish firm will stand out as the chosen representative of the excesses. For where an ambiguous Christ is needed to take upon himself the full burdens of human degradation, where could one more properly look for such a figure, within the conditions of a Christian corporate identity, than among the Jews? And though a Christian businessman had not been near a Church for thirty years, when would he be most likely to think of himself as a Christian, than when fear that the law might catch up with him put him in a penitential mood? If, at such a moment, another Jewish Christ could be found to suffer in his stead, then he would indeed be purified; what's more, he would be *safe*—for usually, when a scandal breaks, the public does not demand punishment for all; the public asks only for a representative victim; and once this victim has been chosen and sacrificed, further prosecutions become anti-climactic, hence un-newsworthy. For dramatically, ritualistically, once the victim has been sacrificed, the world is ready for a New Era, it is the time for the proclaiming of a general amnesty.

We began this section on the "corporate" with reference to bureaucracy: with its organizations, themselves composed of persons variously in agreement and at odds, their roles all participating in a function or purpose common to the organization as a whole, the purpose for which the organization is the agency, and which gives the organization its corporate personality. There are devices typical of these special conditions, devices of "man as bureaucrat," dispositions characteristic of people, not simply as individuals but rather as participants in the identity of the bureaucracy as a whole.

When the editor, for instance, speaks in terms of the "editorial we," he works in an order of motives that may be quite distinct from his motives as an individual. In his role as "we," he may affirm views or accept manuscripts which, as an "I," he would thoroughly despise. And he comes bureaucratically perfect in proportion as the motives of his office, be they good or bad, become "his" motives; the compleat bureaucrat would be the man who could not even sleep with his wife except in his capacity as "spokesman." He becomes a creature of the organization that employs him; he becomes an "exponent" of the interests he serves in his official capacity; the question of his intrinsic substance retreats behind the kind of substance he derives from the public agency that supports him. He is made up of two distinct portions: a large portion of bureaucratic functioning, a small portion of "pure personality" that seems like a survival from prehistoric times, but actually takes shape in dialectical opposition to his job. Vacational, in contrast with the vocational, it is generally under the sign of license, and finds expression and solace in a not very imaginative imagery of sin, crime, and violence (though, heaven knows, there are plenty of other ways to arrive at these).

Organizational amplification is in one sense a concealment, since the powers of the organization are ascribed to its representatives, as though these were personal properties of the representatives themselves. But there is an order of reality here too, in that special aptitudes are needed for best adjustment to the conditions of a particular organization. Hence, the several invitations to rhetoric, which can (1) merge individual and organization, to his advantage; (2) merge them to his disadvantage; (3) dissociate them to his advantage; (4) dissociate them to his disadvantage.

The political party chooses a leader, in the hopes that his prestige with the people will redound to the credit of the party, and then uses the resources of the party to build up the prestige of the leader. Once the rhetoric of the build-up has been developed, not even the man's bitterest opponents can really know to what extent his very character is a mere function of this rhetorical enterprise. Trotsky's attacks on Stalin are interesting in this regard, since Marxism recognizes the need of a centralized party in the organizing of a revolution, so that Trotsky must find ways of rating Stalin as a mediocrity while at the same time endowing him with positive traits that equipped him to gain control of the party organization. The underlying form of his argument seems to have been like this: The conditions of revolution demand a strongly led, centralized party; but the material conditions prevailing generally at a given time may have a bad effect upon the quality of the political organization itself; in Russia, certain factors that would make for the best criticism of party leaders were weak (the workers, for instance, were "backward"); hence the situation favored an inferior type of personality, as best equipped to gain control of the party organization itself handicapped by adverse social conditions.

Where industry is highly developed, the interlocking network of organizations is so complex that one inevitably works along the connections which they provide. Let some individual start a wholly new enterprise, for instance; and insofar as it grows to any size, it will do so by becoming woven into already existent organizations: the mails, the banks, the railroads, the educational institutions, the advertising mediums, the markets, etc. Hence, in a secondary way, we are "bureaucrats all," engaged in acts much more affected by this labyrinth of agencies than we can ever clearly discern. (The "Existential" philosophy, it would seem, is an attempt to reaffirm a ground of motivation more substantial than this, wherein the properties of an individual man "as man" would be distinct from the organizational properties so persistently calling for the rhetorical *nostrum,* and even endowing them with a genuine kind of reality, in the order of Agencies (a preponderantly instrumental emphasis at which the pragmatism of the modern world arrives through Stoic doctrines of service to the political community, Christian servitude to God, and the cult of utility in the philosophies of business and applied science).

Once, while Mussolini was at the height of his power, and was getting both the financial and the "moral" support of prominent interests in the United States, I saw a photograph of him dressed as a coal miner, surrounded by vociferously applauding admirers—and his smile of asinine complacency made it apparent that he was somehow being exceptionally clever in this performance, that no other man in Italy could have done this act with such brilliance. And I recalled, years before, an incident on a ferry carrying a boatload of clerks and stenographers on the way to their offices. On the back of one man's coat, some pranksters had pinned a sign, saying, "I am a fool." He did not know it was there; but his companions did; and gradually all about him people began looking at him with amusement—particularly since he began to blossom under the attention he was getting, and in bantering with his companions unknowingly made remarks that referred ambiguously to the sign on his back. Everyone roared—and he must have thought himself suddenly transformed into a remarkable wit: he enjoyed the lights of a Bottom translated.

Was the underlying situation much different with Mussolini? Was he not thinking that there was something inordinately skillful in his performance *per se,* whereas the whole effect derived from a *double entendre?* His relation to the national power was an amplifying device, converting the slightest risibility into the uproarious.

When I first began reading newspapers, I could not understand why there were so many dull statements by businessmen featured in headlines. The books I was reading had startling things to say, yet they were quite ignored, even in the book sections, while these platitudes by literary dullards who would not produce one good sentence in a lifetime were presented as though they had been uttered by a cross between a Biblical magistrate and a Delphic oracle. It took me many years to understand that the representative dullness of an idiot, when magnified by the total organization of the press, is practically God Himself, for it is *history.* So the time came when I carefully watched the news, knowing that it was a true report of what the Agencies wanted me and my countrymen to believe.

Everything here is under the aegis of Agency. The bureaucratic Agencies are the scene of man's Acts, reducing the conception of serious action itself to this circumference (with other orders of action admitted only as outlaw); in terms of these Agencies he conceives of human Purpose; and his personality as Agent is defined by the properties, both material and social, that best equip him for adjustment and advancement in such roles.

But though we are all at least indirectly identified with the corporate personality of Agencies, under the present head we should consider only the rhetorical resources of direct identification, culminating in devices whereby the bureaucrat uses his position as a kind of *conspiracy.*

There is first of all the mild conspiracy of the personal letter written on the organization's letterhead, a rhetoric so spontaneous, and so slight, as to seem like no rhetoric at all. It is worth noting only for its symbolic value, particularly as with those who would use the letterhead by turning the paper upside down and over.

Others have noted the kind of courage that gives itself to moral indignation when approval is assured. But a closer observer suggested a subtle improvement here; he conceived of a speaker who does not merely follow the line, praising what the faithful take as praiseworthy and damning the damnable, but rather skirts the thin edge of "revisionism," so that the hearers tell themselves, aghast, "Now he seems about ready to go too far to the right," "Now he seems about ready to go too far to the left," "Now he seems about to uphold a view that was correct last year but is incorrect this year," etc., yet each time, just at the last moment, he swings back into line, so that the properties are saved.

Bureaucrat's Creed:
(But let us not look simply for satire here, for there is a good flair for dialectic, too, in a good bureaucrat.)

I believe that one should seek to take credit for the good work of others, and pass the blame to others for bad work of one's own. (Where possible, I shall alembicate this by blanket acknowledgment of my indebtedness, when it can be done in ways that do not arouse the imagination, since they are not specific enough to incriminate me, while the vague gesture can stand as a testimonial to my probity.) I believe that as, in the fourteenth century, the bondsman sought to break his bonds, so in the twentieth century the free man should seek to establish connections. Learn to use the connections already there. Do no new thing, if it endangers the connections. Ignoring the connections is like stumbling through the woods; following the connections is like speeding along a highway. I believe that, whereas there used to be a Manichean battle between Vice and Virtue, there is now an ecological balance between the Vice Rackets and the Virtue Rackets. I believe in the Quietus: "wait till he sticks his neck out"; up to that point, the Quietus; then, "frank and open discussion," which is to say, chop. Otherwise, if a man is obnoxious as you think he is, someone else (some damned fool poet, probably) will blurt it out for you. Through fearing to tread where fools rush in, one can come to feel like angels. The truly accomplished pussyfooter doesn't merely pussy-foot: he also knows when to come out in the open, when to ringingly "challenge" a weak minority in voicing the prejudice of a strong majority. Otherwise, attack nothing, unless you know that, if you do not attack it, it will attack you.

By connections, the Quietus is made sound. And it remains so, until the course of destiny itself breaks the connections. Where the Quietus is not absolute, it may still be there in effect, if it be relatively predominant. The resources of the comparative Quietus are endless, given the will for it. The subject takes us into the area of the *fait accompli,* discussed elsewhere. Finaglings that disfranchise certain classes of citizens, or neutralize their votes, are aspects of the Quietus. Gerrymandering, for instance, or splitting a reform vote by putting up rival reform candidates, are devices on the outer rim of the Quietus, as variants of the *fait accompli,* in the rhetoric that transcends mere verbal eloquence by devoting its attention to a stage further back, in setting up conditions that guarantee the ineffectiveness of a purely verbal rhetoric. And here, surprisingly enough, as the paradoxical ultimate of the Quietus, belongs the *Filibuster*, whereby legislators use *unending talk* to prevent a bill from coming to a vote.

Hence, here also we move into all devices for so setting the rules that (by the scene-act ratio) the conditions for a desired kind of policies are implicit in the situation. Hence, the struggle in the United Nations Council over the right of veto, and over the ways of distinguishing "substantive" and "procedural" matters (with the parliamentary finagling for classifying issues under one head or the other, depending upon the kind of decision wanted). Here also we move into the setting of the rules to be glimpsed behind the delays before a nation withdraws from an occupied country. If the bureaucratization has been effective, when the time comes, the occupying nation can make a great show of giving the occupied nation its total freedom, while the rules are such that the occupying *nationals* can enjoy all the advantages which their *nations* have formally renounced. If you can set the rules for the nurturing of foreign investments in a country, you can then grant it conditional independence in the name of absolute independence. This can be done by protecting, in the occupied countries, those domestic interests which, in protecting themselves, by the same token uphold the kinds of law and representation that uphold the foreign holdings; since the bureaucratic identity is essentially public, *what it is* is much less important to it than *what it is thought to be*. Hence, above all, the bureaucrat is constantly in quest of "face-saving" devices. These are countered by "smear campaigns." And the nature of such an organization fits it above all to a bland use of the "leak" either for releasing information by which it hopes to profit but which it would disclaim, or for enlisting the public's support for a certain faction within the bureaucracy.

But these are bold devices. The bureaucrat is most effective in his day-by-day tithing as support for this way of life, in his pious concern not to overlook even the humblest kinds of finagling. I thus once saw the relative Quietus used in this modest wise: There were two resolutions to be voted on at a public gathering; the committee in charge of the voting wanted to discredit one of these resolutions; as a result, while the resolution favored by the committee was presented in a clear copy, the mimeographed copies of the unloved declaration looked like this:

Whot kind of throat nood Amorico moko? Only a throat that sho would stand behind tho troditions on which our notion is founded. The kind of throat involvod in tho cloor doclorotion that this constantly oxponding monaco is viowod as itself a throat, and will no longor bo tolorotod.

It was issued as an appeal to the Amoricon pooplo, against the gruosomo powors of aggrossion.

Youth shows its growing aptitude for enrollment in the service of the bureaucracies when blandly canvassing the local merchants for funds in support of the local ball team: goodwill purchased under an implicit threat, as when political clubs solicit "subscriptions" to various functions. And though campaign funds are a kind of honest bribe that our business interests gladly give to political parties, as advance payment for services rendered, when a concern gets around to the point of giving funds to rival factions, so as to be in a position to ask favors regardless of the outcome, a large percentage of this is *functionally* a device whereby the political order levies tribute of the commercial order. And further along, in the same direction, we find "protective agencies" which, working in connection with gangsters, nominally offer their services to guard property *against* the gangsters, a rhetorically happy way of stating the real situation in reverse, the "protection" money in reality being exacted as a charge for calling off the gangster allies, so that sums change hands "lawfully" which would otherwise change hands in terms of crime. Here we have, in effect, an organization to *redeem* crime.

Completion of Bureaucrat's Creed:

The less work, the more secretaries.

If you are in danger of being dismissed, do not become bellicose, unless there is a rival faction waiting to take up your cause. Make it easy for your superior to shunt you into other connections, maybe even better-paying (as with those who are "kicked upstairs").

Through connection A, make connection B, through connection B make connection C, and so on. Hence, even if you are the kind that quickly wears his welcome out, you can keep a step ahead of your own collapse: when connection L has gone sour, you are already making fresh advances along connection M, and so on, as with those who get better incomes from a series of bankruptcies than most men get from sound businesses. If a concession should be granted, but you refuse it to one man, lest others ask for the same concession, refuse it on the grounds that, in granting it, you would be unfair to the others.

Attack nothing that doesn't endanger your vital interests, except when the attack upon a weak or harmless object can deflect criticism that would endanger your vital interests.

Lest routine kill the smile, routinize the smile.

Prepare for the landslide; for that which slid you in may, in the next phase, slide you out.

Search for the Poetic Order of Motives:

The search for the poetic order of motives behind or beneath rhetorical motivations is the search for the *state of innocence,* or original insight, out of which a given bureaucratization developed. The Agencies are means to an end; but in their accumulation, development, and transmission from the original inventors to mere receivers, or cultural heirs, they produce a new situation, with motives peculiar to its own nature. Instead of being means to the original end, the agencies thus become the ground of a new end. The sense of this reversal is behind fantasies like Čapek's *R. U. R,* depicting the revolt of the machine, or any other satires suggesting that man is being enslaved by his machinery (in either the technological or sociological orders of bureaucratization).

The bureaucratization of an insight, then, means the translation of a Purpose into a structure of Agencies having a nature of their own, distinct from the nature of the original human Purpose behind their invention. In this respect the Bureaucratization bears the same relation to the original insight that religious *ceremonies* bear to the religious *feeling* expressed in them. The ceremonies can in time come to be, not a *way of recovering* the original feeling, but rather an *alternative to* it. At this stage, we can expect strong signs of demoralization, inanition, alienation, in the social sphere, until some new Pietistic radicalism arises, attempting to recover the original motive behind the ceremonies, and finding that, to do so, it must transform the ceremonies themselves.

Whitman was in this sense "Pietistic." He sought to affirm an order of motives that *transcended* the merely pragmatist exploitation of capitalism's financial and industrial resources. While the bureaucratizations steadily mounted, in both the political and business orders of government (or "administration"), he sought to see them as the ritualizing, in material terms, of a universal human elation (here paralleling the Transcendentalist search for the respects in which even the most utilitarian of acts could be viewed as emblematic of deeper or higher motives).

True, his Pietistic search was ambiguously motivated. (Malcolm Cowley has recently made this obvious beyond question.) There was more going on here than the usual Protestant urgency to find godly motives in even the most worldly of acts. There was a special reward for himself hidden in his gospel. For expressions that, on one level, were designed to reaffirm the poetry behind the traffic, were on another level implying, roundabout, the sanctioning of his homosexuality. Democracy, as rejection of the king, was a symbolic rejection of the father; and the resultant solidarity of the sons united by this conspiracy made democracy equal a kind of brotherly love that equaled indirectly a cult of homosexual promiscuity. Hence, the quasi-Biblical tonalities of his prophecies were somewhat akin to the hot evangelism of Gide's *Nourritures Terrestres,* calling men to a kind of persuasion that could be more persuasive generally if its full significance were left vague. And we may take it as a rule of thumb that there are always likely to be such complicating factors in men's attempts to see more deeply into the world of merely pedestrian motives. One is less likely to accept the everyday terminology of motives when himself goaded by some urgency which they do not recognize, or do not express in the desired tonalities. So his search for a "return" to "original" motives (which is a way of designating, in temporal terms, what might in non-temporal terms be called a search for the *essence* of motives) would be sharpened by such complications whereby its idealism is grounded in a *furtive* realism. And the clamor is justified because, after all, homosexuality itself is not a primary motive, though the accidents of stress in a given society may lead its champions to become as preoccupied with it as though it were. In the case of Whitman, for instance, I should myself want to contend that the homosexuality was but the translation of his insight into terms of sexual promiscuity, as the cult of democracy was the translation of the same insight into terms of political relations. Principles of personalization would be prior here; and the restless confusions in his own poetic statement of his motives would be a more exact representation of his true situation than would a sharp reduction to homosexuality as primary motive in the total evangelical recipe.

In any case, whatever may be the true order of motives, or however our own attempts to discover them universally may be confused by our own personal involvements, it is clear that the mere order of instrumentalities cannot be primary. Indeed, even when you begin with such a world of sheer contingencies, where each task is set by the logic of the "connections" in the Agency itself, you must look for *essential* motives, asking yourself "what it all adds up to"—and the mere posing of this question takes you beyond the very order of contingencies which it is designed to consider. For it is a summing up, whereas the contingencies are to be taken piecemeal, as with the secretary who answers the phone rather than the buzzer because it was the phone not the buzzer that rang.

Considered from the standpoint of our present speculations, the bureaucratic routines are seen rather to be an inferior kind of ritual. They take on this nature, for there must be a "song" behind their function as sheer traffic, if only the song be a mean one, marked by intense irritability, as with the worker whose work eventually gives him ulcers of the stomach. In the past, as regards civilizations, usually at the point where the "neo-ritualization of routines" became prominent, the society was ripe for invasion from without; eventually, it was overrun by barbarian tribes whose structure of Agencies had not developed so far from the ways of primitive piety, hence were not psychologically crippled by the archaicizing attempts to make routine itself serve as ritual. Today, however, the power in the routines of technology is so great that there is no opportunity for the invasion of tribes with more direct ways of living. The primitive demoralization in the face of Western "progress" is aptly symbolized by the caricature of the jungle king, in loincloth and high hat, sporting a big cigar and a jalopy. Such people can be powerful only insofar as they master technology themselves (which means that the only threat to Western technology is in its own power to blow itself up).

Hence, civilization now thrives on attitudes that would have meant the extinction of earlier societies. The high degree of indirection in the modern economic structure makes it absolutely imperative that millions of men resign themselves to social cooperation, if they are merely to exist. The resources of accountancy make it easy to direct such cooperation by endowing every job with a "rational" (hence, "human") motive, no matter how intrinsically repugnant the work itself may be. Thus, it would not greatly matter if technology proved to be a good moralizing principle for only a relative handful of experts (who incidentally didn't stop to ask themselves just what it might mean that they relaxed by reading murder mysteries, whether for instance the presence of such motives might also be indicated in their constant upbuilding of sinister material powers). Even though every single job in our society were drudgery, the acceptance of the grind would continue; for there is an alternative only in exceptional cases.

Hence, men's demand for the rhetorical nostrums that can keep their unwieldy industrial structure going (and developing towards still greater unwieldiness). Hence their complicity in any assurances that can "spiritualize" this vast body, and can seem to breathe into its dead bulk the appearances of personality. Hence also the surprising zeal atop the boredom, while the high rate of change in technological methods keeps routines themselves from lapsing fully into ritual, as men are constantly being aroused with a jerk by the discovery that they are out of step with the newest conditions, and even where a concern might somewhat mellow with age, the friction of other organizations is usually enough to keep it rubbed raw, prodding it to new efforts, for new men would step lively in it where old men would let it dawdle (and, in any case, it must either be laved in rhetorical unction or be charged by a rhetorical injection). And whatever the nostrum may be, and however abysmal it may be as judged by poetic or philosophic standards, the urgency at least is genuine: the desire to see behind the bureaucratization is just; the demand for an order of motive transcending the piecemeal motives of the Agency itself is imperative.

Bureaucratization of the Imaginative:

In an earlier work (*Attitudes Toward History*), I proposed the term, "bureaucratization of the imaginative," to name in general the historical process whereby the means for carrying out a purpose become themselves a new motivating condition that conceals the original purpose, or even opposes it. Beginning in the "esthetic" tradition, I had long tried to persuade myself that there were certain areas of human action where this process did not occur. But I finally came to see that it necessarily, or universally occurs, that in this sense "the dialectic" is "inevitable," though no particular series of modifications can be called inevitable until it has occurred (for the past inevitably has to have been as it was, a fact so drastically true that men would apply the same strict pattern of inevitability to the future, considering the future incongruously in terms of the past, the very condition the future most emphatically is not).

The realization was forced upon me, in all its forcefulness, during the period of "proletarian" or "propagandist" art in the thirties. For the insistence of the Left, that all writers enlist their services formally in the cause of political and economic reform, made me realize at least how writers willy-nilly figure *somewhere* in political choices, as even the "purest" of "pure" art becomes identified with certain political and economic choices, not unambiguously, to be sure, but "by and large," "in the aggregate," so that what is on its face a poetic program is covertly or by implication a rhetorical one. At that point, I began to see, or at least to think I saw, the *ubiquity* of traffic, the *inevitability* of organization. Even the most uncompromising of artists would remain unheard, if his work could not somehow fit in with the genius of our vast book-manufacturing and book-distributing bureaucracies, unless he wanted to go forth like a new Johnny Appleseed and recite his work for nothing, leaving little germs behind as he passed from one community to another, and perhaps somehow preparing the way for a literary movement so immediate that it would need no publishers' organizations to spread it, any more than is necessary to the spread of an apt slang term or a good dirty joke.

Deciding that bureaucracy was ubiquitous, as typical of "business government" as of "political government," as typical *mutatis mutandis* of tiny magazines as of large ones, I decided that one must resign himself to it. And I began to look for the "comic" devices whereby this might be accomplished; for I thought it essentially comic that men should be required to "resign themselves to progress."

So, as a badge of my resignation to what I considered a universal predicament, I saluted the "bureaucratization of the imaginative," that process whereby the track through the virgin forest becomes a highway (or the tremulous, sensitive adolescent, after a whole series of affairs, finally matures into the perfection of a "line"). And I began to ask myself what could be salvaged, by critical correctives.

However, at this point rhetorical sophistication was forced upon me with an almost traumatic insistence. For when my book was reviewed, I found how my proposed resignation to the ubiquity of bureaucracy could itself be interpreted in purely rhetorical terms. Elsewhere in these pages I have discussed the formula, "extension for prevention," that a critic might use against me. All he needed was sufficient ill will to make it worth his trouble; and the nature of the Stalin-Trotsky controversy at that time provided the ill will.

For the Trotskyite rhetoric had a vested interest in the *restricted* use of the term "bureaucracy." Here the term was given special application to the Stalinist bureaucracy—and some of its persuasive resonance with capitalist liberals would be sacrificed if the strict interpretation were exchanged for a broad one. This was particularly the case in that most Trotskyites, in insisting upon a wholly secular or naturalistic terminology of motives, had given technology the role of godhead (in treating the methods of applied science as intrinsically and unambiguously a power for universal betterment); yet I proposed to treat the scientific laboratory as itself a prime instance of bureaucratization. And the advertisers' rhetoric of the testimonial, with picture of the man in white flanked by jars, Bunsen burner, and test tubes, with a slogan about science offering proof positive, seemed to me little different in essence from the God of Technology as He is usually worshipped.

Since then, I am happy to say, our analysts of social trends have shown greater friendliness to the broad or universalized interpretation of bureaucracy, rather than attempting to preserve the purity of its strict interpretation for use as a weapon in the armory of anti-Stalinist rhetoric. The broader usage seems necessary to me, precisely because the intricate structure of vast, unwieldy corporate organizations *is* all about us, *is* a major aspect of our reality, hence a major source of our motivations. And however urgently some anti-Stalinist partisans may feel the need of their handy rhetorical convenience (whereby those who felt oppressed by the prevalence of bureaucracy everywhere could be persuaded to work off their resentment by centering all their attention upon one particular bureaucracy among thousands), such restricted usage would offer false promises, in suggesting that in getting rid of this one we should be destroying the bureaucratic principle at its very source. On the contrary, what is needed is a terminology which permits us to contemplate the issue in its entirety.

The bureaucracies of technology and accountancy are here in both their rational and irrational aspects. It is a fact that they make a high degree of social labor both possible and necessary. It is a fact that, whatever divisiveness resides in their hierarchic structure and in their maladjustments with one another, rhetorical nostrums "unitary" in spirit are justified, not merely as "beneficent illusions," but precisely because the vast interlocking of production, distribution, and consumptions is concretely there. The particular nostrums may be nauseous; they generally are; but I see nothing "in principle" against the relevance of the nostrum here.

To be wholly realistic, however, we dare not let the nostrum divert our attention from the many divisions into the *meum* and the *tuum* that mark the world of traffic at every step of the way. A purely unitary rhetoric here must become false to the facts (being as if the Ins, once they were In, called upon the Outs to collaborate with them permanently for the common good, their willingness to remain Out being taken as the test of collaboration). And this must necessarily be true of socialist traffic quite as it is of capitalist traffic. The mere fact that somewhat socialist modes of ownership and control may be a much better fit with the nature of the modern productive forces is not by any means a guarantee against the wrangles of the traffic itself. In many countries it can, in variants adapted to local conditions, ease some of the more dangerous tensions that now beset us. But the Babel-wrangle of the traffic-wrangle can be expected to continue, along with a heavy investment in rhetorical nostrums ranging from the almost simple truth to the almost total lie.

As for the traffic itself, which I almost identify with rhetoric: Whatever may be its discordancies and unwieldiness, I confess that I would not, if I could, have it vanish. The Scramble, the Turbulence of the Human Barnyard, the periodic outbursts here and there, the quirks and crotchets and foibles of a communizing indeterminately cooperative and cut-throat—all this is by no means merely something to decry. Veblen has said that man is best suited to a state of mild savagery: perhaps the Scramble, in its happier phases, is our nearest equivalent, under complex modern conditions, to such a state.

And as I have heard it said that people suffering from certain kinds of uneasiness, or threatened with unbalance, may find it curative to contemplate the antics of the animals in the Zoo, so the thought of the Scramble may be restorative. For the basic motives of human piety are dreadful; rationality itself gives us awesome glimpses beyond its borders; and when the ultimates of contemplation threaten to become too exacting, the lore of the traffic can be an easement. At such times, it is good to think of ourselves as children, playing together like little angels one moment, flaring into a noisy squabble the next, and then, lo! back once more, all one, in a kind of hum.

A friend once told me of an aquarium, with both water and a beach. And along with fish and water plants, he had two frogs, a big one and a little one. They were companionable frogs, often sitting on a rock side by side. Until one day, on looking into his aquarium, he noticed that the little frog was missing. But when he looked at the big frog, sitting stolidly alone on the rock, he noticed two small frog's legs protruding from his jaws. He had been in time; he pulled out the little fellow, who was as good as ever; and the next time he looked into his aquarium, there the two were, companionable as ever, sitting side by side on their rock.

Here is the average fable of trafficking mankind, with its shifts among alignments. Here is the "normal" state of divergency (though, for the fable to be perfect, big frog and little frog would be reunited as cronies, not merely by letting bygones be bygones, but by a sudden realignment which provoked them to join in common cause against, let us say, a heron). It has its own menacing moments: at its worst, it can mean death, starvation, emotional deprivation, and with the perfecting of modern war, even perhaps such devastation and desolation that the traffic will have abolished itself, and human action will have disappeared from all the universe, leaving only that eternity of motion to which men themselves, in perversely systematic moments, would persuade themselves prevails already (as they well might, seeing that all their mighty technological plant is in the order of motion, and in its rational perfection ironically invites them, as an order of being that must strive ever after rationality, to make themselves over in the image of their so totally rational machines).

But if we can appreciate the traffic in its less ominous aspects, if we can remember that, precisely in its wrangles and deceptions, it proves itself a field of *action,* reaffirmed even as men unintentionally vow themselves to service in the drastically dehumanized world of sheer motion, perhaps by such hypochondriac appreciation we can go towards a milder traffic than is allowed by the present cults of empire implicit in the frantic development of technological power for its own sake. Confronting the gruesome pieties of the laboratory, the human squabbles of the Scramble are like a loud laugh in church—and if there is mockery in the laugh, that is because the cult itself is a mockery, leading to neo-pagan forms of devotion that will, in time, lead us to see just what all is indicated in the fact that experimental science, as emerging in the Christian scheme, had its start in *black* magic.

CHAPTER 4

[Notes toward] The Rhetorical Situation

This chapter is entitled "[Notes toward] The Rhetorical Situation" to signal
that it is based on incomplete, unrevised drafts and notes available in Burke's
papers at Penn State. The numbers in brackets at the end of each paragraph
are Burke's penciled-in additions: they are calibrated to the numbers in the
"Outline of 'The Rhetorical Situation'," a facsimile of which is included in
this volume as Appendix 1.—Eds.

The essential rhetorical situation resides in the *constancy of the invitation to war*. "Property is theft," our anarchists tell us, following Proudhon. And the statement is even truer than they meant it to be. For they referred only to the nature of private property as exemplified in the role of a privileged "ruling class." But the basic incentive to militancy that resides in "property" is much wider in its application. [1]

Beginning at the highest level of generalization, we see the problem grounded in the metaphysical relation between the whole of the universe and its parts. For the identity of any part is twofold: first, there is its nature as participant in the universal nature in which it is grounded; and there is its nature as a part distinct from other parts. Its nature as *distinct* is, in effect, an *exclusion*. The lamb, for instance, can "logically" persist in its nature as a lamb only so long as it avoids incorporation into the body of a lion. And even the lion that devours the lamb could not persist in his nature as a lion if he did wholly merge with the nature of his victim. So, in the most general sense, there is an "invitation to war" in the sheer division of totality into the partisanship of partiality. [2]

Now partiality, in this most general sense, is the same as "property," or "mine-own-ness." As we observe the use of the term "property" in Aquinas, for instance, we can readily see why the Churchmen are so disturbed at the Marxist view of property. For a common "mine-ness" is felt to be a contradiction in terms. And even that which is "appropriated" to one Person of the Trinity is thereby distinguished from appropriations to the other two Persons. Such is all the more the case in the divisive realm of creatures, where the part continues to be itself only insofar as it reserves properties to itself (a kind of logical exclusion that is a "theft" insofar as one living thing can be itself only by preventing something else from being itself, since all assimilation involves the destruction of the assimilated). [3]

We are not by any means embarrassed by the fact that the situation, when considered in terms so universal, is not clear-cut. Though some particular existing animal, for instance, can maintain its "properties" as such only by the assimilation of alien substances, the species of such animals could not continue to exist if all the species of such other substances were destroyed. Hence, there must be a "sharing" as well as a "theft." Lions, for instance, can continue to exist only by an ecological balance whereby they suffer much of their prey to go uncaught, depriving themselves and their progeny accordingly. Indeed, "essential" distinctions are "peaceful" in that they simply *cannot* steal from one another. That is, the essential nature of a thing thoroughly excludes all other essential natures; its definition, for instance, cannot "appropriate" any property alien to that definition. A nature can be what it is only by excluding all that it is not. Its private nature involves privation ambiguously, as it both deprives itself of other things and deprives other things of it (a situation that besets the poet who, having constructed a method of expression before his complete intellectual maturity, may rule out further intellectual development lest it cause the disintegration of his method). And the existential nature of a thing (as some particular animal) can be maintained only insofar as other things are allowed to go on maintaining their existential nature. So that, in both cases, at this abstruse level of generalization, there are "pacifist" elements intermingled with the "militant" ones. [4]

In brief, we here find, intermingled, a state of affairs which, in terms less formal than the part-whole relationship, could be treated as a competition-cooperation ambiguity (with neither capable of prevailing to the total exclusion of the other). A generic term for both could be "action," which could then be subdivided specifically into competition (or war) on one side and cooperation (or peace) on the other. But here again the ambivalent nature of the ground term (action) might be expected somehow to inspirit both of its specific offsprings. And since the generic term contains implicitly division into *both* war and peace, we may legitimately expect to look for warlike elements in peace and peace-like elements in war. That is, when the "pure" distinction between the nature of war and the nature of peace is brought down to embodiment in specific cases, we may expect some degree of imperfection, as were our terms rather "peace-like war" and "warlike peace." As indeed we readily find them: for consider the great invitation to the competitive that resides in some great project of social cooperation (as with rivalry in candidacy for office or in matters of policy); and similarly, consider what an astounding degree of cooperative organization is required to conduct a war under modern conditions. [5]

Why then, if the warlike and the militant are, by the nature of the case, ambivalent in the very nature of action itself, why do we single out the invitation to *war?* Particularly inasmuch theology already suggests a happy solution for us in treating "good" as an efficiency and "evil" as a mere deficiency, whereby good can be proclaimed the ultimate ground, underlying evil. "Every actual being is a good; and likewise every potential being, as such, is a good, as having a relation to good. For as it has being in potentiality, so it has goodness in potentiality. Therefore, the subject of evil is good." Aquinas, *Summa Theologica,* Q. 48, Art. 3. I was about to say: because in peace there is no problem. But that is not quite the case. For in peace there *is* a problem: perhaps the most terrifying problem of all. The simplest indication of this is to be found in our own recent history, where the mighty efforts needed to transform our economy from peace to war were managed with far less of the intestine brawls that marked our period of reconversion after the end of hostilities. For men are unified by *purpose;* and war readily supplies unity of purpose, whereas a state of peace threatens to deprive men of all purpose whatsoever, and certainly of all *urgent* purpose, except insofar as they may, by neurosis or overweaning ambition, restore for themselves a set of distressing conditions that serve as the "moral equivalent of war." [6]

In general, then, there is the invitation to war lurking even in peace. This is transcended mainly by the factor of *human interests*. Metaphysically, for instance, it is "war" for men to blast a tunnel through a mountain. Or if such concern with the natural integrity of a mass which probably is not at all interested in continuing to "be itself" may seem too squeamish or pedantic, at least one can discern the element of "war" in, let us say, a project for mosquito extermination, where men would destroy a kind of existence that is interested in continuing to be itself. But the matter of interests transforms such metaphysical destruction of natures into peace insofar as the aim of the destruction is itself pacific (as judged by human standards). In brief, we can cause peace, rather than war, to be the essence of the peace-war ambivalence (or coopera-tion rather than competition to be the essence of the ambivalence we disclosed in the generic concept of "action") by infusing the entire enterprise with a pacific, or cooperative purpose, as the Allies in the last war were more essentially peaceful than the Nazis, since the Nazis were explicitly aiming at a state of permanent subjection of other peoples, whereas the Allies were explicitly aiming at a state of equality (though, alas! there were many tendencies towards subjection *implicit* in their ways, as was eventually revealed by the British treatment of India and the Indonesians, and our own treatment of the Negroes in the South or aid to the reactionary elements in China). [7]

But though there is an element of destruction in any act of construc-tion, one would be pedantic indeed who did not recognize that some enterprise like our Tennessee Valley Project is *essentially* constructive, as judged by the interests of mankind. Or perhaps we had best put it this way: *Insofar as there are no deceptions involved,* any constructive-destructive act undertaken for the good of men is to be interpreted as constructive (as being infused with the spirit of the purpose). [8]

Our reservation, the words "insofar as there are no deceptions involved," can allow for a great deal of haggling. However, at this point we are trying to formulate a principle, not to treat of its application in specific cases. In fact, a major reason for our point about the "invitation to war" is precisely the fact that there so frequently are deceptions involved. Indeed, ironically, one might even lay it down as a rule of thumb that the criterion of exclusively *human* interests would defeat itself if followed with too great strictness. Show me that man who, in the engrossment in his own peculiarly human purpose, has no concern for the integrity of alien substances, and I'll show you a man who lacks sympathy with mankind itself. Those demons of diseased ambition (and maybe all men are such) who can destroy a countryside without com-punction, if there but be a certain quick profit to be gained by the dev-astation (like some early pioneers, so unconcerned with the true per-centage of things, that they would kill a buffalo for his tongue), are but letting loose a brutality of motivation that in the end comes back to plague mankind itself. Much of the "imaginal" danger in the modern demoralized use of the powers of applied science is of this sort: a way of life that, in the end, invites the user of such powers to treat mankind itself in the same terms. Those who do not feel a certain distress even in the chemical eradication of bacteria harmful to human life, open the way for those who will treat human life itself as mere bacteria. [9]

I remember once, at a world's fair, in a Miracle Hall of Magical Science, or something of the sort, a demonstration of a newly invented electric ray, its powers here exhibited to those who were meant to admire it for its death-dealing properties. On a screen there was projected a globule of water, greatly magnified. The water was contaminated by a myriad of microscopic organisms that went scurrying back and forth across the surface of the screen (and in their magnified projection looking, as I recall, about the size of large ants). Then the demonstrator shot his new ingenious ray through this liquid, for the fraction of a second. And immediately all the scurrying organisms stopped dead still. And through the audience ran an exclamation of *pity*. And in that pity, I felt, there resided some hope—hope not for the silly little bugs, who were unquestionably on the way out, but some hope for mankind. Power in itself is impersonal and pitiless. And to see mankind in its terms would be to treat men quite as that ray treated the microscopic bugs. And this is what I have in mind when saying that even an approach to the world from the standpoint of exclusively human purposes would defeat itself, becoming inhuman, except insofar as non-human things are treated with humanity. Otherwise, human things will be treated without humanity. The atrocities committed by Nazi physicians, in the name of scientific experimentation, upon prisoners of war and the inmates of concentration camps are a gruesome indication of what we mean. The ultimate horror is in this possibility: that those who tortured their prisoners in sadistic delight were nearer to the wells of human pity than those who went about their work of infection and destruction without emotion, acting sheerly with the methodological precision of the specialist. [9a]

Or the dangers of peace may be glimpsed in the ironies that have beset the progressive development of scientific power. Power and knowledge being attributes of the godhead, and the striving towards greater rationality being par excellence a mark of human goodwill, nothing could be on its face a fuller exemplar of peace, cooperation, and construction than the work of the scientist, applying his senses, imagination, understanding, and intuition to the greater perfection of instruments. Yet the *application* of scientific principles has regularly made its greatest strides forward under the urgency of war. And there is a profound justice (from the imagistic point of view) in the fact that the resources of atomic fission had their formal inauguration in three great blasts, marked wholly by an awesome spread of death and desolation. The scientists themselves, we have learned after the fact, had for some time been effectively suppressed by those who would teach us to take pride in our freedom from censorship, petitioned that the Japanese be informed of the bomb, and be given evidence of its powers, and then be called upon to surrender as the alternative to its use in war. Their own work was essentially peaceful. For left to their own resources, they would find it enough to join with their colleagues throughout the world in the cooperative development and perfection of their theory and its application. Such engrossment in the solution of problems is probably as very great a satisfaction as men can ever get from creative work in a collective enterprise. [10]

But where there is power, there is the invitation to intrigue. And where the power is fantastic, men awake with the sudden terrorized realization that the intrigue may be correspondingly fantastic. And so, at every step, the scientists found themselves exiled from their realm of intellectual freedom and confined in a metaphorical concentration camp (nor was it so metaphorical at that, for many were afraid to utter not only the professional knowledge of their subject, but not even their private views on matters of politics and morals, lest they be literally sent to prison on the grounds that they were divulging military secrets). [11]

Even mere considerations of ceremony might well have been enough to make them dislike the idea of introducing their newest triumph under such hellish auspices (the expert sizzling of thousands upon thousands of human beings at one clip, and without even a chance to surrender before the new instrument of rapine and torture was set loose upon them). But no use: the power was there, and so the invitation to intrigue was there. And the bombs were dropped, apparently as a "dramatic" way of detracting from the effects of Russia's imminent entry into the war. The bombs were used, in brief, as a bit of *infernal rhetoric,* mainly as a device for robbing one of our Allies of full credit for its help. In itself it was perfected purely by theories evolved in terms of *motion.* But here's how it was quickly adapted to an inferior terminology of *action.* [12]

But the ultimate irony was to be disclosed a bit later: for after the bomb had thus been used rhetorically as a rather heavy-handed bit of rhetorical "actualization" in accounting for the Japanese surrender, it was next discovered that Japanese politicians were using it exactly the same way, but for their own purposes. That is, once it became apparent that the world was horrified by the use of the device, the Japanese promptly gave it full credit for terminating the war. Whereupon, our local word-slingers had to get busy again, this time excoriating the J*** for publicly proclaiming the bomb as important a factor as *our* spokesmen had done. They were accused of trying to put too much stress upon the effect of this latest importation from hell, thereby detracting from our other preparations and victories. Or, as stated in the *New York Times:*

> Japan's attempt to save face by attributing her capitulation mainly to the atomic bomb was brushed aside by Secretary of State Burnes, who declared that Tokyo had admitted defeat before the first new bomb fell and had appealed to Premier Stalin to intervene for peace at Potsdam. [13]

Still remaining at high levels of generalization: we'd say that the essential irony (the profoundest kind of intestine discord goading to relief in outward aggression, as one might feel homicidal to avoid feeling suicidal) arises under those circumstances when a purpose which was (from the standpoint of the agent) essentially peaceful has come to reveal, by a change of circumstances, traits essentially militant. Science, or knowledge, as a purpose is unambiguously a *good;* but applied science is an ambiguous agency, capable of being used for both good and evil; and insofar as the evil potentialities gain expression, there is a corresponding frustration at the very roots of the ethical. For when conditions are such that one can be reasonable only by abandoning a strict interpretation of rationality, he may feel as though he were invited to be rational by the abandoning of reason, a suicidally reflexive state, an intestine brawl for which the natural relief is some act of aggression (either out-and-out destruction, or translated into construction). [14]

You might think it too recondite of us to be looking for evidences of war in such out-of-the-way places, at a time when millions of people lie suffering from the results of war in its most brutally obvious form, as far from the battlefields as it is possible for one to be under conditions of total war. Yet a situation far from the battlefields has its own way of demonstrating the ravages of war. For it is by the war of words that men are led into battle. And there is nothing recondite about this, except in the accidental sense that men may not have paid sufficient attention to it. Recently a traveler over Germany, observing not only the ruins of cities but also the beauty of the countryside in the areas that had been spared, asked himself: "What made these people so crazy? When they had so much, what more did they want?" And this at least must be granted by everyone: That while Russia, still painfully pulling itself out of the mud, asked for nothing but the right to go on improving the lot of its people, a Germany felicitously laden with the accumulation of many centuries of industrious upbuilding was avid for foreign conquest. And if, by a sudden magical granting of a wish, the German people could be given back just what they had before they began listening to the insidious goadings of their Hitler and his diseased band, nothing more but just what they had, while feeling so deprived, would they not now think their nation blessed by a very miracle of bounteousness (as indeed it was)? And is there not a similar fallacy, beginning in mere triviality and lack of imagination, among those of our own nation who now talk of another war, able to conceive of construction at home only when undertaken as an incidental aspect of destruction abroad? [15]

Were a sudden magical restoration of Germany possible, would the German people recognize the extent of their bounty? They probably would. Many of them might even feel piously exalted enough to give thanks to God. But the next day, I am sure, they'd be at it again, proclaiming themselves terribly put upon, pressing for recognition, quite as before complaining of deprivation while deliberately allocating a large percentage of their productivity to preparations for war, plotting throughout the world for the vindication of the Nazi philosophy, or its analogue, and alas! finding plenty of allies who would help to build them up to the point where many of these same allies might then decide to knock them down again, as with the blowing-hot and blowing-cold that imperialist movements in Germany have traditionally encountered among the British Tories, and our own. (The difference being that, with the latest improvements in weapons the very center of the earth would feel the vibrations of such a war, and when it was over, the face of the earth might not even be a fit habitat for bugs.)[16]

If you would ponder these matters, I submit, you will find the answer not on the battlefield, but in the study. And you will find it when looking for the wide range of war, as revealed by the analysis of human speech. Perhaps we do not realize how deep the motives of war do really go. Language is a miraculously subtle instrument. And in its subtlety, miraculously devious. So that, for every goad to war explicit in our calling the enemy a fiend, there are many goads to war implicit in our calling the enemy a darling. There is war in the best that any religion or any philosophy could ever have to offer: there is war in forgiveness, and in charity. [17]

I am not, at this stage, prepared to say whether any state of national existence is possible without a strong invitation to war. But at least everyone will admit that in nationality there is a ready invitation to war.

Next, one must begin to ask himself whether certain doctrines and conditions of nationality may contain greater incitements to war than others. And just as it is the very essence of the ethical and the rational to *universalize* a moral principle (as with the Christian universalizing, at least in precept, of the golden rule), so we may legitimately look for something essentially ethical even in a crude doctrine of national domination, which would universalize a principle of sovereignty. [18]

Science itself likewise seems to call for the unification of all human society, its eventual inclusion in a world-order, whatever degree of economic autonomy the complete development of technology may eventually make possible, reversing the trend towards the universal market by developing within each political unit a self-sustaining economic plant that compensates for the lack of some raw materials by producing synthetic substitutes for them, and setting up artificial conditions for the growth of certain foods not indigenous to the climate. And any trend towards world unification which the conditions of technology call for in itself invites to war so long as the situation is considered in nationalistic terms. [19]

It is also quite possible (still keeping on an almost indiscriminatingly high level of generalization) that "healthy nationalism" is naturally and inevitably *expansionistic* in one way or another, though such expansionism may take many forms, some of them much more pugnacious than others. Judged purely as imagery, a national doctrine of purely internal development would seem quite suspect. One can get the point by asking himself how such doctrines look when considered as the translation of an *individual* psychology into *political* terms. In this form, a sincere theory of autonomy and national isolationism looks simply like the nationalist analogue to the ideals of a "shut-in personality." It is in-turning, and narcissistic. As an actual fact, such isolationist doctrines have usually operated rhetorically as a way of enlisting personally retiring people in behalf of policies which have latently aggressive implications (as our sincere advocates of a nationalist indwelling could be enlisted, by "America First" movements, in policies that interfered with the struggle against Fascism). The German doctrine of "autarchy," for instance, while suggesting something of this sort to many people, was a rhetoric of expansionism, the least "autarchic" policy possible. Yet imaginally, it had the lineaments of retirement to endear it to people who did not follow the minutiae of politics. Hence: in every country, there are active and passive elements; and in our country the passive element still feels cheated because she was not yet raped by Hitler. [20]

I should guard against possibilities of misunderstanding here. I am not by any means trying to treat of nationalistic aggression in terms of merely "natural" impulses, and as a mere transmogrified replica of individual development. On the contrary, I am suggesting that the *imagery* of individual development may be rhetorically enlisted as a way of recruiting, in jingoistic policies, scrupulous but unsuspecting persons who would otherwise be much against their government's meddling abroad in behalf of its "nationals." But one knows that, as an individual, one *must* "expand" in some way or other, and that when one ceases to do so, one is profoundly on the road to death. Individually, such expansion may but take the form of clearing the brush about the house, or learning a new language, or adding a new commodity to one's sales list, or travel, or getting some new furniture. But as translated into a simple nationalistic analogue, it amounts to a vicarious sense of vigor and power got by one's identification with images of national prowess. [21]

And, ironically enough, though the "nationals" whose special interests abroad are protected by general public taxation, themselves otherwise transcend nationalism by reason of their deals with the international cartels, it is the deprived persons at home who, impoverished because so much of the national effort is turned to the resources of foreign aggression rather than to the improvement of domestic conditions, it is precisely these *victims* of nationalistic aggressiveness whose fervor is most readily enlisted through the imagery of sheerly *vicarious* participation in the power of our nationally subsidized corporations abroad. [22]

In sum, then, the invitations to war which we have considered so far are: the purely metaphysical problem of part and whole; the ambiguous involvement of competition in the cooperativeness of action; the frustration of rationality insofar as even the applications of science itself must be distrusted; the aggressiveness that arises when the ethical tendency to universalize a principle is applied to the principle of national sovereignty; the conflict implicit in the fact that technologically engendered world unification must now be considered in terms of national integers; the deceptions that arise from too naïve an identification of the individual with nation. [23]

Still considering the invitation to war broadly, we may thus note a whole cluster of motives, mutually reinforcing one another, and beginning not in such "evil" as malice, envy, or the lie as their ground, but in "virtue" (the very word for which, in the old Greek and Latin texts out of which Christian thought was developed, was a synonym for the power and valor of the warrior). The detailed analysis of such a cluster would belong rather in our book on Symbolic. But here we should consider it broadly, in its general totality, in order that, when we see some fragment or another of it in any particular poetic or rhetorical expression, we may have an intuition of the ways in which this fragment ties back into the cluster as a whole. [24]

One might begin by noting the imaginal kinship of weapons, tools, and genitals, as revealed in popular speech. I would suggest that such kinship, on the level of the Symbolic, provides a basic resource for instigation on the level of Rhetoric. The relation indicates a constant potentiality of the human mind, to be actualized when anyone would "morally" persuade others or himself to any aggression ranging from indignation to slaughter, by relating it to the assertions of sex and work. The call to convert swords into plowshares indicates a reverse readiness to convert plowshares into swords. [25]

One can see how quickly devious resources arise here, when considering the medieval division of men into those who work, those who fight, and those who pray. For, since those who pray were celibates, they intended that a kind of verbal assertion would replace the sexual motive—as it did, insofar as bodily cohabitation could find an equivalent in doctrinal insemination. But here we find many other possibilities opening up. For prayer has its counterpart in the oath, as in the resounding rhetoric of the *Excommunicatio* translated in Chapter XI of *Tristram Shandy,* calling down God's damnation upon the unrepentant, cursing him "inwardly and outwardly," cursing him "in his temples, in his forehead, in his ears, in his eye-brows, in his cheeks, in his jaw-bones, in his nostrils, in his fore-teeth and grinders, in his lips, in his throat, in his shoulders, in his wrists, in his arms, in his hands, in his fingers," and even visiting wretchedness upon him *mingendo, cacando, flebotomando.* The formula by which the gentle Spinoza was laden with the curses of his church are equally resonant, showing how readily the prayer, in lending itself to oath, leads into ramifications of the cloacal ambiguity, so that the prayer in reverse, besides equaling war, equals a befouling with excrement (as we shift from the sexual to the excretory aspects of the "demonic trinity"). The blood let in battle may equal the semen let in sexual union or the fertilizing rain upon the soil. War itself is analogous to the morality of work or harvest, as there is promise that the time of sacrifice will be followed by a time of bounty (as it was indeed, in primitive war, in the "formal recognition" that to the victors belonged the spoils, in both women and goods—and as is informally the case with the "fraternizings" and the loot by purchase that accompany modern armies). [26]

Add now the purely financial ways whereby the sacrifice-booty pair can figure, as soldiers dying on the battlefield get the sacrifice and big industrialists selling to the government at a fantastic profit get the booty, with the dissociation being healed by a vast nationalistic identification whereby "all" can share "spiritually" in the grand total of sacrifice and profit, the possibilities of suasion here being greatly increased by the fact that sons of the profiteers too died in battle. [27]

Broadly, there is the invitation to war in the fact that any adjustment between the property structure and the conditions of production and distribution involves redistribution of ownership. Indeed, some such redistribution takes place inevitably, even if all the world were uniformly agreed on preventing it, since the changing nature of production itself adds up, willy-nilly, to changes in the allocation of opportunities and necessities, involving apparent or concealed taxation (the latter kind including excess prices paid by consumers, acquiescence in unsatisfactory living conditions, in brief all sacrifices asked of some members of the community and not of others). Increased technological productivity, without a corresponding change in the financial structure, invites to war in forcing a choice between more marketing abroad and fewer hours of work at home. It is not necessary here to consider in particular the many incentives of this sort. Besides, each cause we singled out would itself be a moot issue, itself a subject for rhetoric, for any material interest can be presented in terms of some corresponding ideal, given the will to do so and sufficient control over the main sources of public information to see that the will has its way. [28]

The overall generalization that concerns us here is the element of war implicit in all such ideals, whenever the situation is such that the ideals are used for purposes of alignment. For in every such case, though they have the peacefulness and prayerfulness of heavenly intent, they are weapons in the war of words. And such a resource is so ubiquitous that we must expect to find traces of war even in a benediction. Rhetorically, any man is a fool who proposes to fight for a mean reason, since there is available a "noble" reason for just about anything. But our point at the moment is this: so long as one can shift from ideal to ideal, there is a "peaceful" version of every interest, no matter how discriminatory. And since there are different material alignments implicit in given situations, every ideal is implicitly warlike. So, when you find us many thousands of miles from home, meddling in the policies of other countries, you can depend upon it, in advance, that we are doing so for the best of reasons, insofar as the policy is thought, rightly or wrongly, to favor the interests of the faction which the given spokesman represents. No nation has ever gone to war for an ideal; but no nation has ever gone to war without one. [29]

The quickest way to appreciate the compulsion of the weapons-tools-sex cluster is to think of the obstacles that immediately present themselves the moment one attempts to eliminate war. The sexual analogue is the choice between absolute anarchy, a total communizing of sexual relations, and the vow of chastity (the only two ways of avoiding sexual discrimination). Unless sexual relations are as free as the air, they possess the ingredients of war. For the more we grant the success of St. John Chrysostrom's prescriptions for merging the mine and thine in Christian marriage, the more forcefully must we recognize that the union itself is a divisiveness, separating itself off from all the rest of the ownership in the world—and so calling for resistance to any trespasser who would poach here. Similarly, one who would translate the eradication of war into sexual terms, without favoring total promiscuity, can do so only by symbolic castration. [30]

And the elimination of war, as translated into terms of work, calls for the elimination of ambition, the basically competitive virtue of capitalism. And where the struggle for the predominance of one plan or policy or doctrine over another is conducted under the mimetics of peace, we are admonished to look beneath it for the traces of war, though they be found lurking only in a *forcefulness* of imagery or in the compulsions of logical *cogency*. [31]

However, we must guard lest our discovery of the ubiquity and universality of war, as disclosed by treatment of our subject on such a high level of generalization, be interpreted as an argument for a simple conclusion that "war is the essence of all existence," and that, accordingly, by the logic of the scene-agent ratio, "man is essentially a fighter." And particularly if such a view is taken as ground for an out-and-out philosophy of war, as with doctrines having individual or national aggrandizement as the principal motive of morality (a temptation, we cannot too often repeat, that is implicit in the very etymology of our word for "virtue" itself). [32]

One must be continually ready to narrow the scope of his generalizations when confronting particular situations calling for particular policies. And when doing so, one immediately discovers that, in every case, there is cause for *discriminations* which, though there be an element of war in every discrimination, will assist in the choice of policies relatively more warlike or less warlike—or where the nature of the "war" motive itself is farther along in the direction of peace, as the enslaving of a conquered people would be essentially more "peaceful" than the killing of them, and a treaty would be more peaceful still, etc. And though we have, in recent decades, had much evidence of the war implicit in commercial ambitions, it is obvious that only certain forms of such ambition lead to war proper. [33]

Indeed, our very thoroughness in proclaiming the ubiquity of the incentive to war is intended rather as an answer to those who would base the principles of morality in war itself. For as soon as one has granted that there is war *everywhere,* one must recognize that, by the same token, there is *peace* everywhere. For not even self-aggrandizement could be possible without the destruction of the individual unless many cooperative acts accompany it, somewhat as a Machiavellian prince, to be strong in dominion, would have to build up the strength of his subjects, and at the very worst such upbuilding requires a furthering of the production and distribution of goods. [34]

The United States is (or at least was) fabulously rich in natural resources. Naturally, the first settlers had to be quite considerate of their Indian hosts, living on honorable terms with them, until the white population was well enough entrenched to feel that it could risk breaking faith. Thereafter, despite hardships and setbacks, the white immigrants could extend their empire steadily at the expense of the natives. The despoiling of the natural resources on a grand scale (along with much transference from collective ownership to private ownership) could become synonymous with "progress." The incentives to destroy the forests, squander the minerals, pollute the rivers, and deplete the soil could be looked upon as an exceptionally bright and new motive in human culture, an "American way." And the fact that, with so much vast natural wealth being thrown about, nearly everybody could, if he used patience and cunning enough, and didn't have too great a run of hard luck, contrive to pick up enough at least to keep him alive, was interpreted as the evidence of some miraculous trait in the culture itself. Furthermore, since more people kept coming from the East, nearly any piece of land was likely, for a time at least, to increase in monetary value, as sheer real estate, if you held it long enough—and this too could seem like the reward for some exceptional virtue, a sign that the owner of the deed was one of God's elect, or in any case, one of society's elect. [35]

All told, the rhetorical opportunity here was atrocious. In fact, it was so overwhelming that Americans may never be brought to question it radically until far too late. The situation was purely and simply this:

Unless moral vigilance, national self-criticism, critical intelligence, and economic imaginativeness were universally at their greatest (and they were not!), men were invited to make asses of themselves and one another by assuming that the squandering of this natural bounty indicated the presence of some special genius peculiar to this particular citizenry, as individuals and as a nation. A profusion of *materials* could be interpreted as an endowment of *spirit*, somewhat as though a man considered himself a genius for having stumbled over a well-stuffed pocketbook to which no one else could establish a claim. [36]

Here resides the essence of our coxcombry as a nation. This is the situation out of which arises, as rhetorical strategy, our spontaneous and indoctrinated belief in the "American way." And this failure to distinguish between matter and spirit is carried, almost suicidally, a momentous step farther when, in the secularizing of religion that marks modern life as a whole, we locate the criterion of the ethical in the cult of material commodities, seeing both "freedom" and "propriety" in terms of purchased things. [37]

And the rhetoric here threatens to become a nightmare, when we realize that, by now, an *excessive devotion* to such materialism is necessary, to us as a nation, if we are but to be able to keep ourselves at work. For if we have been indoctrinated to believe that the impoverished should not be housed and otherwise aided at government expense, and if in their condition as poor customers there is no incentive for private enterprise to build them up as consumers of essentials, if indeed there is even much incentive to keep them impoverished, as a source of cheap service for the financially more fortunate, and if we cannot manage beyond a certain limited amount to force our wares upon foreign customers in the face of competition from other nations, tariff barriers, inability to meet the payments on debts, and the like, then our productive plant can only be kept going at a high enough rate to keep a large percentage of our population within the orbit of capitalism (that is, earning *money*) if those who do have money to spend squander it largely on *trifles,* on things they *do not need* and *cannot use.* For, to the extent that our industrial productivity is not to provide *necessary* accommodations for people short of money, to that extent it can only be kept going by providing *unnecessary* accommodations for those having money. Insofar as anyone can afford to buy beyond his essential needs, he must be induced to desire passionately all sorts of trivial things that can bring him no genuine rest. This is what Veblen had in mind when he called advertising "creative psychiatry." [38]

The material that is not used for a poor man's house must be used for a rich man's gadget, if those whose income is derived from this material (as workers, managers, investors) are to continue receiving this income. Or else, if it does go to constructive ends, it must go to satisfy the one sure economically useless customer, *war*. For though, our property structure being what it is, we can without anguish build whole emergency cities for workers in a munitions plant, to be scrapped or abandoned as "ghost cities" after the crisis, a rhetoric infused with the ideals of the National Association of Manufacturers would be let loose in earnest, and throughout the length and breadth of our press (peculiarly blessed, in its freedom from "government control") upon any project for housing this same population, in quarters of no greater cost, for permanent peacetime living. [39]

Two other points:

1. insofar as we squander here, "need" for us to get resources elsewhere to squander—new irony: though we produced a fairly large percentage of purchasers by our squandering at home—the squandering abroad can work the other way: we can keep the population wholly impoverished, simply by working in league with a small ruling class there. this too we can take as evidence of our genius. we can add to their wretchedness, until they are almost devoid of hope—and then we can cite their hopelessness as evidence that they are essentially inferior, and not worth anything but exploitation. [40]

2. another aspect of secularization—the possibility that there is actually a "psychological need" for an inferior class, unless we are exceptionally just, critically intelligent, and imaginative in admonishing ourselves against such temptations (and as we have said, national morality is a kind of conspiracy, or conniving, a casuistry of conscience made easy, avoiding indictment for injustice by making the injustice national, as per Burke's notion that one can't indict a nation), a poor class "needs" a poorer class—and ironically, this particular bastardized survival of religion in capitalism is, like all true religion, inimical to capitalism: in the South, for instance, the pressure to keep down the income of workers in general and Negro workers in particular means in the long run an effort on the part of that region itself to make sure that that region gets a smaller percentage of the national income. the low income may be a good bait for drawing capital to a section, but the high income is better, capitalistically, once the capital is there. [41]

Facsimile of the Outline of "The Rhetorical Situation"

Figures 4a–d present a facsimile of the Rhetorical Situation Outline. The numbers from 1 to 41 correspond to the paragraph numbers provided by Burke in the margins of the manuscript of his draft, and for the convenience of the reader we reproduce those numbers in brackets in "[Notes toward] The Rhetorical Situation," chapter 4 of *The War of Words*. Source: This outline of what Kenneth Burke had in mind for "The Rhetorical Situation" follows the manuscript of "The Rhetorical Situation" in box 5, folder 17, of the Kenneth Burke Papers at Penn State.—Eds.

Situational   -   Outline

1 - essential rhetorical situation: - constancy of the
invitation to war - "property is theft" cd. be interpreted
much more extensively than it is by the anarchists

2 - beginning at highest level of generalization: relation of
part to whole - identity of any part, as part of whole, as part
of whole - lamb, to persist, must exclude the lion - and even
lion cd. not persist if he included nature of lamb - hence,
invitation to war in division of totality into partiality (partisanship)

3 - partiality as property, mine-own-ness - "property" in
Aquinas, as not possible to two Persons - ~~xxxxxxxxxxxxxxxxxx~~
a creature to assimilate must destroy the assimilated

4 - admittedly, the situation as so generalized is not clear-cut -
there must be a "sharing" as well as "theft" - ecological
balance - sense in which essential distinctions are peaceful,
and can't steal from one another - its appropriation as
privation (depriving self of others, and depriving others of it)
- things can exist only by letting other things exist

5 - in brief: cd. treat as competition-cooperation ambiguity,
with the generic term, action - action cd. then be subdivided
into war and peace - but we might expect that the genius of the
tertium quid wd. give us, rather, "peacelike war" and "warlike
peace" (as embodied in the imperfections of existent cases) -
and this we find: as per the ~~xxxxxxxxxxxxxxxxxxx~~ rivalry
in cooperative enterprises, and the great amt. of cooperation in
modern war (

6 - if war and peace are ambivalent, why single out invitation to
war? particularly since theology offers us a solution, in
proclaiming good as efficiency, evil as deficiency - was about
to say: because it can peace there is no problem . but there is -
as indicated in our recent history: ~~xxxx~~ so much greater ~~xxxxxx~~
smoothness in conversion for war than in reconversion for peace
- for men are unified by purpose

7 - how factor of human interests transcends the ambiguity -
it is "war" to blast a tunnel or to exterminate mosquitoes -
but factor of human interests can transform such destruction into
peace - infusing enterprise with peaceful purpose -
Allies more peaceful than Nazis in last war - (explicitly at
least, though implicitly there were many elements of war, as per
India and our treatment of Negroes)

8 - TVA essentially constructive, as judged by interests of mankind.
hence our principle: Insofar as there are no deceptions involved,
any construction-destruction act undertaken for the good of
men is to be interpreted as constructive (as infused with the
spirit of the purpose).

9 - haggling possible via our reservation ("insofar as there
are no deceptions involved"). but here we are trying to
formulate a principle, not treat of application to specific cases
- the major invitation to ear is precisely that there are so many
deceptions involved - danger in test of exclusively human
interests (eventual invitation to treat men likewise in terms of
the treatment for non-human victims of human interests)

FIGURES 4a–d. Facsimile of the Rhetorical Situation Outline. The numbers from 1 to
41 correspond to the paragraph numbers provided by Burke in the margins of the
manuscript of his draft. Source and credit: The Kenneth Burke Literary Trust.

9 a anecdote of the episode at world's fair - destruction of
the bacteria, shown on screen - the audience's cry of pity -
in this cry there was some hope - otherwise, an absence of
pity or consideration for non-human things ~~months~~ affects our
attitude towards ~~hum~~ mankind itself - as per atrocities committed
by Nazi physicians in name of scientific experimentation -
~~sadid~~ sadists were probably nearer to human pity than the specialists

10 - dangers of peace , revealed in science (wisdom and godhead -
rationality as mark of goodwill - yet application of science has
made its greatest strides under urgency of war) - imagery of the
inauguration of the ~~bomb~~ atomic bomb

11 - where there is power , there is invitation to intrigue -
scientists, for freedom, suddenly find themselves confined - ~~even~~
~~considerations of ceremony might have made them dislike the~~
~~inauguration under such hellish auspices~~

12 - even considerations of ceremony might have made them dislike
inauguration under such auspices - but the~~b~~ bombs were needed as
a bit of infernal rhetoric, to rob Russia of credit for entering war -
- developed by theories of motion, here's how it was transformed
into terms of action

13 - but the ultimate irony was disclosed later - Japs began
making same claims for bomb as our spokesmen had - hence ~~there~~
the next move was to deny what had been asserted - cite from NY Times

14 still remaining at high level of generalization: essential
irony (of intestine discord goading to outward aggression, as per
feeling homicidal to avoid feeling suicidal) arises when a peaceful
purpose ~~mischonus~~ begins to reveal militant traits - the
suicidally reflexive (as were one to be rational by abandoning
reason - a ~~xx month~~ suicidally reflexive state)

15 - not recondite to be looking for such out-of-the-way aspects
of war - war is contrived by words - the traveler over Germany,
asking, "what more did they want?" - Russia wanted internal
development, while the Germans wanted conquest - similar trends
in US

16 - if Germany cd. be magically restored, Germans wd. appreciate
their bounty for a eay, and then resume their plotting (aided by
British and US Tories, who wd. again build them up to the point where
they had to knock them down again). except that ~~th~~ the next time
wd. make the world uninhabitable

17 - these matters have to be pondered in the study - wide
range of war, revealed by study of human speech - we may not realize
how deep the motives of war do really go - explicit goad to war,
in calling the enemy a fiend - implicit goad to war, in calling him
a darling - war in forgiveness, and charity

18 - not prepared to say whether any state of national existence
is possible without strong invitation to war - at least, nationality
is a strong invitation to war - ethical ~~tm~~ motive in tendency to
universalize a ~~month~~ principle, and the same may apply to the
principle of national sovereignty - ~~xxixxxexiikawixxxxsaxxxxx~~
~~xi~~
19 - ~~hitherto~~ science likewise seems to call for unification of
all human society - (however, there are are trends towards
self-sustaining units) - any ~~xixx~~ scientific trend towards world
unification invites to war so long as it is encountered in nationalist
ic terms

20 -   imagery of expansionism - imagery ofxx purely internal
national development mayx be the analogue of the "shut in personality" - doctrinesxf of autonomy enlist personally xxxx
xxxxxxxxx retiring people in behalf of aggressive policies -
as isolationism in US aided Fascism - Nazi doctrine of
autarchy, a rhetoric to xxxxxx cloak.expansion -   active and
passive elements in every nation, and passive element in US
feels cheated because she was not raped by Hitler

21 -   we are not trying to treat of nationalistic aggression
in terms merely of "natural" impulses - but we are trying to
show how imagery of individual development can be rhetorically
utilized for jingoistic purposes - individualistically, failure
to "expand" equals death.   expansion may take many forms in
individual , but in nationalistic terms xx there is identification
with national prowess
                                          with
22 - ironically, the "nationals" xxxxe special interests abroad
transcend nationality, while supported at govt. expense   - it is
the deprived at home who enjoy national prestige vicariously

23 - in sum, on invitation to war: metaphysdcal relation btw.
part and whole ; ambiguous involvement of competition in cooperative
action ; frustration of rationality, insofar as even science may
be distrusted ; aggression in universalizing of ethical principle,
when that principle is nationalism ;   conflict implicit in
fact that technologically engendered world unification must be
considered in terms of nation ; deceptions that arise xxxx from
too naive identification of individual with nation

24 - whole cluster of motives, mutually enforcing one another,
beginning in "virtue" - detailed analysis of this cluster wd.
belong in Symbolic, but here we can treat it broadly (getting
intuition of ramifications)

25 - imaginal kinship of weapons, tools, genitals, as revealed
in popular speech - indicates tendency to equate agressiveness
in militant with assertions in sex and work - reverse conversion,
of plowshares into swords   -   xxxxxxxxxxxxxxxxxxxxxxxxxxxxxx

26 - those who work, fight, pray - in celibacy, the sexual
becomes the verbal insemination-   the Excommunication in
Tristram Shandy -   action of cloacal ambiguity, demonic trinity
- blood in war, semen in sex, fertilizing rain for crops -
war and harvest, sacrifice and bounty

27 - financial ways whereby sacrifice-booty pair can figure,
as soldiers sacrifice and investors get bounty - complicated by
sacrifice of profiteers' sons

28 -   invitation to war in all redistribution of ownership (such
as any change in production involves)   - this takes place even
inevitably -   but not necessary here to consider the many individual
situations making for this , each of which wd. be a moot question

29 - over-all generalization; element of war implicit in all
such ideals, no matter how peaceful their appearance - there
is a noble reason for every war - our meddling abroad, bound to
be for a "good" reason - no nation ever goes to war for an
ideal, and no nation ever goes to war without one

30 - quickest way to appreciate compulsion of weapons-tools-
sex, is to think of the obstacles that arise at attempt to
eliminate war - sexual analogue to warlessness is either
promiscuity or castration - St. John Chrysostom's view of
marriage involves divisiveness, resistance to poacher who wd.
trespass - ~~translated into terms of work, elimination of war~~

31 - translated into terms of work, elimination of war wd. equal
elimination of ambition - and every attempt to recommend
one policy over another involves discrimination, using forcefulness
of imagery or compulsions of logical cogency

32 - however, our position does not involve us in saying
simply that "war is the essence of existence" and "man is
essentially a fighter"

33 - we must be continually ready to narrow the scope of our
generalizations, when confronting particular situations -
- always grounds for discrimination btw. policies - though such
discrimination is itself warlike, it may help to choose policies
less warlike - enslavement less warlike than desrruction, treaty
less warlike than enslavement - war implicit in commercial
ambitions, but in varying degrees

34 - our purpose in thus broadly generalizing is to obstruct
the "man a fighter" doctrine - for it is as true to say that
peace is everywhere - a Machiavellian prince can't be strong
in domination without building up strength of his subjects

35 - situation underlying rhetoric in US - the great natural
wealth available for squandering - empire-building and destruction

36 - great moral vigilance, ~~criticalminitekhigmeney~~ national
self-criticism, economic imaginativeness required, so ~~motmim~~ as
not to interpret this profusion of materials ~~xxx~~ as endowment of
spirit

37 - danger of coxcombry - opportunity for rhetoric of "American
way" - failure to distinguish btw. mateer and spirit~~xx~~ also
due to secularization of religious

38 - rhetoric now threatens to become nightmare , as successive
devotion to materialism is now necessary - need for people to
be made to passionately desire trivial things - "creative
psychiatry"

39 - if not gadgets, then war

40 - squandering opens up ~~mew~~ need for getting new sources to
squander - hence, exploitation of foreign sources

41 - possibility that a submerged class is psychologically necessary -
national morality a connivance - irony of region's maintaining
low income rate

Foreword (to end on)

We provide in Appendix 3 a facsimile of the "Foreword (to end on)," which offers some of Burke's reflections on *The War of Words;* to assist the reader, we first include here in Appendix 2 the word-for-word transcription of the contents. Based on evidence in the archive, the editors date "Foreword (to end on)" in the early to mid-1970s. It may have been composed in anticipation of publication of the *Devices* by the University of California Press.—Eds.

FOREWORD (TO END ON)

Though most of this material (except for incidental minor revisions and the Appendix) was finished some decades back and attained the hopeful stage of a fair copy, I laid the MS aside while I worked on Grammar of Motives and Rhetoric of Motives, that I then judged to be needed as a preparatory grounding.

This notion was all wrong. The books should have been published exactly in the order in which they were written, with the Devices as preparation for what followed.

Though I did use the material in the classroom and in public talks, the only portion I ever published is the article, "Rhetoric—Old and New" (Journal of General Education, April 1951). It is reprinted in the collection, New Rhetorics, edited by Martin Steinmann, Jr., Scribner's 1967. But if I may borrow a word beloved of the media, in recent years we have seen quite a "spate" of specimens that would be classed under the same head as my Devices (largely a kind of "poor man's Machiavelli").

The originating impulse behind the project was an effort at self-cure. Since I seemed to be seeing more signs of plotting, deviousness, and duplicity than were good for me, I tried to work out "comic" ways whereby, as far as possible, a measure of fun might be derived from such observations. Also, despite myself,

I sometimes felt downright mean. At the time when the United Nations was being founded, for instance, under conditions when mankind needed a constant appeal to the greatest possible exercise of reasonableness and patience, precisely then the parties in power and leading journalists vied with one another in their zeal to play upon people's rancors and suspicions. It was a fateful stage in the annals of "global" relationships—and it was being zealously botched. And the trends that were to reach a kind of ad interim fulfillment in the McCarthy era, with surprising new twists in the Kennedy, Johnson, and Nixon years, were already inexorably emerging.

Thus I also kept delaying publication because I saw many places that would profit by reference to subsequent developments. Then lo! I suddenly awoke to the realization that, if I left things pretty much as they were in my original MS, the sheer course of history has brought it about that readers can of themselves readily profit by the "pathos of distance" in both seeing the original circumstances and seeing around the corner of those circumstances.

. . .

Just where place the Devices, with regard to the Motivorum project as a whole? The Grammar was designed to consider the universal aspects of human thought (as coming to a focus in paradoxes of the term, "substance"). The Rhetoric focussed on modes of partisanship and their transcending (as coming to a head in the term, "identification"). The Symbolic (in the restricted sense of the term) centers on individual "identities" (involving "equations" as revealed either in particular works of art ("Poetics") or human characters ("Ethics")).

Insofar as the Devices involve their use for "ulterior purposes" (to advocate a policy, for instance), they are clearly in the field of Rhetoric. But often they are employed as an aspect of one's character. In this regard, whatever their function as rhetorical "ploys," the Devices overlap upon the field of Ethics. Here is an illustration that occurs to me, since I happen to be writing these pages at a time when there is much talk of persons who, being entrusted with the task of enforcing the law, by the same token tend to think of themselves as above the law, and will readily adopt illegal methods to spy on persons suspected of illegality.

Consider thus the rural policeman who invariably parked his car on the wrong side of the road. And when, along with several other local citizens who were not thus "within" the law, he was taking a test on first aid, he quite unabashedly opened his book to copy out the answers, whereas none of the others dared to do anything of the sort, all properly expecting that, by the rules of the test, when they didn't know the right answer they would simply get marked "wrong."

In this sense the Devices tend to become implicit self-portraits, in representing the character of the user. Thus, there is a tendency for a given agent to favor certain Devices not just for some ulterior practical purpose, but for their own sake, by way of "self-expression," as with the stick-up man who didn't kill in order to rob, but robbed in order to kill (through sheer love of the kill as such). Or there was a news story of a subway "rapist" who, having demanded that a girl give him her purse, and having been given the purse in compliance with his demand, sliced her to death anyhow.

I have used extreme examples to sharpen the point; but the anecdote of the rural policeman would set the ideal tone for the Devices as a whole (at least to the extent that ideally we'd surround sinister specimens with a context of comic analogues).

Not until now did it occur to me that whereas, in my <u>Rhetoric of Motives,</u> I list some typical devices in Machiavelli's <u>Prince</u> and Ovid's <u>Art of Love,</u> my view of them as characteristic fragments of human characters (hence as embodying motives that move us from Rhetoric to Poetics and Ethics, enactments in and for themselves) may have its roots in the Flaubert of <u>L'Education Sentimentale,</u> though he certainly would have had no sympathy with my valiant effort to grin.

Facsimile of "Foreword (to end on)"

A word-for-word transcription of this "Foreword (to end on)" is included as Appendix 2.—Eds.

Foreword (to end on)

Though most of this material (except for incidental minor revisions and the Appendix) was finished some decades back and attained the hopeful stage of a fair copy, I laid the MS aside while I worked on my Grammar of Motives and Rhetoric of Motives, that I then judged to be needed as a preparatory grounding.

This notion was all wrong. The books should have been published exactly inthe order in which they were written, with the Devices as preparation for what followed.

Though I did use the material in the classroom and in public talks, the only portion I ever ﬁﬁﬁﬁﬁﬁ published is ﬁﬁ the article, "Rhetoric - Old and New" (Journal of General Education, April 1951). It is reprinted in the collecﬀion, New Rhetorics, edited by Martin Steinmann, Jr., Scribner's 1967. But if I may borrow a word beloved of the media, in recent years we have seen quite a "spate" of specimenﬀs that would be classed under the same head as my Devices (largely a kind of "poor man's Machiavelli").

The originating impulse behind the project was an effort at self-cure. Since I seemed to be seeing more signﬂl of plotting, deviousness, and duplicity than were good for me, I tried to work out "comic" ways whereby, as far as possible, a measure of fun might be derived from such observations. Also, despite myself, I sometimes felt downright mean. At the time when the United Nations was being founded, for instance, under conditions when mankind needed a constant appeal to the greatest possible exercise of reasonableness and patience, precisèly then the parties in power and leading journalists ﬁﬁﬁﬁ vied with one another in their zeal to play upon people's rancors and suspicions. It was a fateful stage in ﬁﬁﬁﬁﬁ the annals of "global" relationships - and it was being zealously botched. And the trends that were to reach a kind of ad interim fulfillment in the McCarthy era, ﬁﬁﬁﬁﬁﬁﬁﬁﬁﬁﬁﬁﬁﬁ with surprising

FIGURES 5a–c. Facsimile of "Foreword (to end on)." Source and credit: The Kenneth Burke Literary Trust.

Foreword - 2

and
new twists in the Kennedy, Johnson,/Nixon years,were already inexorably
emerging.

   Thus I also kept delaying publication because I saw many places
that would profit by reference to subsequent ~~developments~~ developments.
Then lo! I suddenly awoke to the realization that, if I left things
pretty much as they were in my original MS, the sheer course of history
                    has
~~has~~ brought it about that readers can of themselves readily
                                              in
profit by the "pathos of distance" ~~by~~ both seeing the original circumstances and seeing around the corner of those circumstances.

                                *

   Just where place the Devices, with regard to the Motivorum project
                                       consider the universal
as a whole? The Grammar was designed to ~~treat of universal~~
aspects of human ~~thought~~ thought (as coming to a focus in paradoxes of
the term, "substance"). The Rhetoric focussed on modes of partisanship
and their transcending (as coming to a head in the term, "identification"). The Symbolic (in the restricted sense of the term) centers on
                                                   as
individual ~~side~~ "identities," (involving "equations" a revealed either
in particular works of art ("Poetics") or human characters ("Ethics").

   Insofar as the Devices involve their use for "ulterior purposes"
(to advocate a policy, for instance), they are clearly in the field
of Rhetoric. But often they are employed as an aspect of one's
character. In this regard, whatever their function as rhetorical
                                                      Here is
"ploys," the Devices overlap upon the field of Ethics. ~~Here is~~
an illustration that occurs to me, since I happen to be writing these
pages at a time when there is much talk of persons who, being entrusted
with the task of enforcing the laws, by the same token tend to think
                                                 adopt
of themselves as above the law, and will readily/~~adopt~~ illegal methods
to spy on persons suspected of illegality.

   Consider thus the rural policeman who invariably parked his car
on the wrong side of the road. And when, along with several other local

Foreword - 3

citizens who were not thus "within" in the law, he was ~~mutaningmanawana~~ taking

~~two~~ a test on first aid, he quite unabashedly opened his book to copy

out the answers, whereas none of the others dared to do anything of the

sort, all properly expecting that, by the rules of the test, when they

didn't know the right answer they would simply get marked "wrong."

In this sense the Devices tend to become implicit self-portraits,

in representing the character of the user. Thus, ~~thmm~~ there is a

tendency for a given agent to favor certain Devices not just for some

ulterior practical purpose, but for their own sake, /~~aamamihfm~~ by way of "self-

expression," as with the stick-up man who didn't kill in order to rob,

but robbed in order to kill (through sheer love of the kill as such).

Or there was a news story of a subway "rapist" who, having demanded

that a girl give him her purse, and having been given the purse in com-

pliance with his demand, sliced her to death anyhow.

I ~~uaa~~/have used extreme examples to ~~chamify~~/sharpen the point; but the anecdote of

the ~~trural~~ rural policeman would ~~bm~~ set the ideal tone for the Devices as a

whole (at least to the extent that ~~ihfdmahwaysmwantmtmmdudutm~~ ideally we'd surround sinister

specimens with a context of comic ~~mmamm~~ analogues).

Not ~~m~~ until now did it occur to me that whereas, in my <u>Rhetoric</u>

~~mmmmpmmmm~~ list some typical devices

<u>of Motives</u>, I ~~rdnsomasmbhamdmutaes~~/in Machiavelli's <u>Prince</u> and Ovid's

<u>Art of Love</u>, my ~~viewm~~ of them as characteristic fragments of human

characters (hence as ~~mm~~ embodying motives that move us from Rhetoric to

Poetics and Ethics, enactments in and for themselves) may have ~~had its~~

~~smamtmfmam~~ its roots in the Flaubert of <u>L'Éducation Sentimentale</u>, though

he certainly would have had no sympathy with my valiant effort to grin.

List of Textual Emendations and Explanatory Notes

PAGE	LINE	TEXT	EDITORS' EMENDATIONS AND NOTES
43	—	*Introduction*	Added before Burke's introductory text.
45	—	*Chapter 1*	Added before "The Devices."
46	31	*dozen pennies*	Deleted ten lines after "dozen pennies" that Burke had crossed out in pencil.
47	4	*Misses Preen*	Added "and Prone." This formulation was offered in Burke's penciled changes to the carbon copy version of the manuscript.
48	21	*will prove it*	Deleted six lines after "prove it" that Burke had crossed out in pencil.
49	4	*Iranian controversy*	When the U.S.S.R. refused to relinquish Iranian territory in 1946, after agreeing to do so at Potsdam, the case went before the United Nations Security Council.
50	4	*Tartuffe*	The title character in the 1664 play by Molière.
51	2	*UNRRA*	United Nations Relief and Rehabilitation Administration.
52	20	*And there is*	Accepted the formulation added by Burke on the carbon copy version of the manuscript.
52	33	*good n******	This offensive term is spelled out in the original manuscript.
53	1	*Likewise,*	Accepted the formulations added by Burke on the carbon copy version of the manuscript.

55	27	*Deputy Minister Vishinsky*	Andrey Vyshinsky headed the Soviet Union's United Nations delegation between 1947 and 1953.
55	40	*Other heads*	Here Burke deleted a paragraph in his original manuscript.
59	28	*get a conviction*	In July 1942, Attorney General Francis Biddle indicted twenty-six American fascist leaders on charges of violating the 1917 Espionage Act and the 1940 Smith Act in what became known as the Great Sedition Trial of 1944. In 1946, the charges were dismissed.
65	36	*Where there is no retreat*	Deleted a proverb in this paragraph.
68	12	*Arthur Krock's formulation*	Arthur Krock won the Pulitzer Prize for his journalistic coverage of Washington politics.
70	8	*as in the awful thing*	This reads "when the awful things" in the manuscript.
78	18	*Governor Dewey*	Thomas Dewey was the Republican candidate for president in the election of 1944.
83	14	*borrowing on a liability*	Accepted the formulations added by Burke on the carbon copy.
83	33	*the Sacco-Vanzetti trials*	Nicola Sacco and Bartolomeo Vanzetti, anarchists, were convicted of murder in a controversial 1921 trial and were executed in 1927.
85	32	*the Adler*	The Adler Shoe Company manufactured shoes with lifts.
86	21	*the Italian elections*	After the Communist coup in Yugoslavia in February 1948, the U.S.-backed Christian Democratic Party defeated the Soviet-backed leftist coalition in a fiercely contested election.
88	17	*Federal Trade Commission*	Burke wrote "Federal Trades Commission" and had an unclosed parenthetical mark before "Federal."
89	33	*nothing is more futile*	Inserted "is" after "nothing."
90	39	*When the Communists assumed power in Czechoslovakia,*	When the Communists in a coup assumed power in Czechoslovakia in February 1948, Foreign Minister Jan Masaryk (a liberal non-Communist) committed suicide—or was murdered. In his funeral oration, Klement Gottwald claimed that Masaryk was pressured by Westerners into leaping to his death.

98	18	*Roger Babson*	Babson (1875–1967), an entrepreneur and business theorist, was known for his inspirational sloganeering; he ran for president in 1940 on the Prohibitionist Party ticket.
99	14	*Recall the previously mentioned*	Amended "previous" to read "previously."
100	39	*"Western Union"*	The alliance, formed after the 1948 Treaty of Brussels, is considered a precursor of the more familiar North Atlantic Treaty Organization (NATO).
101	13	*literary battles of the Thirties*	This refers to infighting among left-leaning writers (including Burke) who gathered around the League of American Writers.
103	33	*normally*	Burke's manuscript uses the word "properly."
105	1	*The words are*	Changed "They are" to "The words are."
106	24	*a "stern warning*	Inserted "a" before "stern."
110	19	*"Duffy's Tavern"*	*Duffy's Tavern* was a popular radio show that ran on several networks during the 1940s.
111	25	*Mr. Blane . . . Miss Pettengill . . . Joe McQuade*	Blane, Pettengill, and McQuade are all Burke's creations.
114	26	*rats*	Accepted "rats" instead of "vermin" from the carbon copy version.
114	28	*Franklin Delano Roosevelt . . . Theodore Roosevelt*	Changed "F. D. Roosevelt" to "Franklin Delano Roosevelt" and "T. R. Roosevelt" to "Theodore Roosevelt."
114	39	*Montgomery sought to neutralize*	Field Marshall Bernard Montgomery was Chief of the Imperial General Staff of Great Britain from 1946 to 1948.
122	31	*Interpreting vexatious contradictions*	Changed "vexations" to "vexatious."
126	9	*Cut In from Another Angle*	Changed "Any" to "Another."
127	27	*a bright young man*	Changed "bring" to "bright."
128	27	*quite successful*	Changed "quietly" to "quite."
130	8	*expression is there*	Inserted "is there" after "expression."
131	19	*malignly*	Inserted "malignly" from the carbon copy version.

133	27	*P. M.*	*PM* was a left-leaning newspaper published daily in New York City throughout most of the 1940s.
133	18	*Churchill made his speech at Fulton*	Winston Churchill delivered his famous "Iron Curtain" speech, condemning the Soviet Union, at Westminster College in Fulton, Missouri, on March 5, 1946.
135	18	*However, in other respects*	Reads "Yet" in Burke's original.
137	22	*in brief, the epideictic*	Added an opening parenthesis.
137	35	*(the fear of others) and would*	Added "and."
137	36	*for insofar*	Substituted a parenthesis for a comma.
138	1	*the very issues*	Changed "these very" to "the very."
138	22	*each of whom*	Changed "which" to "whom."
141	10	*the British Tories decided to end that routine*	The British Tories backed Neville Chamberlain's negotiations with Hitler in 1938.
145	7	*Let them be bred . . .*	Block quotation from Burke's *Towards a Better Life*.
145	27	*Harold Rosenberg*	Harold Rosenberg's words were delivered to Burke at the 1935 meeting of the League of American Writers.
151	2	*show signs*	Inserted "show" before "signs."
151	23	*"Preface to Decision," by Donald Davidson,*	Davidson's essay is historically notable as a defense of Jim Crow.
153	1	*an association*	Changed "as association" to "an association."
154	19	*Empson*	William Empson's *Some Versions of the Pastoral* appeared in 1935.
155	10	*When is one conditioned*	Inserted a question mark at the end of this sentence.
158	3	*has the nunlike Isabella*	Changed "Arabella" to "Isabella."
159	14	*A Rhetoric of Motives*	The carbon copy version of the manuscript substitutes "A Rhetoric of Motives" for "a Science of the Human Comedy."
160	32	*Or if Q is returning*	Changed from "Or is Q returning."

165	7	*Pujo Investigation*	In 1912–13, a congressional subcommittee under the leadership of Arsene Pujo investigated Wall Street bankers and financiers.
169	1	*Chapter 2*	Added before "Scientific Rhetoric."
213	29	*George Seldes' . . . In Fact,*	George Seldes, a muckraking journalist, published his newsletter *In Fact* between 1940 and 1950. Burke references *In Fact* in chapter 2.
179	1	*editorial policies).*	Inserted closed parenthesis after "policies."
179	11	*"adult education")*	Inserted closed parenthesis after "education."
179	14	*anti-Nazi Protestant minister*	This is likely a reference to Martin Niemöller (1892–1984).
182	24	*John L. Lewis*	Lewis led the United Mine Workers union from 1920 to 1960.
183	4	*Oxnam Holds War*	Garfield Oxnam (1891–1965) is the Methodist bishop to whom Burke refers.
183	21	*"marked by bluntness*	Added open quotation mark before "marked."
188	14	*Recall the occasion*	On December 12, 1937, Mae West and Edgar Bergen (as Charlie McCarthy) engaged in a suggestive radio skit that resulted in West's being banned from radio shows for over a decade.
190	12	*De Gasperi*	Alcide De Gasperi, who founded the Christian Democratic Party, was prime minister in Italy from 1945 to 1953.
191	1	*Henry Wallace*	Henry Wallace, Franklin Roosevelt's vice president (1941–45), founded the Progressive Party and served as its presidential nominee in 1948.
192	16	*what nation*	Changed "nation's" to "nation."
192	16	*might belong*	Changed "might be" to "might belong."
223	1	*Chapter 3 . . . [Notes toward]*	Added before "The Rhetoric of Bureaucracy."
229	40	*Bottom translated*	Refers to a famous scene in Shakespeare's *A Midsummer Night's Dream.*
232	24	*foreign holdings;*	Substituted a semicolon in place of a comma after "holdings."
234	7	*Search for the Poetic Order of Motives*	Inserted before the section that opens "The search for the poetic order of motives."
237	15	*Bureaucratization of the Imaginative*	Inserted before the section that opens "In an earlier work."

238	28	*provided the ill will*	These paragraphs allude to Sidney Hook's scathing 1937 review of *Attitudes Toward History*.
242	1	*Chapter 4 . . . [Notes toward]*	Inserted before "The Rhetorical Situation"
248	34	*may not have paid*	Deleted "not" after "may not have."
250	25	*how such doctrines look*	Inserted "how" before "such doctrines."
252	36	*there is promise*	Deleted "of" before "there is promise."
252	39	*as is informally*	Inserted "is" before "informally."
255	4	*had much evidence*	Changed "had made evidence" to "had much evidence."
255	16	*distribution of goods*	After "distribution of goods," Burke inserted in pencil, "might insert on Machiavelli here."
257	14	*Two other points:*	Burke scratched these words out, but we restore them in order to assist the reader; these two points are in outline form, not in paragraph form.

Index

CPSIA information can be obtained
at www.ICGtesting.com
Printed in the USA
LVHW020s0710241018
594635LV00001B/6/P